LAUER SERIES IN RHETORIC AND COMPOSITION

Series Editors: Catherine Hobbs, Patricia Sullivan, Thomas Rickert, and Jennifer Bay

LAUER SERIES IN RHETORIC AND COMPOSITION

Series Editors: Catherine Hobbs, Patricia Sullivan, Thomas Rickert, and Jennifer Bay

The Lauer Series in Rhetoric and Composition honors the contributions Janice Lauer Hutton has made to the emergence of Rhetoric and Composition as a disciplinary study. It publishes scholarship that carries on Professor Lauer's varied work in the history of written rhetoric, disciplinarity in composition studies, contemporary pedagogical theory, and written literacy theory and research.

Other Books in the Series

Ancient Non-Greek Rhetorics

Edited by
Carol S. Lipson
Roberta A. Binkley

Parlor Press
West Lafayette, Indiana
www.parlorpress.com

Parlor Press LLC, West Lafayette, Indiana 47906

SAN: 254-8879

Library of Congress Cataloging-in-Publication Data

Ancient non-Greek rhetorics / edited by Carol S. Lipson, Roberta A.
Binkley.
    p. cm. -- (Lauer series in rhetoric and composition)
Includes bibliographical references and index.
ISBN 978-1-60235-095-3 (hardcover : alk. paper) -- ISBN 978-1-60235-
094-6 (pbk. : alk. paper) -- ISBN 978-1-60235-096-0 (adobe ebook)
    1. Rhetoric, Ancient. 2. Rhetoric--History. I. Lipson, Carol. II. Binkley,
Roberta A., 1941-
PN183.A53 2009
808.009--dc22
                                    2009008640

Cover design by David Blakesley.
"Works of the Fields" in the Tomb of Paheri. Osiris.net. Used by permission.
Printed on acid-free paper.

Parlor Press, LLC is an independent publisher of scholarly and trade titles
in print and multimedia formats. This book is available in paper, cloth
and Adobe eBook formats from Parlor Press on the World Wide Web
at http://www.parlorpress.com or through online and brick-and-mortar
bookstores. For submission information or to find out about Parlor Press
publications, write to Parlor Press, 816 Robinson St., West Lafayette,
Indiana, 47906, or e-mail editor@parlorpress.com.

Contents

Acknowledgments

The editors wish to acknowledge the support of the College of Arts and Sciences at Syracuse University, which provided funding to help offset publication costs and also provided leave time, enabling efforts to bring this project to fruition. It has been a joy working with the talented contributors, as well as with dedicated staff members at Parlor Press; Tracy Clark and David Blakesley deserve special kudos.

We dedicate this book to Monica, Marissa, and Gretel, as well as to Edward, Michael, Daniel, Doree, and Benjamin.

—Carol Lipson and Roberta Binkley

Ancient Non-Greek Rhetorics

1 Introduction

Carol S. Lipson

*[T]he study of human rhetoric is not complete if it does not in-
clude the rhetorical traditions of non-Western cultures. . . .*

(Xing Lu ,1998, Introduction, p. 1)

In recent years, rhetorical scholars have shown increasing interest in
extending understanding of practices and theories to cultural territory beyond the boundaries of Western frameworks. Challenges to the
parochial and situated nature of Western paradigms have arisen from
various directions: due to recognition of the global nature of communication in contemporary society, and due as well to recognition of
the heterogeneity of rhetorical frameworks within America itself and
the Western world more generally. As Jackie Jones Royster queried in
2003, "What if we treated what we know about the history of Western
rhetoric as it were merely what we know best rather than what *is* best?"
(166). Such a shift is by no means a trivial or simple one, given the difficulty of putting aside both the theoretical lens and related values and
apparatus through which Western scholars have come to view human
communication.

COMPARATIVE RHETORIC, AND COMPARATIVE STUDY IN RELATED FIELDS

Much of the work involving rethinking of the field of rhetoric in relation to other cultures, particularly non-Western cultures, has taken
place under the rubric of comparative rhetoric, a field which by definition compares principles and practices of one culture with those
arising from classical Greece and Rome. Much of that work has ex-

amined the questions of appropriate methods and ethical practices. As LuMing Mao points out in "Reflective Encounters," the study of non-Western rhetorics requires that a scholar begin with familiar concepts and terminology, but the scholar must attempt to move toward a more *emic* analysis, developing enough understanding of the culture and the historical context to view the phenomena as would a member of the society being studied. Bo Wang points to the increasing move in comparative scholarship to examine rhetorical practices within their particular historical contexts (171).

Our interest in this volume involves recovering and examining the ancient rhetorics in non-Western cultures and other cultures that developed independently of classical Greek models. Scholars trained in fields of rhetoric and composition face particularly high hurdles in attempting such work, for academic programs in rhetoric rarely offer specialization in the ancient languages and cultures of non-Western societies—whether China, Egypt, Mesopotamia, Japan, India, or indeed Western rhetorics such as those in Mesoamerica and South America. Such problems face not only rhetoricians, but also philosophers who begin study of such ancient cultures. The late philosopher David Hall makes a limited case for the value of such participation despite a philosopher's unfamiliarity with the ancient language. He writes that the main contribution of such a "comparativist is in the recovery of *traditions*" (20). Hall has contributed to the understanding of similarities and differences between Chinese and Western thought. In an essay published posthumously, Hall defends the contributions of a scholar who is not a Sinologist, and who does not have the ability to read ancient Chinese. His particular argument takes the direction of advocating collaboration in composing translations and in conducting comparative work. In his case, since he is concerned with Chinese philosophy, he argues for the need for collaboration involving a specialist in philosophical traditions of the west and one familiar with the ancient Chinese language, with the goal of producing translations of ancient philosophical texts that could be meaningful to contemporary philosophers. Hall's essay is a passionate defense of the value of collaborative participation, alongside a language expert, by a scholar who may be an amateur in the culture and language being examined, but is an expert in the subject being compared; his main concern was the translation of ancient Chinese philosophical texts.

In the case of rhetorical study, the examinations of ancient non-Western rhetorics are mainly conducted by scholars who do not have expertise in the languages and perhaps in the historical cultures involved. Such scholars are not involved in translating texts, but in studying texts based on translations to determine the rhetorical principles underlying such texts. Many such rhetorical scholars have inevitably been faced with the question as to whether they are fluent in the ancient language involved. At this stage, most are not.

Another philosopher, Paul Goldin, addresses the issue of appropriate methodology in studying the texts of ancient cultures—in his case, classical Chinese philosophical texts. He argues for a paradigm involving thick description, based on earlier work by Gilbert Ryle, who had himself built on work of Clifford Geertz. Acknowledging the popularity of the method for cultural anthropologists and ethnologists, he finds the method just as applicable for cultural history in determining the meanings within an ancient culture and its operative cultural codes. In his view, knowledge of the classical language is extraordinarily valuable in understanding linguistic dimensions suggested, for instance, by resonances created through similarities in related words that sound alike (1–3; 17–18).

Philosophy is not the only discipline concerned with the methodological issues involved in comparative work on ancient cultures. A Stanford project on comparative history of the Ancient Chinese and Mediterranean Empires (ACME) notes that the two cultures exhibit many similarities (Scheidel 3), including "ideological unification through monumental construction, religious rituals, and elite education; the creation of a homogeneous elite culture and corpora of classics; the emergence of court-centered historiography; ideologies of normative empire sustained by transcendent powers . . . and a philosophical and religious shift in emphasis from community values to ethical conduct and individual salvation" (3). Yet despite the similarities, the two civilizations differed significantly in the specifics of their cultural manifestations. The Stanford project is based on the premise that a huge gap is left in scholarly understanding when the "two largest agrarian empires of antiquity" have not been examined comparatively (6). The scholars involved attribute the lapse to the complications of the language issues, and to the limitations imposed by academic specializations.

The scholars leading the Stanford study outline several approaches to such historical inquiry that are considered responsible in their field. The first involves comparing equivalent units, and then attempting to determine explanations for the similarities and differences. The second approach examines equivalent units in light of a predictive theory. Work of the second type attempts to assess theory, while the first approach seeks to examine the relation between the cultural and political contexts, and the differences in units being compared. A third, macro-level approach looks at convergence or differences found in units being examined, in order to generate new historical theories. The project scholars show concern that comparative history not simply assemble sets of data about differences and convergences, but seek explanations and meaning based on the data. To do so responsibly, they point out, requires collaboration among experts in the different areas. They also point out that in actual performance, comparative history generally applies more than one approach, assembling and studying details of case studies with some determination of significance.

Since the middle of the nineteenth century, the field of religious studies has also shown a strong interest in comparative studies of religion. The early writings showed concern that such study be characterized as scientific, and mainly examined homonymous phenomena—which, as Arvind Sharma states, "appear similar but are really different" (25). Sharma advocates a new comparative practice, "oriented toward making synonymous comparisons" between religious traditions, "examining phenomena that appear different but possess similar significance in each tradition" (25). Such comparisons, in his view, reciprocally illuminate both traditions.

While comparative religion is commonly taught, comparative study has not been uncontroversial. Much has been written on both sides of this issue. A 2001 article by Robert Segal titled "In Defense of the Comparative Method" addresses and attempts to counter a variety of objections to problems and limitations of the comparative method in religious studies. Segal lists the objections to the method as follows: the method tends to link phenomena in later time periods with evolution; the method focuses on finding only similarities; the method at times confuses similarity with identity; the method can lead to generalizations that are too broad and premature; the method facilitates taking phenomena out of context; and finally the method can lead to studies that do not generalize at all (346–48). Notably, while there is great concern in the field's writings on methodology for accuracy and for proper choice of equivalent elements to compare, the list of objections does not cite dependence on translations as a problem. In fact, religious studies comparative scholarship commonly uses translations of the various texts it examines. Segal does acknowledge that good comparisons must examine phenomena in their contexts, using the writing of an early oft-maligned comparative scholar, James George Frazer, to help advance his argument. But Frazer's quote notes the need to live among the peoples being studied, and to gain fluency in their language; such contextual knowledge is not required of scholars in comparative religious studies. A 1985 review of a set of essays on the comparative method in religion notes that the essays vary "from the more traditional 'comparative method' by focusing less on individual comparisons, and by showing "a greater concern to place the entity being discussed in its total context" (220). This review by Dennis Pardee, in the *Journal of Near Eastern Studies,* points to the need for close attention to the historical and cultural context in such examinations, which he does not always find satisfactorily present in comparative studies in religion.

As part of his argument for the value of the comparative method, Segal claims that it "simply categorizes phenomena, but the categorization prompts the quest for an explanation of the similarities or the differences found among cases of the category. . . . In providing the categories on which accounts rest, the comparative method is indispensable" (373). Segal's defense here displays the particular analytical bent of comparative religious studies, in the value of categorization as an optimal mode of analysis. In fact, in a 2006 *Blackwell Companion to the Study of Religion,* edited by Robert Segal, methodology in religious studies in general is addressed by Segal in his introduction. Segal claims that the common method used can be termed "taxonomy at the descriptive level . . . the classification of professedly religious beliefs, practices, and objects" (xiv). Comparative methodology in religious studies is discussed in an early chapter in this volume by Paul Roscoe, who suggests that Segal's 2001 defense does not address epistemological issues (25). Roscoe attributes the humanistically inclined critique of the comparative method to objections that "cultures, by their nature, cannot be compared," and that classification and generalization involve unwarranted, distorting, and controlling impositions (26). That is, he claims that the debate is not really about the method, but "about the validity of the comparativist assumption that the surface manifestations to be explained are all expressions of the same" meaning (29), and that "comparativists do not take enough meaningful context into account" (42). The same Frazer quote that Segal used appears here, as well—but that is the only appearance of reference to language familiarity as being an important part of interpreting the context in comparative studies, or of determining the meaning.

As in the field of philosophy, collaborative studies are also looked to in religious studies as a possible way to address the problems with the comparative method. Robert Cummings Neville organized the Comparative Religious Ideas Project, based at Boston University. Introducing the project in one of the resulting volumes, Neville refers to the dismay about the imperialism in prior comparisons and comparative theories, which undermined the credibility of the activity (xvi). He assembled a group of six specialists, each an expert in a particular religious tradition, each well grounded in historical context within that specialty. Four generalists in religious studies were also included in the project (xvii). Senior outside advisors joined the group at the end of the first year, and at the end of the fourth year. SUNY Press has published three volumes representing the work of this collaborative team. Much of the effort of the participants involved collectively selecting and justifying categories for comparing the different religions: Chinese religion, Buddhism, Judaism, ancient Christianity, Islam, and a particular text in the Vedanta tradition of Hindu India. Not unexpectedly, the specialists tended to resist anachronisms or distortions applied to their periods and areas of expertise. As Wesley Wildman writes, no religious studies scholar is prepared "by training or scholarly experience" to do scholarly work across traditions and cultures (278–79). Wildman and Cummings Neville describe resistance and dismay among participating specialists about the project of comparing and its scholarly viability. Yet, the project reached its end, with the cautious conclusion that comparison can prove productive and responsible if done "carefully and vulnerably," by bringing to the foreground questions and issues that might otherwise have gone unnoticed (17). On the one hand, the organizer deems the collaboration of specialists from different areas useful; yet, the elaborate structure and process could not be sustained without substantial funding. For the purposes of the field of rhetorical study, the Comparative Religious Ideas Project would of necessity require translation to small-scale collaborations.

While comparative religion focuses on ideas and phenomena, comparative rhetoric, in contrast, is intimately tied to interpretation of language, and most recent writings on comparative rhetoric all emphasize the value and need for rhetoricians to gain knowledge of the original language and culture. But there is also realism about the current situation. Similar to Paul Goldin, Sue Hum and Arabella Lyon indicate that a scholar without detailed familiarity with a culture and its language is less likely to do harm if that scholar simply describes a text without attempting to develop theoretical conclusions, though this approach would gain limited knowledge (in press). They point to the small amount of scholarship, analysis, and theorization as a major deficit in the field of comparative rhetoric, but also acknowledge the dangers of theorizing based on the limited scholarship available and on the restrictions involved when studies are conducted by non-specialists. In their view, narrower studies describing particular sources in their local historical settings would be more ethical than larger-scale studies that oversimplify or that lack crucial grounding. In the area of non-Western and unfamiliar rhetorical studies, they advocate the value of examining "fragments" in local historical contexts. They claim that such study, while it may not fully represent the culture's rhetorical nature, would be preferable to scholarly inattention to the rhetorical traditions of non-Western cultures. In *Rhetoric in Ancient China, Fifth to Third Century BCE: A Comparison with Classical Greek Rhetoric,* Xing Lu pronounces the work of the first generation of scholars of non-Western rhetorics as useful, while also advocating the need for future scholarship to base itself on knowledge of the ancient Chinese language along with knowledge of the cultural and historical contexts (39). In a later article, "Studies and Development of Comparative Rhetoric in the USA: Chinese and Western Rhetoric in Focus," Lu proposes as the ideal approach to comparative rhetorical study collaborations involving Western and Chinese scholars of rhetoric (115).

ISSUES IN STUDYING ANCIENT CULTURES AND RHETORICS

While recent years have seen a good deal of work on the rhetoric of ancient cultures, on the whole such study remains at early stages. Ancient China has received the most attention, generally with a focus on Confucian rhetorical principles. Other ancient cultures have not been examined much with a rhetorical focus. This is true for Near Eastern cultures such as Mesopotamia or Egypt, as well as for other

Far Eastern cultures such as Japan or Korea. This is equally true for
cultures arising in the Indus valley or in the Americas.

Mesopotamian History and Rhetorical Study

One of the earliest literate cultures arose in Mesopotamia, which covered approximately the same territory as Iraq does currently; writing
here began in southern city-states within Sumeria. Sumerian was the
language of southern Mesopotamia, while Akkadian was spoken in
the north. Not only did the languages differ, but cultural traits did as
well (Liverani 6). In the mid-third millennium BCE, Sargon of Akkad
conquered the Sumerian south to establish a large state, in fact considered the first empire (Chavalas 43). At first, Sumerian was still used for
literary texts, and in temples for rituals and chants, but not for everyday
writing (Baines and Yoffee 221, 248). By the middle of the second millennium BCE, Akkadian translations of Sumerian texts were taught
in scribal schools. The Sumerian system of cuneiform was adapted
to accommodate the Semitic Akkadian language, which was used for
Sargon's public inscriptions and monuments, in the royal court, and
in the administration of the empire (Baines and Yoffee 221). Sargon's
daughter, appointed by her father as high priestess for the moon god
in the temple of Ur, took a Sumerian name (Enheduanna) and wrote
in Sumerian (Melville 243); she herself claimed she had been chosen
by divination and by divine action (Westenholz 542). When after 150
years, the Akkadians were defeated, Sumerian again became the language of administration. Eventually Aramaic, in the first millennium,
became the language for daily activities, while written Akkadian using
cuneiform script dominated Mesopotamian history for the next 2,000
years (Kuhrt 46).

Mesopotamian history involved the rise and fall of a series of kingdoms, often city-states expanding their territories, with some periods
of strong empires; but overall, the region was characterized by diverse cultures, languages, political orders, and religious beliefs. This is
partly due to the lack of geographic boundaries and to the permeable
mountains to the north and east (Snell 5). The various cultural groups
included Amorites, Maris, Hittites, Elamites, Babylonians, Assyrians,
and finally Persians. Thus, expertise in Mesopotamian rhetoric would
involve knowledge of multiple languages and mixtures of languages
(Michalowski 176–77) as well as a complex set of cultural and political
changes. Even during periods of strong empires, powerful city-states

in the region preserved some distinct cultural and political structures while absorbing some aspects of the dominant culture. As political and cultural conditions changed, the city-state inhabitants maintained some independence, not always using the ruling language or abandoning the old. For example, Sumerian continued to be used for literary texts for 600 years (Kuhrt 46). Simply identifying the language of early cuneiform Mesopotamian texts carries complications; the region evinced considerable contact between different societies with different languages, and thus became quite multilingual. But all the Mesopotamian languages were written in variants of Sumerian cuneiform. For instance, an existing cuneiform text might be in Sumerian, Akkadian, or a patchwork of both, as well as possibly in Hittite (Fischer 53).

Without doubt, the overall body of texts from Mesopotamia is quite large, and the discipline of Mesopotamian studies remains quite preoccupied with developing text editions. William Hallo has estimated that cuneiform texts "provide the most abundant archival documentation before the European Middle Ages" (192). The large group of texts also encompasses diverse languages and a succession of differing cultural and political conditions. As Snell points out (114), training for expertise in Mesopotamian language and for cultural study more generally is both long and esoteric. Baines and Yoffee note that few scholars of Mesopotamian civilizations undertake comparative work (203). And, I might add, training for comparative studies involving Mesopotamian rhetoric, on top of general training in fields of rhetoric and composition, would involve commitments far beyond the average time allotted for doctoral study and support. Snell notes that ancient Near Eastern studies as a field therefore involves few scholars but many texts, with most of the energy thus far involved in establishing archives (115). For a number of the texts, there do exist translations by ancient Near Eastern specialists. Is it any surprise that the first generation of rhetorical scholars taking on study Mesopotamian or ancient Near Eastern rhetorics would have turned to translations? Though expert knowledge of the original languages would have been preferable, such scholars base their work on a belief that our field can learn from studies involving an immersion in the culture and history surrounding the texts, along with consultation of expert translations of the texts.

Hall's response to such a situation would likely be mixed, despite his advocacy regarding the value of non-Sinologists participating in translating Chinese philosophical texts. Hall states that

> Absent the combination of Sinological and Western philosophical skills in a single individual, successful translations of texts such as the *Analects* and the *Daodejing* into Western languages require collaboration between Chinese and Western specialists. *Such collaboration from the Western side is usually only minimally and inadequately accomplished, as when an individual ignorant of the Chinese language consults a number of different translations of a given text and seeks some broad understanding of the history and culture of the period that contextualizes the work he is seeking to understand. Without some such initial concern, as inadequate as it may be, the Western interpreter of classical Chinese texts is guaranteed to present a superficial and distorted interpretation* (23; italics added).

The situation described by Hall as "inadequate" and minimal is in fact a common situation among rhetoricians beginning to study ancient Mesopotamian texts, though certainly not universally so. It is a situation that may be superseded by a second or third generation of rhetorical scholars, but it currently exists as the only possible way to attend to the ancient rhetorics of an important part of the world in which writing developed very early.

Studying Ancient Chinese Rhetorics

The situation for rhetorical study of ancient Chinese appears somewhat different from that of Mesopotamia. In fact, the majority of the studies of ancient non-Greek rhetorics address issues of ancient Chinese rhetoric, and many of the authors are fluent in modern Chinese. Though the earliest Chinese writings date from approximately 1200 BCE, in the late Shang era, these inscriptions on bones record a language that is reasonably similar to classical Chinese, and readable to those familiar with modern Chinese. Before the Emperor of Qin unified China in 221 BCE, different areas within China had developed variations in scripts for writing (Kelly 21; Fischer 174). With the Emperor's authorization of the Qin script as the official script for writing, Chinese writing became standardized, and has undergone relatively little change. These Chinese characters as authorized in the Qin period resemble modern Chinese characters. Though it is not clear how the logograms were pronounced, the many rhetorical scholars who can read modern Chinese are able to read the ancient Chinese texts that follow the Qin reform.

Yet the situation is not entirely simple, for as philosopher Paul Goldin points out, the similarities in the characters "obscure a lot of changes. This makes [an ancient text] seem less alien than it actually is."[2] He argues that the difficulties in analysis thus apply to native Chinese speakers as well as to scholars dependent on translation. In *After Confucius,* he writes, "Chinese has never been considered an easy language (along with Arabic, Japanese, and Korean it is commonly reckoned as one of the hardest languages for an American to learn), and the archaic idiom in which classical Chinese philosophy has been transmitted is more demanding than the modern vernacular" (3). And due to the difficulty and at times the impoverishment of much translation, the English texts "fail to convey to a foreign reader the world of concerns of the original text in its culture" (18). In his view, citing philosopher Willard Van Orman Quine, translation must go beyond "transposition of a set of words in one language into another set in another language," but must try to convey the worldview of the ancient culture (18).

Ancient Egyptian History and Rhetorical Study

Rhetoricians facing study of ancient Egypt do have the advantage of examining a relatively stable long-term empire, with changes in ruling dynasties, but not the same degree of changes in culture and language as is the case in Mesopotamia. Ancient Egyptian civilization was prominent in the region for over 3,000 years. Over that period, the development of writing saw a series of different scripts, with hieroglyphics remaining in use for public and monumental texts throughout Egyptian history. Normally, an individual text would use 200 to 300 different hieroglyphs (Junge 260), while scholarship indicates a total of approximately 4,000 hieroglyphic signs over the entire corpus. The more cursive hieratic script, designed for use with a brush and ink on papyrus, was used for letters, records, and administrative documents. Given the variations in the cursive scripts over time, between types of texts, and between different local areas, the decipherment of cursive hieratic texts proves quite challenging even for expert Egyptologists. At the beginning of the Late Period, another version of cursive script called demotic came into use, primarily for legal and administrative texts, but also for some literary texts in the vernacular (Junge 262; Wente 208), in fact becoming the normal script in everyday uses from the seventh century BCE. A later variant of demotic script was developed for use in religious texts (Wente 209). Middle Egyptian was used as the language for literature and other significant texts even while the language was no longer spoken or familiar, from the twenty-third century BCE to the fourth century AD. Late Egyptian was in use from the fourteenth to the seventh centuries BCE. Hyksos, Hittites, Nubians, Libyans, Assyrians and Persians all invaded Egypt and ruled as pharaohs, yet most invading cultures maintained Egyptian customs on the whole, including matters of textual and visual decorum. For rhetoricians to master the various ancient Egyptian dialects, as well as to develop full understanding of 3,000 years of history and culture, clearly becomes a massive undertaking. In fact, most universities do not have resident Egyptologists on faculty. For most graduate students and faculty in the field of rhetoric, access to Egyptological expertise is rare.

Conditions Impacting Ancient Japanese Rhetorical Study

Writing first appeared in Japan in the Chinese language—the only written language known to the ancient Japanese—after Chinese writing was introduced to Japan via Korea around 370 AD (Fischer 196). The earliest extant examples of such Japanese writing are from the fifth to sixth centuries (Borgen 200). Even after developing its own writing system, Japan still deferred to Chinese as the language of choice for a range of writing genres. Since women were not taught Chinese, texts by women were written in the Japanese language. However, early writings by males were written in Chinese, even when transcribing Japanese words (202). Since the Chinese script was used to write the Japanese language as well as the Chinese language, it can be difficult at times simply to distinguish the language of a text. The Japanese court sent students to China, who brought back Chinese notions of centralized imperial rule. Extensive attention was given at court and at universities to the study and composition of poetry in Chinese (205). Chinese models became sources for legal and administrative systems, as well as for city planning (206). A major criterion for choosing officials involved knowledge of Confucius.

Thus, Chinese ideologies and rhetorical principles proved attractive to Japan's rulers, in reinforcing their political power and the cultural practices and ideals they promoted (Fischer 196). The allegiance to Chinese language and literature models declined in the ninth century, as the development of a phonetic script for Japanese enabled texts to be written in the Japanese language. Chinese classics continued to be taught, remaining as powerful ideological influences.

Such a historical situation renders the study of ancient Japanese rhetoric an even more labor-intensive project than the study of ancient Chinese rhetoric, since it calls on knowledge of the two ancient languages and the two scripts, as well as the history of political contexts of the two cultures, whose relations changed over time. Not surprisingly, there is a dearth of rhetorical scholarship on this early culture.

Ancient Rhetoric and the Indus Valley

One of the largest gaps in knowledge of ancient rhetorics within the field of rhetorical studies involves ancient India, or more precisely the ancient Indus Valley area more generally. The Indus Valley civilization is at times called Harappan culture for one of the large cities prominent in the third and second millennia BCE, located in what is now northeastern Pakistan. Relatively contemporaneous with ancient Mesopotamia and ancient Egypt, the entire Indus Valley civilization included most of Pakistan, the western area of India, and northern Afghanistan. The Indus Valley civilization involved urban centers, and had trade relations with Sumeria. The civilization covered approximately a million kilometers—a huge area (Possehl 261). This is approximately the size of Western Europe, larger than Egypt, Mesopotamia, or China. This was quite an accomplished culture. Cities were built in grid patterns, with systems for sewers and drainage available in all houses, not just in homes for leaders. The architecture was impressive, involving large citadels, protective walls, and storage buildings. No palaces or temples have been found. Seals and pots reveal a large number of symbols and brief inscriptions; while controversy exists among scholars as to whether these hieroglyphs constitute a writing system or non-linguistic signs, the signs are nevertheless taken as communicative in nature. The language has not been deciphered, but the seals seem to show different levels of communication—script at the top for the elite, and designs below for those who lacked literacy (Kenoyer 90–91, 100). The civilization's decline can possibly be attributed to climate change, around 1900 BCE, leading to the rise of regional cultures. In many ways, the Indus Valley culture appears remarkably different from other

ancient cultures of the same period. As Possehl states, the civilization
showed no evidence of a cult of personality surrounding kings; there
are no depictions of kings or elite among the archaeological finds (288).
The language used by the Harappan civilization, currently identified
as related to Dravidian, has been deciphered only partially.

After the Harappan age, what is now known as the Vedic period
arose in the second and first millennia BCE. Various kingdoms rose
and fell in the area encompassing the northern and the northwest section of the Indian subcontinent. This period saw the composition of
the oldest religious Hindu texts —the Vedas, which include narratives
as well as dialogues, arguments, and debates. The *Rigveda,* the oldest
of the Vedan texts, composed over a lengthy period, was completed
by 1500 BCE. The Mahabharata and Ramayana epics, composed in
classical Sanskrit, are considered post-Vedic, appearing after 500 BCE.
The Vedas record ritual chants and practices, often involving sacrifice.
Oral recitation, based on memory, formed the major system for passing on the Vedas and their teaching, in classical Sanskrit. The oldest
fully decipherable preserved forms of the language of the Indus valley
occur in the Vedic religious texts (1500 BCE to 200 BCE).

Vedic Sanskrit differs considerably from classical Sanskrit. Both
were restricted to learned and elite religious groups, and did not represent the spoken language of the people. Though Sanskrit remains a
valued language for Hindu prayer, for temple practices, and for mantras, it is no longer widely used as a spoken language. Notably, Sanskrit
writing was not under the control of a single strong empire, as was
the case with writing in China and Egypt. Many of the major Sanskrit texts arose outside the ruling authority systems, and spread across
states in the overall region. Writing was used for different purposes
and in different ways than in China (Sen 176), and in the Near East
I would add, and the rhetorical principles and practices within the
Indus Valley ancient cultures merit close attention and much broader
understanding. They reveal a tradition of argument and dispute as
well as a tradition of persuasion via stories (Sen 3–4, 65). Academic
fields such as religion, literature, and philosophy have all studied major
Indus Valley texts, but little has been done in the field of rhetoric.
Given the scope, influence, and significance of this ancient civilization, this omission seems highly problematic.

Ancient Israel and the Study of Rhetoric

Just as Indus Valley rhetoric principles arose in a very different political and cultural environment than is the case with other contemporaneous early cultures in the Near East, Israelite writing arose in a quite
different political and cultural environment as well. In fact, ancient
Israelite writing arose without being embedded within the confines of
a state. Ancient Israelite writing, most prominently identified within
the Pentateuch— the first five books of the Hebrew Bible—has been
considered as serving to create, reinforce, and recreate the identity of a
people that did not form a state (Sanders 7–8). A great deal of the rhetorical attention to the Hebrew Bible has been concerned with examining the literary tropes and the rhetorical devices. Rhetorical criticism
was advocated in 1968 by James Muilenburg in his presidential address
to the Society for Biblical Literature, published in 1969. He called the
enterprise rhetoric, and the method rhetorical criticism—or more specifically, form criticism intended to understand the Hebrew Bible as a
Hebrew "literary composition," including its structural manifestations
and literary devices. As George Kennedy has noted, the terms rhetoric
and literary style are often used interchangeably in biblical studies (3).
There has also been active discussion about the meaning and value of
rhetorical criticism of the Pentateuch as differentiated from literary
criticism. Much of this scholarship has raised questions as to whether
and how much the inquiries termed rhetorical criticism are truly rhetorical. In recent years, Erika Falk described a set of rhetorical principles, morally and ethically based, as presented in the Hebrew Bible;
these principles pronounce certain types of speech acts as negative and
to be avoided, and offer positive mandates for other types. Other types
of rhetorical studies have turned to examining the Hebrew Bible as a
persuasive rhetorical text, but as Laurent Pernot observes in an article
focusing on pagan and Christian religious texts, on the whole "many
academic circles remain reticent and unenthusiastic when it comes to
rhetorical readings of ancient religious texts. . . . Things are changing, but slowly. There are brilliant exceptions, but they are rare" (235).
Attention has been given to the persuasive nature embedded in the
structure of the Hebrew Bible (Watts, Metzger), and to the cultural
context in which the Pentateuch was read and made available to its
audience. Attention has also been given to the ancient Israelite theory of rhetoric as embodied in the Hebrew alphabet, focusing on the
epistemic assumptions and effects (Katz). As is the case with studies of

religious rhetoric in general, such rhetorical study of ancient Israelite
religious texts often does use translations.

Western Non-Greek Rhetorics

Rhetorical Study of Ancient Ireland

Some Western rhetorics developed independent of Greek classical rhetoric, and merit study. One involves ancient Ireland, which was not part
of the Roman empire, though trading contact did occur. The Romans
did conquer Britain in 431 AD, but Ireland remained independent,
maintaining its cultural basis. Through contact with European Celts,
Ireland adopted Celtic culture and language. While writing arrived in
Ireland along with Christianity, in the fifth century AD, an early alphabetic script, used in the fifth and sixth centuries, involved a system
referred to as *ogham* (Christin 276–77; Fischer 157–59). This system
consisted of notches and lines on stone, such as tombstones or monuments; in some instances, the script was used on wood, for letters,
and on shields. All such texts are very brief, and are written in the
Irish Gaelic language. Later the Latin alphabet, brought by Christian
monks, was used to write Gaelic, with literary works dating from the
seventh to eighth centuries (Fischer 253–54). Since the Latin alphabet
did not always readily correspond with or transfer Gaelic pronunciation, the act of translation involves much ambiguity. Many of Ireland's
early oral texts were recorded in writing, particularly involving history,
genealogy, legends, sagas, and religious documents. Only in the eighth
century AD was Ireland invaded by Norwegians and Danes, losing its
cultural independence.

Since Gaelic has been kept alive in Irish schools, scholars from Ireland may be well prepared to address rhetorical study of ancient Irish
texts in the original language. This is unlikely to be the case, however, for rhetorical scholars of American origin. Here the choice lies
between offering no sense to Western scholars of this early Western
rhetorical system that arose quite independent of classical rhetoric, or
working with translations to examine this early rhetoric.

Ancient Mesoamerican and South American Rhetorical Study

One additional ancient Western cultural group has received insufficient attention in rhetorical studies: the early Mayan, Aztec, Zapotec,
Mixtec, and Moche pre-Columbian civilizations. The lack of atten-

tion to these cultural rhetorics in this volume is not intentional. The Mesoamerican cultures were never politically unified (Joyce 64), but involved shifting states and political units. Yet, a shared set of values formed a major element of the Mesoamerican cultures (Longhena 66–67; Baines and Yoffee 248). For instance, across cultures it was understood that the fate of maize deities depended on the behavior and practices of elites in the Mesoamerican civilizations. Across the cultures, rhetorical elements involved relief carvings on public monumental platforms, books of bark, as well as similar calendars—with a year of eighteen months, each with twenty days, supplemented by five extra days (Coe 26–27). The inscriptions and books make clear that architecture, art, and clothing functioned rhetorically, communicating messages of power, privilege, and exclusivity (Joyce 72). The art presented some humans (all male) as links to the divine. The different subcultures thus possessed a common vocabulary of ritual performance and common motifs (Joyce 72).

The Zapotec civilization in Mexico is now understood as developing "the most ancient form of a true, proper writing system in the Mesoamerican area" (Longhena 166–67). Some of the symbols have been deciphered, but much remains to be understood. Relationships have been found between the Zapotec script and the Mixtec script, which in Mixtec documents seems quite secondary to images and pictographs. Neither of these two scripts has been fully decoded. Few Mayan texts have survived, but a Russian scholar—Yuri Knorosov—famously deciphered the phonetic pronunciation of the Mayan hieroglyphic code as his doctoral research in 1963. Maya writing is by far the best known among the Mesoamerican scripts, since the recent advances in its decipherment have attracted much scholarly and general attention. Elizabeth Hill Boone has described Maya hieroglyphs as predominantly phonetic, while the Mixtec and Aztec systems are largely ideographic (18). Some Aztec codices do exist, and have largely been deciphered. In the fourteenth century, Aztec scribes combined text with illustration, using a script very different from that of the Zapotecs or Mixtecs (Martin 26). They wrote laws, maxims, myths, tax documents, rituals, and calendars. Understanding of the Aztec script was aided by virtue of the continued use of the Aztec's Nahuatl language by some Mexican tribes. A 72-page codex—the Mendoza Codex—offers historical discussion up to the point of the Spanish conquest, along with records of taxes given to the Aztec kings and discussion of the education and duties of an Aztec warrior. This codex was commissioned by a high official from Spain in the early sixteenth century, to be sent as a gift to the king of Spain. The illustrations demonstrate the extent to which the culture used clothing, decoration, and color rhetorically (Joyce 69).

In South America, particularly in Peru, ancient sophisticated cities and large pyramidal temples have been found in the Supe Valley 120 miles north of Lima (Anitel, Fountain). Radiocarbon dating "confirm[s] the emergence and development of a major cultural complex in this region during the Late Archaic period, between 3000 and 1800 calibrated calendar years BCE" (Haas 1020). Close by, two ancient murals have been discovered, dated 4,000 years ago. Remains have been discovered of what may be a very ancient *quipa* or *khipu* (elaborated knotted strings) used for recordkeeping by the Inca Empire. *Khipus* are still undeciphered, but the *Khipu* Database Project at Harvard, established in 2002 by anthropologist Gary Urton and mathematician Carrie Brezine, serves as a central storehouse and online repository for information. According to Urton, Spanish chroniclers repeatedly indicated that the Inca state records were kept in *khipus;* between fifteen and twenty transcriptions were done by the Spanish, but as yet no direct link exists with a particular *khipu* (Urton, Conversations). As Elizabeth Hill Boone notes, "Clearly visual systems of permanent communication in the New World functioned differently from those in the Old World" (20).

The writings and rhetorical principles of the ancient Mesoamericans and South Americans have not been influenced by Greek classical rhetoric; these cultures present grammars and rhetorical principles based on a supralinguistic approach to communication, and merit close attention by rhetoricians.

Do Studies of Ancient Rhetorics Need to be Comparative?

While many strong and insightful studies of ancient rhetorics have been conducted under the rubric of comparative rhetoric, a number of scholars bristle at any requirement for comparison. As much as possible, they would like to examine the texts and rhetorical approaches of an ancient culture within that culture's own framework, in its own terms, yet are often pressed by reviewers to address the similarities and differences with respect to approaches in classical rhetoric. Contemporary studies of ancient cultures and their rhetorics inevitably depend on some degree of comparison, since scholars cannot totally escape the frameworks of their cultural makeup. Yet, much recent scholarship in history, religion, and philosophy, as well as in rhetoric itself, attempts to address the conundrum by advocating approaches that can facilitate and honor such work, and undergird its reliability. The previously cited work of philosopher Paul Goldin, advocating the method of thick description, supports the intents of those rhetorical scholars who wish not to impose classical Greek categories on texts from other cultures for the sake of comparison. Similarly, Sue Hum and Arabella Lyon argue for a deeply descriptive methodology, situating a text in its cultural and historical milieu, holding back on theorizing in early stages of study. In addition, a 2000 article by Robert Shuter advocates what he calls an intercultural approach to rhetorical criticism, meant to enable more accurate analyses of cultures. The fifth of his five proposals to achieve this goal involves a method that "resists comparative rhetorical criticism, opting instead for discourse analysis within a country or coculture" (Shuter 16). He goes on to explain that the scholar should develop "a deep understanding of the culture that produced the discourse," and thus be prepared to "observe nuances in the discourse." Based upon such "grounded studies," he argues that responsible rhetorical theories about other cultures can be developed (16).

The example from Mesopotamian studies can be instructive for rhetoricians who undertake study of ancient non-Greek cultures. In Mesopotamian studies, the main effort has involved what is called 'establishing the archive' (Snell 115). The effort is based on a positivistic sense that the phenomena under study need to be fully listed and described, before meaning can be made of the evidence. As Roberta Binkley and I discovered in putting together the first volume addressing ancient rhetorics in 2004, this approach can lead to eighty-page articles that simply list and descriptively characterize items on a particular subject, with no attempt at making meaning of the phenomena under discussion. Such long, descriptive lists are common in that field, and can be placed in Mesopotamian studies publications without any problem. In our case, one such lengthy article would overwhelm a collection with page limits imposed by the publisher,, and such a list would not prove of much interest or significance to readers in the field of rhetorical studies. In the end, we parted ways with the particular author and essay involved. Within Mesopotamian studies, M. Van de

Mieroop has deplored that field's positivist inclinations as going too
far in discouraging generalization and theorization (304). Hallo has
also urged his Mesopotamian studies colleagues to hazard hypotheses
(188–89). I would hope that studies of ancient rhetorics do not adopt
that particular extreme as a model of scholarship in order to avoid the
very real problems of comparative scholarship. I would also hope that
studies that cross many cultures would continue to be welcomed, as
long as these are done knowledgeably and sensitively, and as long as
these do not jump quickly to large-scale theoretical claims.

If Not Comparative Rhetoric, Then What?

Given the concern about connotations of the term and about effects
of some of the practices associated with comparative rhetoric, a need
arises for an alternate term. Several possibly suitable terms exist to describe rhetorical study that examines rhetorics of different cultures. I
will address here three such terms that offer differing combinations of
culture and rhetoric: cultural rhetoric, rhetoric culture, and rhetorical
culture. As a faculty member in a doctoral program titled composition
and cultural rhetoric, I am inclined to use the term *cultural rhetoric* to
describe the work I do. Yet, I do not do so without consideration of
other possible terms.

The term *cultural rhetoric* has entered the field of rhetorical studies
through the scholarship of Steven Mailloux, particularly in *Reception
Histories* (1998), where he presents a definition of cultural rhetoric with
an underlying political focus: "A study of cultural rhetoric attempts to
read the tropes, arguments, and narratives of its object texts (whether
literary or nonliterary) within their sociopolitical contexts of cultural
production and reception" (186). That is, for Mailloux, rhetoric focuses on texts, and within texts, on the rhetorical practices of tropes,
arguments, and narratives as these reflect and affect social and political structures and practices within cultures. Faculty members of the
Syracuse University doctoral program in cultural rhetoric have widely
differing interpretations of the term *cultural rhetoric*—not all so politically focused, and certainly not all so intent upon tropes, narratives,
or even arguments. But all do see rhetorics as intimately connected to
the cultures they arise in, and as constituting and affecting cultures
as well as being constituted by cultures. So the term has already been
used outside of Mailloux's definition, and he has written publicly that
this "does not bother me" (167).

In recent years, a project within the field of anthropology has adopted the term *rhetoric culture* to describe a collaborative investigation exploring the reciprocal relation and interaction between rhetoric and culture. Begun by Ivo Strecker and Steven Tyler, the project looks at "rhetoric [as] founded in culture, [while] culture is founded in rhetoric" (Strecker 2). The founders announce the intent to explore the ways that rhetoric might explain cultures, and the ways that cultures are performed, contested, and reproduced. According to Michael Carrithers, their project examines international rhetorics and cultures, by turning to the "rich heritage" of rhetorical theories to illuminate understanding of cultures. Their project outline mainly cites works by Greek and Roman rhetoricians, as well as later thinkers such as Von Humboldt, Vico, and Burke. As evidenced in their project outline, much of their concern involves tropes and metaphors in culture. Significantly, Carrithers reports in his discussion of the 2002 project meeting, which included some rhetoricians as well as anthropologists, that the anthropologists were quite uncomfortable with the political and critical orientation of the rhetorical analyses of cultural texts by rhetoricians. The anthropologists' concern was more to speak for and represent the culture under investigation, and its members—not to examine the culture and its rhetorical manifestations critically. The term *rhetoric culture*, as used by the anthropologists, thus defines an approach and intent that may not apply to many projects in the rhetoric field. Additionally, the focus of their term is more on culture than it is on rhetoric, with culture in the prominent nominal position.

A related term connecting rhetoric and culture is used within the field of rhetoric: rhetorical culture. This term is used most prominently by Thomas Farrell in his book *Norms of Rhetorical Culture* (1993). While the book does not explicitly define the term, it does make clear its understanding that a rhetorical culture is "a culture that fosters an appreciative understanding of [rhetorical] practice" (11) and develops condition and conventions that make norms available to practice (7). In particular, Farrell is concerned that such rhetorical practice—which he argues should be based on Greek rhetorical tradition—can produce "a responsible practice of civic life" (11). His goal is a rhetorical culture of *communitas* (12). Thus, Farrell's term *rhetorical culture* calls for a particular kind of rhetorical practice—one that fosters "ethically significant conduct within any culture," (10) and which fosters a culture open to critical reflection of its foundations, to public challenges, and to contestations. This term, then, while attractive in its combination of culture and rhetoric, carries presuppositions that do not and cannot apply to ancient non-democratic cultures.

All in all, Mailloux's term *cultural rhetoric* seems more suitable and applicable for scholarly work that examines rhetorics of different cultures and subcultures, and in the case of this volume, work that examines ancient non-Western rhetorics, when such work gives close attention to the cultural and particular historical settings for each of the rhetorics. The term avoids the potential dangers accompanying the term comparative rhetoric. And since Mailloux has already welcomed some modification of the focus of his term, there would be no violation of Mailloux's prerogative to use it more broadly.

RETHINKING OF CLASSICAL RHETORIC AS RELATED TO STUDY OF ANCIENT CULTURAL RHETORICS.

In recent studies of Greco-Roman rhetoric, scholars have been pointing to the need to examine visual and material elements, as well as performative elements, in addition to text. A 2005 symposium in Pittsburgh, organized by Debra Hawhee and Don Bialostosky, was titled Revisionist Classical Rhetorics. Essays arising from the symposium are published in the spring 2006 issue of *Rhetoric Society Quarterly*. Two of the essays—by Hawhee herself and by James Fredal—illustrate such calls for attention to multiple media, the visual and spatial means for communication, as well as bodily performance. Hawhee's essay builds on her book titled *Bodily Arts,* which argues that in classical times, rhetoric "was and is a bodily art," and just as athletes performed at festivals, so too did rhetors. She points to the powerful performative rhetoric of athletics in ancient Greece, and cites Wayne C. Booth's recent book titled *The Rhetoric of Rhetoric,* which redefines rhetoric as including "the entire range of resources that human beings share for producing effects on one another" (158). Booth's definition thus includes visual media, new media, material elements, as well as human "bodies and faces"—anything that can be used for rhetorical effect. Similarly, based on his book titled *Rhetorical Action in Ancient Athens,* Fredal argues for the need to attend to spaces for rhetorical performance—to structures and locations—as part of the communicative force. And he argues for inclusion of multiple media—spaces, structures, and sight, and more generally "cultural processes for symbolic exchange"—as important components for rhetorical study.

Such arguments are particularly germane for ancient cultures, where literacy rates were low and much was communicated visually. Early societies adopted a wide range of avenues for broad communication and for rhetorical effect. Mary Garrett suggested that traditional Chinese culture supplemented spoken and written communication with a range of "symbol systems, from posture, behaviors, clothing, and ornamentation to music, art, and architecture, . . . to express and reinforce cultural values . . ." (55). John Hammerback, in 2000, argued forcefully for the need to attend to the visual as well as text in studying Near Eastern communication from Mesopotamia (166). I have argued for the rhetorical force of the interrelations of text and visuals in ancient Egyptian public texts (2003), and argue for the rhetoricity of spatial design in ancient Egyptian tombs in this volume. Ancient Egyptian as well as ancient Chinese and Japanese writings are based on characters that have powerful artistic elements (Fischer 205), and that are positioned within communication systems based on strong culturally based principles of decorum. Mesoamerican texts also combine script and visuals integrally. Beyond the combination of script and visuals, architecture and ritual offered powerful means for communication and social effect in ancient cultures, especially since literacy was not widespread. As Baines and Yoffee write of ancient Egypt and ancient Mesopotamia, "High culture is a communicative complex" (236). The wide range of communicative media merit study and consideration as rhetorical in nature, and as carrying the potential to produce significant effects on societal members.

Of course, not all participants in the 2005 symposium were comfortable with such inclusions. Susan Jarratt notes consequences of the discipline's increased emphasis on other areas, away from language. For one thing, given such new directions, rhetoricians will now have to develop expertise in other relevant disciplines. For another, Jarratt notes that the new emphasis seems quite distant from rhetoric's historical concern with the function of rhetorical education in relation to the student/rhetor as citizen, with the traditional aim of rhetorical education "to cultivate a person 'with sophisticated skills in ethico-political thought and speech'" (217).

While I have great sympathy with Jarratt's goal of helping to prepare students for ethical and active citizenship, I would also note that the more students understand rhetorical effect in all its possible forms and media, the more prepared they are to be reflective about such effects on them. I fully recognize the additional demands on scholars and teachers of rhetoric, but am also convinced that such understandings are crucial to thoughtful, critically based participation in what has become a heavily multi-mediated environment.

What's Coming in this Collection?

Included in this collection are a variety of essays presenting new scholarship on ancient non-Greek rhetorics. The major areas of focus include Near Eastern rhetorics, Far Eastern rhetorics, as well as one ancient Western rhetoric that experienced minimal influence from classical rhetoric. This includes new work on religious rhetorics of the ancient Near East, examining genres—especially prophecies and rituals—that have received little attention in rhetorical studies to date, as well as examining material and multimedia dimensions of rhetorical communication. The section on the ancient Near East also includes a new study of the Hebrew Bible, demonstrating its presentation of a particular theory of rhetoric. The volume also includes studies of ancient Chinese rhetoric that move beyond the Confucian period to attend to the rich and diverse historical manifestations over time. One essay also examines ancient Japanese rhetoric, which has not been much studied to date. A third section examines the rhetoric of ancient India, with one essay examining an ancient Hindu narrative text from a rhetorical perspective, another examining the approaches used to present a counter-intuitive argument by an ancient scholar/teacher. Finally, a fourth section offers a study of ancient Irish rhetoric, as found in major cycles of myths. Essays in each of these sections are described briefly below.

Roberta and I very much regret two gaps in this coverage—pre-Islamic Arab rhetoric, and ancient Mesoamerican and South American rhetorics. We attempted to find scholars to write on each, and delayed submission of the manuscript to allow extra time to facilitate this, but in the end we were unsuccessful, largely due to the small numbers of scholars working in these areas and the many writing commitments they already faced.

Religious Rhetoric of the Ancient Near East

The first essay in this section, by James Watts, examines the rhetoric surrounding ritual performance in the ancient Near East, first by looking at ways that texts are constructed to persuade audiences to perform or avoid particular behaviors, as well as then by examining the rhetorical ways that ancient Near Eastern texts use rituals. Watts covers texts from a range of cultures in the Ancient Near East, including Mesopotamia, Babylonia, Assyria, Mari, Egypt, Akkadia, Phoenicia, Lycia, the Hittite culture, and ancient Israel. Given that rituals served powerful cultural functions to strengthen and undergird kingdoms, societies, and beliefs, such attention to the rhetorical action and rhetorical bases of ritual in these ancient cultures is extremely valuable. In his essay, Watts notes that in Greek rhetorical theories, there is no attention to "religious rhetorical genres such as oracles, sermons, ritual instructions and prayers." Yet, these persuasive genres had great impact in the lives of ancient peoples.

The second essay attending to religious rhetoric in the ancient Near East, by Roberta Binkley, responds to the concern raised by Watts, and to the recent (2006) call by Laurent Pernot for the field of rhetorical studies to expand its attention to a broader range of religious genres, including prayers, hymns, and prophecies. Binkley examines the genre of ancient prophecy, generally neglected in rhetorical study. She focuses specifically on the participation of female prophets in the broad range of cultures that form the ancient Near East, including Mesopotamia, Mari, Assyria, and ancient Israel, as well as Delphi.

The third essay, by Carol Lipson, devotes attention to rhetorical communication in one particular ancient Near Eastern culture: ancient Egypt. This chapter examines the beliefs and handling of provincial elite tombs in the eighteenth dynasty (1539—1350 BCE), focusing on the combination of text, visuals, and architectural design as experienced sequentially by the viewer in moving through the public portion of the tomb. Lipson argues that the ancient Egyptian tomb in this period is a fundamentally rhetorical project, aiming to persuade visitors to read the offering formulae in order to preserve the identity and viability of the deceased in the afterlife.

In the fourth essay examining ancient Near Eastern rhetorical culture, Steven Katz looks at the epistemic focus of a philosophy of rhetoric embodied in the ancient Hebrew Bible. Katz terms this a rhetorical theory of uncertainty. Based on analyses by Jack Miles, Katz argues that the order of the Hebrew Bible evinces a withdrawal of God's immediate voice; the basic principles become *written* in the ten commandments rather than *spoken* by God to the Israelites. In the narrative structure of the Hebrew Bible, God's last words are to Job, following which God's voice is silent, leaving a sense of eternal uncertainty and anxiety. According to Katz, the language of the Hebrew Bible becomes a substitute—a rhetorical simulacrum: a sacred language that embodies something of the divine. Katz argues that the Hebrew Bible celebrates "the ambiguity and power of language and the uncertainty of language." Language is presented—in God's use—as having the power to create reality. As Katz points out, the Hebrew word (*dvar*) for 'speak' is also the word for 'thing.' To speak is to accomplish an act in the world with no need for persuasion—a very distinctive and sophistic theory of rhetoric quite different from that of ancient Greece.

Rhetorical Studies of the Ancient Far East

Two essays in this section examine facets of ancient Chinese rhetoric, followed by one that looks at rhetoric in ancient Japan. Scholars have advocated the need for rhetorical scholarship on China to move beyond the fifth to third centuries BCE (Lu, "Influence" 4; Lu, *Rhetoric* 7, 29, 289; Lu in Wang 179; Garrett in Wang 178). As Yameng Liu pointed out in 1996, as "a culturally based rhetoric," Chinese rhetoric "is necessarily multifaceted and its development is correlated with changing social conditions and historical circumstances" (322). Both essays on the rhetoric of ancient China in this volume respond to these concerns.

First, Yichun Liu and Xiaoye You examine Dong Zhongshu's rhetorical theory as it extended and revised pre-imperial Confucian rhetoric, three hundred years following the death of Confucius. Basing his reformulated rhetorical theory on a Confucian text—the *Spring and Autumn Annals*—Dong added heaven as a dominant participant in discourse, advocating state rituals to enact such a relationship with heaven and advocating that the educational system train scholars in this approach. They point out that Dong thus led to a long-lived imperial academy dedicated to the study of Confucius in China, though Dong substantially modified Confucian theory.

In the second essay on ancient Chinese rhetoric, Arabella Lyon moves beyond seeking concepts in Confucian theory that have similarities to concepts in classical rhetoric. She examines concepts that cross different periods and different schools of thought in ancient China, including Confucian thought, Legalistic thought, and Daoism, with differences in the ways that these concepts are understood in each school. The two concepts are quite different from a Western understanding of rhetoric centered on persuasion. Significantly, the concepts she looks at are not textual in nature, are "invisible to the traditions of the West," but are central to understanding Chinese rhetoric traditions in her view. She argues, based on IA Richards, that the effort of understanding a very different culture and conceptual system requires the creation of a third system of thought—outside of the two being compared. Lyon's essay embodies and demonstrates a serious attempt to follow such an approach.

The field of rhetorical studies has not devoted much attention to rhetorical concepts and practices in ancient Japan, though some studies have examined communication in modern-day Japan. We are very fortunate in this volume to include a study of Shinto and Shingon Buddhist rhetoric by Katherine Wolfe. While the earliest writing in Japan followed the exposure to Chinese writing in the fifth century AD, Wolfe argues that the Japanese had agency in the choices they made in adopting principles of Chinese writing systems and Chinese culture, based on fit and appropriateness to Japanese culture, and based on the power benefits to rulers. With no texts existing that directly present a rhetorical philosophy, Wolfe examines the philosophy of language and communication inherent in ancient Shinto and Shingon Buddhist religions, as a window into early rhetorical practices and concepts in Japan. Here, communication practices involved not just human-to-human communication, but ways of communing with the universe. The ancient Japanese rulers are shown to have fashioned myths to promote their legitimacy and power, along with complex ethical principles. They developed associated practices for addressing the gods, since proper style was considered crucial for the power of prayer; in practice, this led to the rise of intermediaries—priests—to present prayers on behalf of ordinary people. Shingon Buddhism built on the Shinto understanding of the power and need for proper style in using language for efficacy, but with different audiences, purposes, and practices, especially involving the possibility of participation by any member of the culture. In both cases, writing was understood to be incapable of influencing the gods and effecting desired results, and in Shingon Buddhism, of capturing essential meanings. At the end of the article, Wolfe relates the principles found in early Shinto and Shingon Buddhist practice to principles and usages in twentieth century Japan.

Rhetoric from Ancient India

Mari Lee Mifsud, in an essay examining Valmiki's epic titled *Ramayana,* focuses on story telling as a rhetorical act. Addressing story telling as a gift exchange in ancient Hindu culture, Mifsud argues that the story is presented as a gift from the god Brahma, as is the verse form; in exchange, Valmiki is asked to create the narrative to bring ancient Hindu culture into harmony with the divine, with *dharma*. Through the story telling, *dharma* is presented in the epic in didactic forms, as the characters work through a dilemma for a *dharmic* end. Mifsud points to the widespread reflexiveness about the act of story telling in the work, so that the epic in part offers a rhetoric of story telling, involving issues of invention, performance, memory, and delivery.

In the next essay, Scott Stroud examines the handling of argument in a particular school of classical Indian philosophy—Advaita Vedanta—as seen in the works of an influential proponent named Sankara. Stroud looks at Sankara's educative rhetoric, particularly his ways of handling methods of rational argument to defend a doctrine that would seem to violate logic—that is, that all objects in the world are illusory. In this tricky situation, Sankara is shown to use experiential arguments, including examples and analogies that bring the reader/listener to experience an illusion as real. That is, Stroud shows that Sankara brings his audience to experiences that confirm the position he argues.

Western Non-Greek Rhetoric: Ancient Ireland

Finally, Richard Johnson-Sheehan contributes an essay that looks at a Western culture that was minimally influenced by Greco-Roman culture. Here, we have collections of writings, with four cycles presenting myths relating historical narratives of gods and men. Each of the four cycles of stories is set in a different province of Ireland. Johnson-Sheehan argues that these stories, as performed by ancient Celtic poets (bards) or priests (druids) functioned to transmit and strengthen adherence to core cultural values and beliefs, particularly the values of courage, loyalty, generosity, and beauty. The narratives, recited by traveling performers, offer numerous examples in which those who demonstrate these values succeed, and those who are deficient in the core values fail. Notably, bards and druids served to judge disputes as part of their duties. Thus, they not only promulgated values and principles fundamental to the culture in the myths they composed, elaborated, and performed, which served also as historical narratives of the culture, but they also served judgments based upon those values and principles, offering further ballast for adherence to the principles. Thus, the prime function of the texts (oral and written) involved reinforcing societal consensus, belief, and action regarding the culture's core values.

NOTES

1. Similarly, Yameng Liu, in a well-known 1996 article published in *Rhetoric Review,* addressed the difficulties arising for contemporary rhetorical study when translators and anthologists have little understanding of and familiarity with the field of rhetoric as understood by current scholarship.

2. As quoted by Soliman Lawrence in 2006 on a website titled Translating Worlds: Studies in early Chinese philosophy, accessed on February 21, 2008: http://www.sas.upenn.edu/home/SASFrontiers/goldin.html.

WORKS CITED

Anitel, Stefan. "The Oldest Construction in America—4,000 Years Old." 13 Nov. 2007. 22 Feb. 2008 <http://news.softpedia.com/news/The-Oldest-Construction-in-America-70677.shtml>.

Baines, John, and Norman Yoffee. "Order, Legitimacy, and Wealth in Ancient Egypt and Mesopotamia." *Archaic States.* Ed. Gary Feinman and Joyce Marcus. Santa Fe, NM: School of American Research Press, 1998. 199–260.

Borgen, Robert. "The Politics of Classical Chinese in the Early Japanese Court." *Rhetoric and the Discourses of Power in Court Culture: China, Europe, and Japan.* Ed. David Knechtges and Eugene Vance. Seattle: U of Washington P, 2005. 199–238.

Boone, Elizabeth Hill. "Introduction: Writing and Recorded Knowledge in Pre-Columbian America." Ed. Elizabeth Hill Boone and Walter D. Mignolo. *Writing without Words.* Durham: Duke UP, 1994. 3-26.

Carrithers, Michael. "Rhetoric? Culture? Rhetoric Culture! A Report," *Durham Anthropology Journal* 13.2 (2005). 31 July 2008. <http://www.dur.ac.uk/anthropology.journal/vol13/iss2/carrithers/carrithers.html>.

Chavalas, Mark. "The Age of Empires, 3100–900 BCE." *A Companion to the Ancient Near East.* Ed. Daniel Snell. Oxford, UK: Blackwell, 2007, 34–47.

Christin, Anne-Marie, ed. *A History of Writing: from Hieroglyph to Multimedia.* Paris: Flammarion, 2002.

Coe, Michael and Justin Kerr. *The Art of the Mayan Scribe.* New York: Harry Abrams Pub., 1997.

Falk, Erika. "Jewish Laws of Speech: Toward Multicultural Rhetoric." *Howard Journal of Communication* 10.1 (1999): 15–28.

Farrell, Thomas. *Norms of Rhetorical Culture.* New Haven, CT: Yale UP, 1993.

Feinman, Gary, and Joyce Marcus, eds. *Archaic States.* Santa Fe, NM: School of American Research Press, 1998.

Fountain, Henry. "Archaeological Site in Peru Is Called Oldest City in Americas." *The New York Times,* April 27, 2001.

Fredal, James. "Seeing Ancient Rhetoric, Easily at a Glance." *Rhetoric Society Quarterly* 36.2 (2006): 181–89.

Garrett, Mary. "Some Elementary Methodological Reflections on the Study of the Chinese Rhetorical Tradition." *Rhetoric in Intercultural Contexts.* Ed. Alberto Gonzales and Dolores Tanno. Thousand Oaks, CA: Sage, 2000. 53–63.

Goldin, Paul. *After Confucius: Studies in Early Chinese Philosophy.* Honolulu: U of Hawaii P, 2005.

Gonzales, Alberto and Dolores Tanno. *Rhetoric in Intercultural Contexts.* Thousand Oaks, CA: Sage, 2000.

Haas, Jonathan, Winifred Creamer, and Alvaro Ruiz. "Dating the Late Archaic Occupation of the Norte Chico Region in Peru." *Nature* 23–30 (Dec. 2004): 1020–1023.

Hall, David. "What Has Athens to Do with Alexandria? Or Why Sinologists Can't Get Along without Philosophers." *Early China/Ancient Greece: Thinking through Comparisons.* Ed. Steven Shankman and Stephen Durrant. Albany: SUNY P, 2002. 15–34.

Hallo, William. "The Limits of Skepticism," *Journal of the American Oriental Society* 110 (1990): 187–199.

Hammerback, John. "Future Research on Rhetoric and Intercultural Communication: Moving Forward from Starosta's 'Intersection.'" *Rhetoric in Intercultural Contexts.* Ed. Alberto Gonzales and Dolores Tanno. Thousand Oaks,CA: Sage, 2000, 163–67.

Hawhee, Debra. "Rhetoric, Bodies, and Everyday Life." *Rhetoric Society Quarterly* 36.2 (2006): 155–64.

Hum, Sue, and Arabella Lyon. "Advances in Comparative Rhetorical Studies." *The Handbook of Rhetoric.* Ed. Jim Aune and Andrea Lunsford. Thousand Oaks, CA: Sage, in press.

Jarratt, Susan. "A Matter of Emphasis." *Rhetoric Society Quarterly* 36.2 (2006): 213–19.

Joyce, Rosemary. "High Culture, Mesoamerican Civilization, and the Classic Maya Tradition." *Order, Legitimacy, and Wealth in Ancient States.* Ed.

Janet Richards and Mary Van Buren. Cambridge, UK: Cambridge UP, 2000.

Junge, Friedrich. "Language." *Oxford Encyclopedia of Ancient Egypt.* Ed.Donald Redford. New York: Oxford UP, 2001. 258–67.

Katz, Steven. "Letter as Essence: The Rhetorical (Im)Pulse of the Hebrew Alefbet." Ed. David Franks. *Journal of Communication and Religion.* Special Issue on Jewish Rhetoric. 26.2. (2003): 126–62.

Kelly, John. "Writing and the State: China, India, and General Definitions." *Margins of Writing, Origins of Cultures.* Ed. Seth Sanders. Chicago: The Oriental Institute, U of Chicago P, 2006. 15–32.

Kennedy, George. *New Testament Interpretation through Rhetorical Criticism.* Chapel Hill, NC: U of North Carolina P, 1984.

Kenoyer, Jonathan. "Wealth and Socioeconomic Hierarchies of the Indus Valley Civilizations." *Order, Legitimacy, and Wealth in Ancient States.* Ed. Janet Richards and Mary Van Buren.: Cambridge, UK: Cambridge UP, 2000. 88–109.

Knechtges, David, and Eugene Vance, eds. *Rhetoric and the Discourses of Power in Court Culture: China, Europe, and Japan.* Seattle: U of Washington P, 2005.

Kuhrt, Amelie. *The Ancient Near East c. 3000–300 BC.* Vol 1. London: Routledge, 1995.

Lipson, Carol. "Recovering the Multimedia History of Writing in the Public Texts of Ancient Egypt." *Eloquent Images.* Ed. Mary Hocks and Michelle Kendrick. Boston: MIT P, 2003. 89–115.

Lipson, Carol, and Roberta Binkley, eds. *Rhetoric Before and Beyond the Greeks.* Albany: SUNY P, 2004.

Liu, Yameng. "To Capture the Essence of Chinese Rhetoric: An Anatomy of a Paradigm in Comparative Rhetoric." *Rhetoric Review* 14.2 (Spring 1996): 318-35.

Liverani, Mario. "Historical Overview." *A Companion to the Ancient Near East,* Ed. Daniel Snell. Oxford, UK: Blackwell, 2007. 3–19.

Longhena, Maria. *Maya Script: A Civilization and Its Writing.* Trans. Rosanna Giammanco Frongia. New York: Abbeville Press, 2000.

Lu, Xing. "Comparative Studies of Chinese and Western Rhetorics: Reflections and Challenges." *Chinese Communication Theory and Research.* Ed. Wenshan Jia, Xing Lu, and D. Ray Heisey. Westport, CT: Ablex, 2002. 105–20.

—. *Rhetoric in Ancient China, Fifth to Third Century BCE: A Comparison with Classical Greek Rhetoric.* Columbia: U of South Carolina P, 1998.

—."Studies and Development of Comparative Rhetoric in the U.S.A.: Chinese and Western Rhetoric in Focus." *China Media Research* 2.2 (2006): 112–16.

—. "The Influence of Classical Chinese Rhetoric on Contemporary Chinese Political Communication and Social Relations." *Chinese Perspectives on Rhetorical Communication.* Ed. D. Ray Heisey. Stamford, CT: Ablex Pub., 2000. 3–23.

Mailloux, Steven. *Reception Histories: Rhetoric, Pragmatism, and American Cultural Politics.* Cornell UP: Ithaca, NY, 1998.

Mao, LuMing. "Reflective Encounters: Illustrating Comparative Rhetoric." *Style* 37.4 (2003): 401–25.

Melville, Sarah. "Royal Women and the Exercise of Power in the Ancient Near East." *A Companion to the Ancient Near East.* Ed. Daniel Snell. Oxford, UK: Blackwell, 2007. 233–44.

Metzger, David. "Pentateuchal Rhetoric and the Voice of the Aaronides." *Rhetoric Before and Beyond the Greeks.* Ed. Carol Lipson and Roberta Binkley. Albany: SUNY P, 2004. 165–81.

Michalowski, Piotr. "The Lives of the Sumerian Language." *Margins of Writing, Origins of Cultures.* Ed. Seth Sanders. Chicago: The Oriental Institute, U of Chicago P, 2006. 159–84.

Muilenburg, James. "Form Criticism and Beyond." *Journal of Biblical Literature* 88 (1969): 1–18.

Neville, Robert Cummngs. *The Human Condition: A Volume in the Comparative Religious Ideas Project.* Albany: SUNY P, 2001.

Pardee, Dennis. "Review: Scripture in Context: Essays on the Comparative Method." *Journal of Near Eastern Studies* 44.3 (1985): 220–22.

Pernot, Laurent. "The Rhetoric of Religion." *Rhetorica* 24.3 (2006): 235–54.

Possehl, Gregory. "Sociocultural Complexity without the State: The Indus Civilization." *Archaic States.* Ed. Gary Feinman and Joyce Marcus. Santa Fe, NM: School of American Research P, 1998. 261–91.

Richards, Janet, and Mary Van Buren, eds. *Order, Legitimacy, and Wealth in Ancient States, New Directions in Archaeology:* Cambridge UP, 2000.

Roscoe, Paul. "Chapter 2: The Comparative Method." *The Blackwell Companion to the Study of Religion.* Ed. Robert Segal. New York: Wiley-Blackwell, 2006. 25–46.

Royster, Jacqueline Jones. "Disciplinary Landscaping, or Contemporary Challenges in the History of Rhetoric." *Philosophy and Rhetoric* 36.2 (2003): 148–67.

Sanders, Seth, ed. *Margins of Writing, Origins of Cultures, Oriental Institute Seminars.* Chicago: U of Chicago P, 2006.

Sasson, Jack, ed. *Civilizations of the Ancient Near East.* 4 vols. Peabody, MA: Hendrickson Pub., 2000.

Scheidel, Walter. The Stanford Ancient Chinese and Mediterranean Empires Comparative History Project (Acme). 19 Oct. 2007 <http://www.stanford.edu/~scheidel/acme.htm>.

Segal, Robert. "In Defense of the Comparative Method." *Numen* 48 (2001): 339–73.

—, ed. *The Blackwell Companion to the Study of Religion*. New York: Wiley-Blackwell, 2006.

Sen, Amartya. *The Argumentative Indian: Writings on Indian History, Culture and Identity*. New York: Picador, 2005.

Shankman, Steven, and Stephen Durrant, eds. *Early China/Ancient Greece: Thinking through Comparisons*. Albany: SUNY P, 2002.

Sharma, Arvind. *Religious Studies and Comparative Methodology: The Case for Reciprocal Illumination*. Albany: SUNY P, 2005.

Shuter, Robert. "The Cultures of Rhetoric." *Rhetoric in Intercultural Contexts*. Ed. Alberto Gonzales and Dolores Tanno. Thousand Oaks, CA: Sage, 2000. 11-17.

Snell, Daniel. "The Historian's Task." *A Companion to the Ancient Near East*. Ed. Daniel Snell. Oxford, UK: Blackwell, 2007, 110-21.

—, ed. *A Companion to the Ancient Near East*. Oxford, UK: Blackwell, 2007.

Strecker, Ivo, and Christian Meyer. "International Rhetoric Culture Project—Outline." Jan. 2003. 31 July 2008 <http://www.rhetoricculture.org/outline.htm>

Urton, Gary. "Conversations: String Theorist." 2005. 3 Feb 2008 < http://www.archaeology.org/0511/etc/conversations.htm>.

Urton, Gary and Carrie Brezine. "The Khipu Database Project."2004. 3 Feb 2008 < http://khipukamayuq.fas.harvard.edu/DatabaseProj.html >.

Van de Mieroop, M. *Cuneiform Texts and the Writing of History*. London: Routledge, 1999.

—. "On Writing a History of the Ancient Near East." *Bibliotheca Orientalis* 54 (1997).

Wang, Bo. "A Survey of Research in Asian Rhetoric." *Rhetoric Review* 23.2 (2004): 171–81.

Watts, James. *Reading Law: The Rhetorical Shaping of the Pentateuch*. Sheffield: Sheffield, 1999.

—. *Ritual and Rhetoric in Leviticus: From Sacrifice to Scripture*. New York: Cambridge UP, 2007.

—. "The Torah as the Rhetoric of Priesthood." *The Reception of the Torah in the Second Temple Period*. Ed. Bernard Levinson and Gary Knoppers. Winona Lake, IN: Eisenbrauns, 2007. 319–32

Wente, Edward. "Scripts: Hieratic." *Oxford Encyclopedia of Ancient Egypt*. Ed. Donald Redford. New York: Oxford UP, 2001. 206–10.

Wildman, Wesley. "Appendix A: On the Process of the Project During the First Year." *The Human Condition*. Ed. Robert Cummngs Neville. Albany: SUNY P, 2001. 267–86.

Religious Rhetoric of the Ancient Near East

2 Ritual Rhetoric in Ancient Near Eastern Texts

James W. Watts

Texts from many ancient cultures describe and prescribe ritual behavior. They also invoke ritual acts and omissions to explain the course of past history and to promise future punishments and rewards. In fact, very many texts assert that ritual performance is the most determinative factor in the success or failure of rulers and nations. Ritual rhetoric therefore pervaded royal propaganda, as well as temple texts. It also provided the principal rationale for criticizing the status quo.

Human rituals tend to be accompanied by a concern with "doing it exactly right," as has often been remarked (Freud 1907; Staal 1979; Smith 1987). Ironically, that concern does not preclude the ubiquity of ritual improvisation and criticism (Grimes 1990). Roy A. Rappaport (36–37, 124–26) has emphasized the role in all ritual performances of the criterion of ritual invariance on the one hand and, on the other hand, the inevitability of both historical change and individual choice.

Ancient Near Eastern texts reflect this common human concern for ritual accuracy. They depict ancient kings justifying their ritual practices on the basis of supposedly invariable tradition and, frequently, on the basis of old ritual texts. Thus, the ritual rhetoric of ancient texts not only provides a window into the rhetorical practices of ancient cultures. The texts themselves were also ritual products—written, read and manipulated to shape ritual performances and to pronounce judgment on the performers.

In what follows, I will first survey the use of ritual rhetoric for persuasive purposes in texts of diverse genres and cultures of the ancient Near East before considering the persuasive function of ritual texts *per se*. I follow Aristotle and Kenneth Burke in defining rhetoric in terms of persuasion because this definition grounds the rhetorical analysis of many ancient Near Eastern texts in one of their most obvious features:

an explicitly stated intention to mandate and/or prohibit certain behaviors on the part of their readers or hearers. On the basis of persuasion, rhetorical analysis of non-Western texts can bypass the quagmire of debates over whether particular texts are, or are not, "literary" and how Quintilian's criterion of "speaking well" can and should be applied to written documents. By starting with persuasion and with texts that state their persuasive goals explicitly, the cross-cultural study of rhetoric finds a firm footing. Once the rhetorical role of ritual has been observed there, it can be evaluated better in the less explicitly persuasive contexts of ritual texts and their ritual use.

Of course, the category "ritual," like "rhetoric," does not reflect an indigenous ancient Near Eastern category. It is, rather, a modern heuristic device for distinguishing and describing certain kinds of human behavior. Ritual theorists disagree among themselves about the definitions and limits of ritual. I find most useful the description of ritual proposed by Jonathan Z. Smith, who argued that rituals draw attention to, and make intentional, otherwise ordinary practices. Thus, ritual turns everyday routines such as washing oneself, entering and leaving a room, and eating meals into deeply meaningful practices by focusing attention on them, formalizing them and, often, by prescribing exactly how they get done (Smith 1987a, 193–95; 1987b, 109; see also Bell 1997, 138–69). Rituals are often religious, but not inherently so. Though ancient rituals usually involved deities or other supernatural spirits in one way or another, many rituals did not (e.g., compare the various Akkadian incantations translated by Foster 2005, 954–1014.) Conversely, though prophets usually demanded ritual payments to the temples of their patron deities, sometimes they required kings to honor their gods by enforcing justice instead (see Mari letters A. 1121/2731 and A. 1968, tr. Níssínen 2003, 19–20, 22). Thus, the categories of ritual and religion overlap to a great degree, but are not congruent either for antiquity or modernity.

By "ritual texts," then, I mean texts that describe or prescribe rituals. By "ritual rhetoric," I refer to a wider range of statements that invoke either ritual behavior itself or the institutions that sponsor ritual behavior (temples, priesthoods, etc.) for persuasive purposes. My argument is that ritual rhetoric, like the categories "political rhetoric" or "legal rhetoric," provides a useful lens for understanding certain themes in persuasive discourse. "Ritual rhetoric" does not here refer to the persuasive impact of the ancient rituals themselves. That is lost to us; all we have left are texts that mention rituals. Therefore all we can reconstruct is the rhetorical use to which those texts put rituals. It is beyond the ability of modern historians to reconstruct whether or not the authors' persuasive purposes matched those of any of the people who performed or witnessed these rituals (Watts 2007, 1–36). Ancient texts, however, frequently employ ritual rhetoric for explicitly stated reasons. I will therefore start with the wider category of ritual rhetoric to lay the basis for understanding the rhetoric of ritual texts per se, as well as the ritual uses of the texts themselves.

Ritual Rhetoric

The standard justifications made by ancient kings to legitimize their rule were that they established peace in the land by repelling enemies, and that they built and/or restored temples, their furnishings and their rituals. Ritual spaces and practices often played as big a role in political propaganda as did military successes. The two themes were frequently conjoined: warfare established the conditions (wealth from booty and trade), as well as the rationale (thanksgiving to the gods) for celebrating and elaborating temple cults, and ritual sometimes provided the pretext for warfare (to return a stolen god to its temple, or to punish a regime for neglecting its gods). Thus, ritual rhetoric reinforced political claims to power.

Royal inscriptions do not always base their claims to a divine right to rule on the kings' activities in temple building and ritual supplies, but they do so often enough and from enough different periods and places to regard this as a standard theme of royal ideology. Philippe Talon (2005, 113) noted about Neo-Assyrian annals that "the inscriptions themselves are part of a well-attested ritual. They represent, in themselves, a ritual by which the king conforms to the ideal model of the perfect monarch." Examples of using ritual rhetoric for political legitimacy, however, extend far beyond that particular period and genre.

The preface to Hammurabi's law code (eighteenth century Babylonian; all dates in this article are BCE) enumerates the king's achievements by matching his military successes with temple building and cultic establishments (Roth 1995, 71–142). In the same period, Iahdun-Lim, King of Mari, claims among other things that "For his own life he built the temple of the god Shamash, his lord . . . May the god Shamash, who lives in that temple, grant to Iahdun-Lim, the builder of

his temple, the king beloved of his heart, a mighty weapon which over-
whelms the enemies (and) a long reign of happiness and years of joyous
abundance, forever" (tr. Douglas Frayne in *COS* 2.111). The Poetical
Stela of the Egyptian king Thutmose III (fifteenth century) has the
god Amun declare his responsibility for all of the king's victories and
concludes with the quid pro quo: "I gave you protection, my son, . . .
who does for me all that my *ka* desires. You have built my temple as
a work of eternity . . ." (tr. Lichtheim 1976, 2:38). The Kadesh Battle
Inscription depicts Ramses II citing his support of Amun's temples
(including "I brought you all lands to supply your altars, I sacrificed to
you ten thousands of cattle, and all kinds of sweet-scented herbs") to
appeal for the god's intervention at a desperate point in a thirteenth-
century battle (tr. Lichtheim 1976, 2:65).

The annals of the Hittite king Mursili II (fourteenth century) establish a cause-and-effect relationship between religious devotion and
military success. They begin by telling how he came to the throne as
a child, then say,

> while I had not yet gone against any of the enemy for-
> eign lands who were in a state of hostilities with me, I
> concerned myself with and performed the regular fes-
> tivals of the Sungoddess of Arinna, my lady. I held up
> my hand to the Sungoddess of Arinna, my lady, and
> said as follows: " . . . the enemy foreign lands who have
> called me a child and belittled me, have begun seeking
> to take away the borders of the Sungoddess of Arinna,
> my lady. . . ." The Sungoddess Arinna heard my words
> and stood by me.

Then, in several battle reports, the turning point is narrated in this
way: "The Sungoddes of Arinna, my lady, the victorious Stormgod,
my lord, Mezzulla and all the gods ran before me." He concludes by
vowing that "Whatever more the Sungoddess of Arinna, my lady, repeatedly gives to me (to do), I will carry it out and put it down (on
clay)" (tr. Richard H. Beal in *COS* 2.16).

Similarly, Nabopolassar's commemorative inscription for his restoration of Babylon's walls (seventh century) begins his autobiography
with:

> When I was young, though I was the son of a nobody,
> I constantly sought the sanctuaries of Nabu and Mar-

duk my lords. My mind was preoccupied with the establishment of their prescriptions and the complete
performance of their rituals. . . . The Assyrian, who
had ruled Akkad because of divine anger and had,
with his heavy yoke, oppressed the inhabitants of the
country, I, the weak one, the powerless one, who constantly seeks the lord of lords, with the mighty strength
of Nabu and Marduk my lords I removed them from
Akkad and cause (the Babylonians) to throw off their
yoke.

He concludes with the advice, "Any king . . . do not be concerned with
feats of might and power. Seek the sanctuaries of Nabu and Marduk
and let them slay your enemies" (tr. Paul-Alain Beaulieu in *COS* 2.121;
see Talon 1993 on the self-deprecating rhetoric of Nabopolasser and
other Neo-Babylonian kings).

This ideology also appears in the sun-disk tablet of Nabu-Apla-Id-
dina (ostensibly ninth century Babylonian, but probably a sixth century forgery). It begins by describing the ritual chaos created by a foreign
invasion after which the god's "ordinances were forgotten, and his appearance and appurtenances disappeared, and no-one saw (them) any-
more." The inscription then narrates developments over three reigns
in which offerings were established, abandoned, then re-established,
while the image remained lost. Finally, it introduces Nabu-Apla-Iddi-
na "who to avenge Akkade, (to) settle cult centers, (to) found divine
daises, (to) form forms, (to) perfectly perform (cultic) ordinances and
laws, (to) establish offerings, (and to) make bread offerings lavish, the
great lord Marduk, a just scepter, (and) performing shepherdship of
humanity, had placed in his hand." Then follows the story of how he
restored the lost knowledge of the proper appearance of the image of
Shamash and sponsored the statue's recreation. The last half of the
inscription consists of detailed grants of provisions to the priest of
the Sippar temple, and ends with the names of witnesses and curses
against anyone who might revoke the king's grants (tr. Victor Hurow-
itz in *COS* 2.135). Thus, the rhetoric of royal authority is used to justify temple and priestly prerogatives, as in most of these texts.

Most royal commemorative and dedicatory inscriptions content
themselves with recounting the king's building activities and grants of
land and tax exemptions to the temples and their priesthoods. A few
go further and claim royal authority for the conduct of rituals and the

amounts of offerings. Thus, Nur-Adad (nineteenth century) crowns his achievements of restoring the city and temple at Ur by building a bread-oven and cauldron to cook food for the gods that "he made for him (the god Nanna) and for his own life. He restored the traditional cleansing rites" (tr. Douglas Frayne, in *COS* 2:99A). Kurigalzu, a Kassite king of Babylon (later second millennium), records that "3 kor of bread, 3 kor of fine wine, 2 (large measures) of date cakes, 30 quarts of imported dates, 30 quarts of fine(?) oil, 3 sheep per day did I establish as the regular offering for all time" (tr. Foster 2005, 366). Azatiwata, the eighth-century king of a smaller Phoenician town, established a more modest calendar of annual offerings: "therein I caused Tarhunza to dwell, and every river-land will begin to honor him: by the year an ox, and at the cutting (?) a sheep, and at the vintage a sheep," and followed this with an ambitious prayer: "Let him bless Azatiwata with health and life, and let him be made highly preeminent over all kings" (tr. J. D. Hawkins, in *COS* 2.21). A stela of Nectanebo I, one of the last native kings of Egypt in the fourth century, after a hymn celebrating the king because he "supplies the altar, heaps the bowls, provides oblations of all kinds" and after quoting a decree specifying incomes for the temple of Neith from import taxes at Naucratis, then continues, "And one shall make one portion of an ox, one fat goose, and five measures of wine from them as a perpetual daily offering . . . My majesty has commanded to preserve and protect the divine offering of my mother Neith and to maintain everything done by the ancestors, in order that what I have done be maintained by those who shall be for an eternity of years" (tr. Lichtheim 1980, 3:88–89).

It is not just texts having to do with the establishment or restoration of temples that emphasize ritual rhetoric. Ritual rhetoric also plays a prominent, sometimes predominant, role in royal annals and lists of royal decrees, such as those from Egypt in the third millennium BCE Whether that is the case because ritual concerns dominated royal propaganda in general, or whether it is due to the accidents of preservation favoring temple records written on stone is hard to say. Nevertheless, the preserved decrees attest to royal concerns with ritual activity; e.g., a twenty-fourth century stela of Pepy II from Abydos: "[My majesty has commanded the offering of half] an ox, a *meret*-jug of milk, and one-eighth portion of an ox for every festival therein (the temple) for . . ." followed by a list of priests and statues (tr. by Strudwick 2005, 106). Several annalistic records from this early period include (e.g., the sarcophagus of Ankhesenpepy) or even emphasize (e.g. the Palermo Stone) ritual concerns to the point of quoting edicts regulating the amounts of offerings, just as in the temple inscriptions. Even if the precise ratio of ritual rhetoric to other themes in early Egyptian royal propaganda can never be known, its dominance in the extant texts suggests its considerable importance.

Nevertheless, self-justification through ritual decrees was not the exclusive prerogative of kings, though it does show up most often in royal texts. In some times and places, lower officials in the ruling hierarchy, or even collective ruling entities, utilized the same rhetoric to buttress their claims to power. For example, the citizens of Xanthos, together with the local Persian satrap, share credit for restoring the temple and rites of the temple to Leto in a fourth century Lycian inscription (Metzger 1979). Ritual rhetoric extended far beyond political considerations, at least of the temporal kind. It regularly supports appeals for an after-life in the admiring memory of human and divine readers (Talon 2005) or, in Egypt's more elaborate eschatology, justifies passage to a glorious afterlife with the gods, even to the point of sharing their offerings. Thus the sixth-century physician and bureaucrat, Udjahorresne, claims credit for convincing the Persian king to sponsor the restoration of temples and their rites in Egypt, which he then carried out himself. His tomb autobiography records these achievements as evidence that he is deserving of a rewarding afterlife (Lichtheim 1980, 3:36–41). Of course, such eschatological desires also buttress claims to power in this life by justifying the privilege and wealth necessary for an adequate tomb, so the desire for an afterlife does not displace the function of ritual rhetoric in reinforcing the political status quo.

Kings did not just command others to make offerings to the gods; they also depicted themselves as models of piety. Their inscriptions frequently narrate their ritual behavior. Thus, ritual rhetoric informs royal narratives, in addition to being the subject of royal decrees. To cite just some representative Egyptian examples: the Annals of Thutmose III (fifteenth century) report that immediately after winning a battle, "his majesty proceeded to the offering storehouse. Giving offerings to [Amun]-Re-Harakhty consisting of oxen, fowl, short-horned cattle. . . ." Another annal reports Thutmose's motivation for lavishing gifts on the god's temple "that I might compensate him (for) his protection . . . on the battlefield" (tr. James K. Hoffmeier, in *COS* 2.2A,

2.2B). When Akhenaton dedicates his new city of Akhet-Aten in the fourteenth century, he reports that "A great offering was caused to be presented—consisting of bread, beer, long- and short-horned cattle, (assorted) animals, fowl, wine, fruit, incense and all sorts of good plants—on the day of founding Akhet-Aten for the living Aten" (tr. Murnane 1995, 83). A first millennium Egyptian forgery of an inscription supposedly by a third-millennium ruler has him claim that, "I made purification; I conducted a procession of the hidden ones; I made a complete offering of bread, beer, oxen, and fowl, and all good things for the gods and goddesses in Yebu whose names had been pronounced," in order to model proper worship in the Khnum temple at Elephantine and justify its claims to considerable land holdings, tenants, and tithes (Famine Stela, tr. Lichtheim 1980, 3:94–103). Inscriptions from all over the ancient Near East often reinforce such verbal descriptions of royal piety with iconographic depictions of the king performing ritual worship before the god. These include several inscriptions already mentioned above, such as the stela of Hammurabi's law code and the Naucratis Stela of Nectanebo I.

Similar ritual rhetoric shows up in non-inscriptional genres, as well. Epics use narratives to model ideal ritual behavior by kings or venerable ancestors—a somewhat less overt, but probably just as effective, means for enculturating support for the political and religious status quo. A widely known example of such model ritual behavior occurs at the end of the flood story, when the heroic ancestor who has survived the flood (Atrahasis or Utnapishtim in Babylonian accounts, Noah in the Bible) builds an altar and makes animal offerings to the god/s (Atrahasis, the Gilgamesh Epic, and Genesis 9). The Ugaritic epics portray pious kings providing elaborate offerings. Daniel conducts a seven-day ritual of food offerings, libations, and obeisance to appeal for divine aid (Parker 1997, 51–52). The god El orders Kirta to prepare for a military expedition by making offerings:

> Enter [a shaded pavilion]. Take a lamb [in your hands]:
> a lamb of sa[crifice in] your right, a kid in them both—
> all your available (?) [food]. Take a pig[eon], bird of sacrifice. Pour wine into a silver basin; into a gold basin,
> honey. Ascend to the top of the lookout; mount the
> city-wall's shoulder. Raise your hands toward the sky.
> Sacrifice to Bull El, your Father. Adore Baal with your

sacrifice, Dagon's son with your offering (tr. Edward
L. Greenstein in Parker 1997, 14, 51–52).

The epic then recounts Kirta fulfilling the divine command word-
for-word to show his fidelity, and as a result, the campaign succeeds
in its objective. His later failure, however, to fulfill a vow of offerings
to another deity causes him to contract a terrible illness, so the epic
illustrates both the promise and peril of ritual performance. Though
the Hebrew Bible does not contain the self-aggrandizing royal rhetoric
of commemorative inscriptions, its stories do characterize the piety of
favored kings by telling of their ritual accomplishments: David's in
bringing the ark of the covenant to Jerusalem (2 Samuel 6; 1 Chronicles
15–16), Solomon's in building and dedicating the Jerusalem temple (1
Kings 8:62–64; 2 Chronicles 7), Josiah's by reestablishing the obser-
vance of Passover (2 Kings 22–23; 2 Chronicles 35)—all accompanied
by lavish offerings. Revered ancestors are also characterized by their
ritual piety: Abraham makes the covenant with God through offerings (Genesis 15) and circumcision (Genesis 17), and his fidelity is
tested by a command to offer a child sacrifice (Genesis 22); Hannah
fulfills her vow by offering a bull as well as devoting her son (1 Samuel
1); Job's superlative piety emerges from his offerings on behalf of his
children (Job 1). This technique of narrative characterization has, of
course, exactly the same method and purpose as do stories of a king's
acts of piety in a royal inscription. The narrative epic or prose contexts,
however, generalize their examples as idealized types for non-royal as
well as royal emulation.

Gods mandate specific ritual instructions far less often in ancient
Near Eastern texts than one might expect from the frequency of such
divine commandments in the Bible (Exodus 12–13, 25–31, Leviticus
1–17, 23, 25, etc.) and from the quotation of Kirta above. In narratives, as well as inscriptions, deities tend to command wars and building projects far more often than the details of ritual worship. These
texts depict humans responding on their own initiative with appropriate worship, which emphasizes their special piety. The suspicion
that this represents an idealized pattern finds confirmation from a few
textual hints of a more directive ritual rhetoric at work orally in royal
courts. Letters from Mari in the eighteenth century and Assyria in
the eighth century report to the royal court the preaching of prophets
to the effect that the king should provide or increase royal supplies
to particular temples. Thus, one prophet appealing for a land grant

to a temple speaks for the god Adad, saying, "Am I not Adad, lord of Kallassu, who raised him (the king) in my lap and restored him to his ancestral throne? . . . Should he not deliver (the estate), I—the lord of the throne, territory and city—can take away what I have given. But if, on the contrary, he fulfils my desire, I shall give him throne upon throne" (tr. Nissinen 2003, 18). A fourth-century Egyptian inscription reflects the fact that King Nectanebo I's cultic actions and decrees originated in prophetic advice. It describes him as the one "who convokes their prophets to consult them on all the functions of the temple; who acts according to their words and is not deaf to their advice" (tr. Lichtheim 1980, 3:88). Such references confirm that religious officials wielded considerable influence over ritual conduct. Prevailing rhetorical norms, however, hid the role of priests and even prophets behind the voice and authority of kings or, sometimes, of gods. For example, though Egyptian ritual texts were always under the control of lector-priests in the temple libraries, over time they were increasingly credited to the authorship of the god Thoth (Schott 1963 and 1972). The Pentateuch's presentation of priestly texts through a divine voice exhibits Israel's distinctive manifestation of this widespread convention of ancient priestly rhetoric to hide behind royal and divine voices (cf. Metzger 2004, 177–78).

Despite these examples of ritual rhetoric in royal inscriptions and epic narratives, which could be multiplied many times over, this rhetoric is hardly universal in historiographical and epic texts from the ancient Near East. Even many royal annals and chronicles emphasize mostly political events (e.g. the Annals of Thutmose III), and battle scenes vie with depictions of ritual worship in royal iconography. The relative importance of ritual themes waxed and waned; Sallaberger (2005) has charted the increasing emphasis on ritual in Mesopotamian texts between 2500 and 1500 BCE Naturally, a focus on temple rites appears more frequently in temple foundation inscriptions than in other kinds of texts.

A rhetoric that claims divine approval because of the king's ritual piety creates, however, the potential for political attacks on the king to take the form of ritual criticism. Ritual theorists have come to realize that using ritual criticism to undermine political and religious elites has been as common in human societies as using ritual to reinforce the status quo (Grimes 1990, 17–18; Rappaport 1999, 36–37, 124–26). A number of texts from a variety of ancient Near Eastern cultures take full advantage of this opportunity to blame their countries' military, social and climactic misfortunes on the ritual infidelity of particular kings. In fact, it is not an exaggeration to say that ritual rhetoric provides the principal vehicle for political criticism in the extant texts.

The notion that gods get angry and abandon their usual abodes, thus bringing calamity on the land, finds mythic expression in stories of droughts being caused by the absence of storm gods who must be found and convinced to return (see the Hittite myths on this theme in Hoffner 1990, 15–29). Where specific deities become associated with particular cities and their ruling dynasties, a claim that the god is absent becomes political commentary. A regular theme in Babylonian royal inscriptions narrates the departure of the gods, especially Marduk, from Babylon out of anger at the city's inhabitants and, especially, its former kings. The current king claims divinely sanctioned rule in order to return the statue of Marduk to Babylon and restore his worship properly (see the inscription of Nabopolassar quoted above and, for more examples, Foster 2005, 360–64, 374–91). Similarly, Nabonidus (Babylon, sixth century), in celebrating his rebuilding of the Ebabbar temple at Sippar, includes among his titulary titles "the caretaker of the Esagil and Ezida" (two temples in Babylon), then begins the historical section by narrating that:

> Ehulhul, the temple of Sin in Harran, where since days of yore Sin, the great lord, had established his favorite residence—(then) his heart became angry against that city and temple and he aroused the Mede, destroyed that temple and turned it into ruins—in my legitimate reign Bel (and) the great lord, for the love of my kingship, became reconciled with that city and temple and showed compassion. In the beginning of my everlasting reign they sent me a dream. . . . Marduk spoke with me: "Nabonidus, . . . rebuild Ehulhul and cause Sin, the great lord, to establish his residence in its midst."

The king politely objects that the temple site lies in Medean territory, but the gods prophesy that the Persian king Cyrus will scatter the Medes and so allow the work to commence. Thus, the inscription explains not just the royal succession, but also the ebb and flow of national frontiers on the basis of divine concerns for the reestablishment of ritual institutions and practices. For this and several other temples, Nabonidus is scrupulous to follow the foundation deposits (designs) of earlier kings whom he names. In one case, he adds that "the regular offerings and the (other) offerings I increased over what they were and I established for her." The king's motives become explicit in the prayer he recites when the temple has been completed: "As for me, Nabonidus, king of Babylon, who completed that temple, may Sin, the king of the gods of heaven and the netherworld, . . . make my ominous signs favorable. May he lengthen my days, extend my years, annihilate those hostile to me, destroy my foes" (tr. by Paul-Alain Beaulieu, in *COS* 2.123A).

The tendency to blame national misfortune on ritual misconduct could be sharpened into political attacks on particular kings. Kings themselves employed ritual criticism prominently to attack their predecessors and rivals (Talon 1993). The Persian king Cyrus used this rhetoric against Nabonidus by citing the Babylonian's impieties to justify the Persian conquest of Babylon:

> An incompetent person was installed to exercise lordship over his country. . . . for Ur and the rest of the sacred centers, improper rituals [ ] daily he recited. Irreverently, he put an end to the regular offerings. . . . By his own plan, he did away with the worship of Marduk, the king of the gods.

Marduk then "searched for a righteous king whom he would support. He called out his name: Cyrus, king of Anshan." Cyrus claims to have taken the city without a fight, then:

> I daily attended to his worship. . . . I returned the (images of) the gods to the sacred centers (on the other side of the) Tigris whose sanctuaries had been abandoned for a long time. . . . I increased the offerings [to x] geese, two ducks and ten turtledoves above the former (offerings) . . . (tr. by Mordechai Cogan, in *COS* 2.124).

Note the similar pro-Cyrus ritual rhetoric of "The Verse Account of Nabonidus" that lampoons Nebonidus as saying:

> "I shall omit (all) festivals, I shall order (even) the New Year's Festival to cease!" . . . He (continues to) mix up

> the rites, he confuses the (hepatoscopic oracles). . . .
> To the most important ritual observances he makes an
> end (tr. A. Leo Oppenheim, in *ANET* 312–315).

The need to legitimize rulers clearly fueled such propagandistic uses of ritual criticism in royal inscriptions. It also led to the composition of "apologies" by kings convicted of their sins against the gods (usually for treaty violations; see Talon 2005 for Neo-Assyrian examples). On the other hand, literary texts written in scribal schools provide a much wider range of explanations for historical change. Some attest to a divinely-ordained cycle of history (e.g. the Prophecies of Neferti, early second millennium Egypt, Lichtheim 1973, 1:139–45, or the Epic of Erra and Ishum, ninth or eighth century Babylonian, tr. Stephanie Dalley in *COS* 1.113), and some simply bemoan human betrayals (Instruction of Amenemhet I, early second millennium Egypt, Lichtheim 1973, 1:135–39) or even the inexplicable nature of catastrophe (Complaints of Khakheperre-Sonb and the Admonitions of Ipuwer, early second millennium Egypt, Lichtheim 1973, 1:145–63; also Ecclesiastes in the Hebrew Bible, mid-first millennium). Historians have tried to link such literature with periods of severe social disruption, but the flowering of works exploring the theme of social chaos may have more to do with developments in the literary histories of particular ancient cultures than with historical events (Lichtheim 1973, 1:149–50).

Nevertheless, even in literary works that admit the influence of uncontrollable and possibly random forces, ritual provides hope for exerting some control over them. The Instruction to Merikare (late third millennium Egyptian) quotes the earlier instruction of King Khety in a context that gives a variety of reasons for the course of events, but the quotation focuses on ritual: "He who is silent toward violence diminishes the offerings. God will attack the rebel for the sake of the temple. . . . Supply the offerings, revere the god, don't say, 'it is trouble,' don't slacken your hand. He who opposes you attacks the sky" (tr. Lichtheim 1973, 1:105). Another example, the Babylonian Erra epic, despite its depiction of extravagant and irrational divine violence on humans, concludes by recommending the reading, recitation, reproduction, and veneration of the epic itself as apotropaic rituals to ward off the catastrophes that it describes. Thus, ritual rhetoric resonates widely even in wisdom and epic literature.

In the propagandistic contexts of royal inscriptions, however, ritual rhetoric exacted a political price: by depicting the king's religious piety in terms of royal sponsorship of temple cults, it ceded influence to ritual specialists—the priests of those same temples. Priests not only appealed for royal support on that basis (see the prophecies cited above), but they also influenced or even wrote chronicles of royal history that evaluated kings purely on the basis of their support for particular temples. Thus, the Weidner Chronicle (sixth century Babylonian) explains the fortunes of a long list of kings by their treatment of the Esagila, the temple of Marduk (Glassner 2004, 263–69). Its lesson is summed up succinctly: "Whosoever offends the gods of this city, his star will not stand in the sky." Then it describes the actions of a succession of rulers who interfered, for example, with fish offerings to Marduk or restored them, or modified Marduk's drink-offerings or preserved their original amounts, in each case explaining their loss or gain of kingship on that basis. Many Neo-Babylonian chronicles, according to Glassner (77), "favored a political line of reasoning that no longer guided the conduct of a ruler but told him what he could or could not do."

In Israel, at around the same time, similar thinking produced a fierce critique of Israel's and Judah's kings in the form of the books of Kings in the Hebrew Bible. The history approves only those kings notable for their singular devotion to YHWH, the god of the Jerusalem temple: David who brought the ark and Tabernacle to Jerusalem (2 Samuel 6), Hezekiah who purged the Jerusalem temple and outlying cultic sites of idolatrous elements (2 Kings 18:3–8), and Josiah who also reformed the temple and suppressed outlying cults (2 Kings 22–23). Some other kings get mixed reviews in words similar to 2 Kings 12:3–4: "Johoash did what was right in the sight of YHWH all his days, because the priest Jehoiada taught him. But the high places [illegitimate sanctuaries] were not taken away . . ." (cf. 1 Kings 15:11–15; 22:43). Most of the kings of Judah and all the kings of the northern kingdom of Israel are condemned, however, "as doing evil in the sight of YHWH" because they sponsored illegitimate temples and rites (e.g. 1 Kings 12:25–33). Though various stories chronicle the moral and political failings of Israel's kings, the explicit evaluations of this book's narrator emphasize exclusively ritual concerns.

Ritual, thus, frequently provided political justifications for royal rule, for military conquest and rebellion, and for priestly critiques. It is sufficiently widespread in the surviving texts to suggest that the mere mention of ritual activity was meant to presuppose a divine-human quid pro quo, even if it is not spelled out. (Aristotle noted that a typical rhetorical argument, the *enthymeme*, employs unstated presuppositions.) Scholarship on ancient historiography often comments on its religious cast (e.g. Glassner 23: "Theology was the end, history the means to the end"). Rhetorical analysis sharpens this observation by noting the persuasive motive for postulating ritual causality behind historical events: here lay the basis for asserting human control over events, and therefore also for assigning specific human blame. Ritual rhetoric presented a catch-all explanation for past events, while the rituals themselves provided a means for controlling the future. This understanding of ritual causality created an ideological basis for political critique.

Royal examples modeled rituals' effects for common people as well. Everyone could try to control the vicissitudes of fate by tending the needs of the gods to the best of their abilities and resources. The tilt toward royal interests in the extant texts probably reflects the conditions of these texts' production and preservation more than it reflects differences between the ritual interests of royalty and commoners. The royal and priestly historiographic texts demonstrate the high stakes felt by ancient peoples in ritual accuracy: not only the city and the dynasty, but also one's health, wealth, and life (and, often, afterlife) depended on ritual accuracy and fidelity. These historiographic texts can therefore help us understand the social situations and rhetorical settings in which ritual texts, more narrowly defined, were written and used.

RITUAL TEXTS

In contrast to the overtly persuasive intentions behind royal inscriptions, temple dedications and even many chronicles, ancient Near Eastern ritual texts usually contain far fewer indications of their rhetorical goals. The category "ritual texts," as used by translators and interpreters, is very heterogeneous and undefined. It usually contains collections of spells, omen lists, lists of offerings, festival calendars, regulations of priests' incomes, and temple inventories, as well as detailed instructions for performing particular rites. Individual texts often contain mixtures of several of these elements. Scholars usually categorize such texts functionally as "archival" or "didactic" texts, in distinction from historiographic or literary texts. We have already seen, however, that similar ritual topics also appear in these other genres and were used to reinforce their rhetorical goals. That observation suggests that ritual texts had persuasive functions, as well, and that the rhetorical role of didactic, and even archival, texts in ancient cultures requires serious reconsideration.

Ritual texts reveal their rhetorical purpose most obviously when they exhort their hearers or readers to perform their instructions. Such exhortations to ritual performance are, however, surprisingly rare outside the Bible (e.g. Exodus 12:1–20; Leviticus 17:1–16; 18:2–5; Deuteronomy 12:1–31). They do commonly appear in the publicly accessible areas of ancient Egyptian tombs, where inscriptions ask for prayers and offerings for the deceased. Thus, an inscription in the tomb of Paheri (fourteenth century) urges, "Just so may you recite the offering prayer in the manner found in the writings, and the invocation offering as spoken by those long dead just as it came from the mouth of God" (Foster 2001, 176–77). A few non-funerary rituals also enjoin their performance: for example, ritual instructions to accompany recitation of lamentations for Isis and Nephthys (Ptolomaic period Egyptian) conclude, "You shall not be slack in reciting this book in the hour of festival" (Lichtheim 1980, 3:116–121).

Somewhat more common in ancient Near Eastern ritual texts are blessings on those who perform or sponsor their ritual stipulations. Thus, several lines further in the prayers of Paheri, reward is promised for the recitation: "Goodness is yours when you perform it, for [you] discover [that it earns] you favor" (Foster 2001, 177). The famous spell 125 of the Egyptian Book of Coming Forth by Day (the so-called "Book of the Dead") concludes, "He for whom this scroll is recited will prosper, and his children will prosper," etc. (Lichtheim 1976, 2:132). Similarly, an Ugaritic drinking rite (fourteenth or thirteenth century BCE) promises that the god will bless a worshiper who offers libations: "Your success he will ask of *Ba'lu*. To what you have requested he will bring you . . ." (tr. Pardee 2002, 193–95). The Marseilles tariff (Punic, fourth century) promises sanctions for ritual transgressions: it mandates monetary fines for non-compliance with its stipulations (*COS* 1:98; *ANET* 502–503).

Sometimes, texts connect the reason for performing a particular ritual with its promised outcome. In a Babylonian text containing several different rituals, one or two ominous omens introduce some of the ritual instructions which then conclude, "If you do all this, no evil will approach the king" (tr. A. Sachs, in *ANET* 340). Other texts, while providing no motivation for the entire ritual sequence, do note the negative consequences of ritual failure for certain parts. For example, the festival calendar for the Babylonian New Year's Festival (*ANET* 331–34, lines 364–65) mandates that the chief priest must be absent while the temple is purified, or else become defiled himself. Another infrequent rhetorical strategy for motivating compliance is to cite the authority of those promulgating the instructions. In some cases, the implications of that authority claim remain unstated, as in the case of a third-millennium Egyptian offering list that emphasizes the royal authority behind it (Strudwick 2005, 87–91). In other cases, an authority claim invokes explicit enforcement mechanisms, as in the case of the first-millennium Punic Marseilles and Carthage tariffs that emphasize their authorization and enforcement by "the thirty men who are in charge of the revenues" (tr. Dennis Pardee, in *COS* 1:98; also *ANET* 656–67).

Nevertheless, rarely do such explicit exhortations or motivations appear in ritual texts, in marked contrast to the royal inscriptions analyzed above. For the most part, ritual texts simply state the order and amounts of offerings, the sequence of ritual actions and liturgies, and calendars of festivals and events. Thus, a common element in Egyptian tombs from the third millennium on is a list of offerings (Strudwick 2005, 87–91). The huge amounts listed in later private tombs ("May they give a thousand of bread, beer, beef and fowl" in the prayers of Paheri, Lichtheim 1976, 2:16) suggest exaggeration, at the very least. The phrasing of the deceased's request for recitations ("Say 'An offering, given by the king'") may indicate that the offering list's effectiveness was believed to lie not in describing actual food gifts, but rather in its oral recitation. (See further below.) Other ritual texts, however, associate actual offerings with verbal recitations: several early and late Egyptian rituals juxtapose ritual actions with spells and longer recitations, e.g. from the third millennium Pyramid Texts: "Osiris Unis, accept the one of the shank, Horus's eye. 1 BOWL WITH A SHANK OF MEAT" (tr. Allen 2005, 23; for his discussion, see page 6); similarly, from almost two thousand years later, the daily ritual of Amun-Re (*COS* 1.34).

Judging from the amount of space given over to it, a preponderant concern for ancient writers of ritual texts was the issue of who gets what. Recipients include deities, their temples, priests, prophets and other temple functionaries. Ritual texts list sizable expenses in a matter-of-fact tone that rarely expresses any overt concern for the financial consequences of their mandates for those who have to pay.

For example, the Emar ritual for the installation of a high priestess describes seven days of offerings, feasts and purifications. The following lines are typical:

> They give the diviner (one?) shekel of silver, and they sacrifice the one ox and the six sheep before the storm god. They set before the gods the ritual portion of beef and the ritual portion of mutton. . . . The officials who give the consecration-gift, the heralds, and seven eat and drink at the storm god's temple. The men of the consecration gift receive one standard loaf and one standard vessel of barley-beer each (tr. Daniel Fleming, in *COS* 1.122; similarly *COS* 1.126).

Different kinds of texts devote different amounts of attention to the various parties to the ritual exchange. Festival calendars tend to focus on which deities get what and/or when (e.g. Emar texts [*COS* 1.123–125]; Egyptian Old Kingdom festival calendars [Strudwick 2005, 87–91]; an Ugaritic calendar for the month of vintage [Pardee 2002, 56–65 = *COS* 1.95]; Numbers 28–29 in the Hebrew Bible). Simple lists of deities may have served a similar ritual purpose: several such lists from Ugarit contain the cuneiform equivalent of check marks in the margins of the tablets, presumably documenting that the rites were performed and in the proper order (Pardee 2002, 12–13, 200). The aptly named "tariffs," on the other hand, seem more concerned with priestly incomes. The Punic "Marseilles" tariff specifies which portions of each kind of animal belong to the priest (*COS* 1.98), as do the ritual instructions of Leviticus 1–7 in the Hebrew Bible. The Punic and Israelite tariffs make clear that various kinds of animals, ranging from the expensive ox to the inexpensive turtledove, may count as the same kind of offering. They thereby provide a scale of graduated payments that implicitly depends on the worshiper's financial resources or willingness to pay.

One stylistic feature of ritual texts that lends them a didactic feeling rather than a persuasive one, at least to modern eyes, is how they introduce their provisions. Calendrical texts begin, of course, with some kind of date formula, such as the first line of the Ugaritic calendar mentioned above, "In the month of *Ra'šu-Yēni*, on the day of the new moon, cut a bunch of grapes for *'Ilu* as a peace-offering" (Pardee 2002, 63). Non-calendrical texts often introduce their provisions by specifying the occasion of their performance with a conditional clause: "If people are dying in the country and if some enemy god has caused that, I act as follows . . ." (Hittite, tr. Albrecht Goetze, in *ANET* 347), "When the wall of the temple of god Anu falls into ruin, you shall prepare . . ." (Akkadian, tr. A. Sachs, in *ANET* 339), "When *'Attartu-Hurri* enters the 'mound'(-room) of the palace: put on a feast . . ." (Ugaritic, tr. Pardee 2002, 71), "When one of you offers an offering to YHWH, you may offer your offering of domestic animals, that is from the herd or the flock. If their offering is a burnt offering from the herd . . ." (Hebrew, Leviticus 1:2–3, NRSV). Such conditional formulas leave modern readers with the impression that compliance is optional. The texts seem to give instructions to those already inclined to follow them, rather than mandating performance in overt imperatives like the inscriptions tend to do. Modern interpreters, therefore, tend to classify rituals as didactic or archival, rather than hortatory. They even debate whether particular texts prescribe the rituals or simply describe them (Levine 1965 and 1983).

Such conditional or "casuistic" formulas, however, are also the most characteristic stylistic feature of ancient Near Eastern law collections. Their use in law indicates their appropriateness for detailing obligatory practices. This conditional or casuistic form reflects the influence of scribal, "academic" reflection on the formation of a text, as Raymond Westbrook (1994, 30) observed:

> The casuistic form was the quintessential 'scientific' type of Mesopotamian literature, as attested in the omen and medical texts. It was the means whereby raw data could be cast into a generalized, objective form, stripped of any connections with circumstances irrelevant to their universal application. It was the nearest Mesopotamian science could come to expressing principles. . . . The choice of form for the individual paragraphs of what was essentially a literary document, belonging . . . to the genre 'academic treatise,' was not a legal one but depended on other factors, perhaps pedagogical or rhetorical.

Those rhetorical factors have been clarified by Carol Lipson's study of an Egyptian medical text in the sixteenth-century, the Smith Papyrus. She argued that its repetitive conditional formulas established not only the anonymous writer's authority but also intended to "direct surgeons, in communicating with their patients, to continue a tradition of treating medical discourse as formalized, ritual oration" modeled after a ritual chant (1990, 399). Thus, ancient experts, like their modern counterparts, often couched their pronouncements in categorical and objective rhetorical forms to reinforce their authority. The frequency of conditional or casuistic phrasing in ritual texts reflects their production and use in the same scribal circles that produced catalogs of omens, medical texts, and collections of laws. Ritual texts in conditional form represent collections of knowledge, and recommended or even mandated practices just as these other genres do.

Such academic origins naturally lead interpreters to assign a primarily didactic function to ritual texts. Why should we look further for a persuasive function? It is the frequent appearance of ritual rhetoric in the contexts of royal inscriptions and decrees that points out the persuasive force of ritual texts in their original social contexts. Inscriptions and decrees illustrate the very high stakes that ancient peoples placed on ritual accuracy and fidelity. The texts that established such ritual standards probably played a very normative role in regulating ritual behavior. Though the texts themselves may not give many indications of this persuasive role, the regulative function of such ritual texts was enforced by the social contexts in which they were used. That is typical of the rhetorical force of lists in general: they gain their power from the social contexts of their use. This observation, however, should not be taken as diminishing their rhetorical effectiveness. As collections of laws, instructions, and procedures, normative lists regulate the lives of those within their social context more extensively than almost any other textual genre (O'Banion 1992, 12; Watts 2004, 202).

Ritual Functions of Texts

We do not, however, have to rely only on such inductive reasoning to ascertain the rhetorical function of ancient ritual texts. There is more direct evidence for their persuasive power, namely, references to using ritual texts themselves as ritual objects.

One might well wonder why ancient temple priests needed ritual texts at all. Functioning as professional and often hereditary guilds of specialists, priesthoods throughout the ancient Near East must have used oral tradition as the primary means for educating young priests.

Since few people outside the scribal and priestly classes could read, ritual texts would have been used almost exclusively by people who were already enculturated in the oral tradition. What use did priests have for ritual texts?

One function of ritual, as well as other texts, was to advance the oral education process itself. Recent research has emphasized the complex interactions between oral traditions and writing, in marked contrast to older scholarship that conceived of orality and literacy in historical sequence so that literacy was thought to have gradually displaced oral ways of learning and thinking. Comparative analysis of ancient Near Eastern and Mediterranean cultures suggests that they all, in one way or another, used texts to buttress and reinforce oral modes of education rather than displacing one with the other (Carr, 2005). Traditions were memorized by being written and copied, and memories were corrected on the basis of written texts. Furthermore, the reading of ancient texts depended heavily on prior memorization because their graphic forms were difficult for even expert scribes to scan immediately. Thus, one function of ritual texts was to ground oral performances, both reading and memorization.

Ritual texts in particular, however, did not just ground oral performances. They were also used to guarantee the accuracy of ritual performances. Just as Nabonidus searched for texts and drawings to reestablish the original designs of temples and statues, so many references indicate that kings and priests used old texts to (re)establish correct ritual practices. Thus, a prayer of the Hittite king Muwatalli II in the thirteenth century claims that when the gods are offended, he not only consults with knowledgeable elders but also that "whatever I, My Majesty, discover now in the written records, I will carry out" (Singer 2002, 83). During one of his predecessors' reigns, a long-drawn out plague motivated a search of archives to find old ritual and treaty texts whose provisions had fallen into abeyance, with the result that the rituals were reinstated and offerings were made to compensate for the treaty violations (Singer 2002, 58–59). The revival of rituals on the basis of old texts receives prominent depiction in the Hebrew Bible (2 Kings 22–23; Nehemiah 8), and also appears in Greek and Roman sources (Watts 2005, 2007).

The use of ritual texts to revive old rituals shows the persuasive value of texts in situations of ritual conflict and change. When external crisis or internal criticism requires ritual change, old texts can be used to buttress the authority for such changes because they appear to be independent of the kings and priests who wield them. Unlike oral traditions, which can only be presented through the embodied voices of those who have learned them and who may therefore be suspected of bias, texts seem to preserve voices out of the past. By appealing to a ritual text, priests and kings could invoke an apparently independent authority for their traditional practices or ritual changes. Never mind the fact that those who control texts, especially in predominantly oral cultures, control their contents almost as completely as oral tradents manage their traditions. The rhetorical force of ritual texts derives from their *appearance* as independent authorities, and ancient kings and priests invoked them precisely to gain that authority for themselves.

This emphasis on the independent appearance of ritual texts was not just figurative. Their role in legitimizing ritual practices sometimes led priests to display texts prominently within the rituals themselves. In Egypt, such practices led to one important functionary being designated as the "lector-priest," that is, the person who is responsible for reading and holding the ritual scrolls. Illustrations of the "opening of the mouth" ceremony often feature the lector-priest displaying an open papyrus scroll in front of the sarcophagus of the deceased (Lorton 1999, 149). Such displays were not limited to this ritual alone, however, as a seventh century papyrus in the Brooklyn Museum of Art shows: it records and illustrates a divine oracle received during the procession of the image of Amun-Re which includes a lector-priest holding up an open scroll. The public reading of books of the law, in which the scroll was displayed as well as heard, played a crucial role in religious reforms in Jerusalem as well (2 Kings 22–23; Nehemiah 8). By the late first millennium, Torah scrolls had become such recognizable symbols of Judaism that some were intentionally destroyed in attempts to suppress Jewish ritual practices (1 Maccabees 1:56–57). In Hellenistic and Roman culture more broadly, book burning became a common method for suppressing religious movements (Sarefield 2007).

The association of ritual texts with ritual performance became so strong that the texts could themselves become stand-ins for the rituals. Instead of doing what the text says, it was enough to recite the text itself in order to receive the same ritual benefit. Though it is tempting to places such ideas at the end of a long historical development, they in fact appear quite early among Egyptian funerary texts. The Pyramid Texts consist of ritual instructions, recitations and spells that were inscribed on the walls of royal tombs in the mid-third millennium. James Allen described the function of these texts: "Originally recited by a lector priest in the role of the deceased's son during rites that probably took place at the funeral, they were carved on the walls of the pyramid's chambers to ensure their ongoing effectiveness" (2005, 5). I have already mentioned wall inscriptions in publicly accessible parts of some Egyptian private tombs that invite visitors to recite "an offering given by the king," apparently in lieu of actually giving offerings. Thus, the Babylonian Talmud (*Menahot* 110a-b) expresses very ancient sentiments when it claims that studying the Torah's rules for the burnt offering earns the same merit as actually performing a burnt offering.

Sometimes, the rituals mandated by a text consisted entirely of preserving and performing the text itself. The Akkadian Erra Epic (eighth century) concludes with the god Erra proclaiming,

> In the sanctuary of the god who honors this poem, may abundance accumulate, but let the one who neglects it never smell incense. . . . Let the singer who chants (it) not die from pestilence, but his performance be pleasing to king and prince. The scribe who masters it shall be spared in the enemy country and honored in his own land. . . . The house in which this tablet is placed, though Erra be angry and the Seven be murderous, the sword of pestilence shall not approach it, safety abides upon it (tr. Foster 2005, 911).

Promises of supernatural blessings on those who honor and preserve the text containing the blessings, as well as curses upon those who do not, appear widely in ancient inscriptions. The negative sanctions in particular echo in later Jewish and Christian literature (e.g. the Letter of Aristeas [Charlesworth 1983, 2:33]; 1 Enoch 104:10–13; Revelation 22:18–19). The Torah, however, presents a more expansive rhetoric containing both promise and threat, within which textual rituals play an important role:

> Keep these words that I am commanding you today in your heart. Recite them to your children and talk about them when you are at home and when you are away, when you lie down and when you rise. Bind

them as a sign on your hand, fix them as an emblem
on your forehead, and write them on the doorposts of
your house and on your gates (Deuteronomy 6:6–9,
NRSV).

Read this law before all Israel in their hearing. Assemble the people—men, women, and children, as
well as the aliens residing in your towns—so that they
may hear and learn to fear the LORD your God and
to observe diligently all the words of this law (Deuteronomy 31:11–12, NRSV).

Thus, various ancient cultures employed ritual texts as talismans to
curry divine favor. Such practices, which are so well attested in later
Western religious traditions (Parmenter 2007), have their roots in ancient Near Eastern ritual rhetoric.

CONCLUSION

All these examples show that a quid pro quo predicating divine favor
toward humans on their assiduous support for the gods' sustenance
and residences is a major theme in ancient propaganda and literature,
as well as in ritual texts more narrowly defined. This ritual rhetoric, as
I have termed it, provided an ideological basis for political criticism. It
also encouraged the manipulation of ritual texts as symbols of fidelity
to the instructions they contain. Thus ritual rhetoric served as a powerful means of persuasion.

One would not know that, however, from classical rhetorical theory.
Greco-Roman theorists of rhetoric provide no analysis of religious rhetorical genres such as oracles, sermons, ritual instructions and prayers.
Religious holy sites and temples find no place in their three-fold division of public civic space between law court, political assembly, and
funeral. Religion, therefore, has no role in the three rhetorical genres
of persuasion. Though these theorists include among their examples of
arguments some that mention the gods (e.g. Aristotle, *Rhetoric* II, 23.4
[1397b], 23.7 [1398a], III.18 [1419a]), they avoid any participation in
the institutional rhetoric of temples and sects. Plato's dismissive attitude towards religious rhetoric seems to typify much of the subsequent
theoretical tradition:

> They produce a bushel of books of Musaeus and Or-
> pheus, the offspring of the Moon and of the Muses,
> as they affirm, and these book they use in their ritual,
> and make not only ordinary men but states believe that
> there really are remissions of sins and purifications for
> deeds of injustice, by means of sacrifice and pleasant
> sport for the living, and that there are also special rites
> for the defunct, which they call functions, that deliver
> us from evils in that other world, while terrible things
> await those who have neglected to sacrifice (*Republic*
> II 364e-365a, tr. Paul Shorey in Hamilton and Cairns
> 1961, 611–12).

This lacuna in ancient rhetorical theory becomes glaring when one surveys the rhetoric of ancient Near Eastern cultures. That is not because of the prevalence there of stories about deities and their activities, which were just as pervasive in Greco-Roman culture. It is, rather, the prominent mention of rituals in ancient Near Eastern texts that points out the theorists' omission. Greek theorists reflect in passing the existence of this rhetoric in their own society (see, e.g., Aristotle, *Rhetoric* I.15 [1377a] on oaths and II.5 [1383b] on the causes of confidence, which may be due to the fact that "we have wronged no one, or not many, or not those of whom we are afraid; and generally, if our relations with the gods are satisfactory, as will be shown especially by signs and oracles" [tr. W. Rhys Roberts, in McKeon 1941, 1392]), but they give it no distinctive function. Such passing references suggest that it would be profitable to investigate Greek inscriptions for traces of ritual rhetoric that could contextualize the distinctive social and ideological position of the classical theorists over against not just the Sophists, whom they often explicitly attack, but also vis-à-vis the rhetoric of temple priests and oracles, whom they ignore.

Laurent Pernot has recently called for expanding classical categories to include the range of genres in ancient religious rhetoric. He starts by giving particular attention to the rhetoric of prayers and hymns (Pernot 2006). Another avenue for exploring the nature and power of religious rhetoric can be found in the pervasive influence of ritual rhetoric in ancient Near Eastern and Mediterranean cultures. Though clearly grounded in the practices of temples and shrines, ritual rhetoric reached beyond those settings to shape the ideological grounds for political power and resistance, and also the less documented struggles of non-elite people in their everyday lives (e.g. Meskell 2002). Study of ancient ritual rhetoric therefore provides insight into ancient peoples' political and social struggles, as well as their religious practices and beliefs.

ABBREVIATIONS

ANET Pritchard, James B. 1969. *Ancient Near Eastern Texts Relating to the Old Testament,* 3rd edition with supplement. Princeton: Princeton UP.

COS Hallo, W. W. and K. L. Younger, Jr., eds. 1997, 2000, 2002. *The Context of Scripture: Canonical Compositions, Monumental Inscriptions, and Archival Documents from the Biblical World,* 3 vols. Leiden: Brill.

tr. translated by

WORKS CITED

Allen, James P., and Peter der Manuelian. *Writings from the Ancient World: The Ancient Egyptian Pyramid Texts.* 23. Atlanta: SBL, 2005.

Bell, Catherine. *Ritual: Perspectives and Dimensions.* New York: Oxford UP, 1997.

Burke, Kenneth. *A Rhetoric of Motives.* 1950. Berkeley: U of California P, 1969.

Carr, David M. 2005. *Writing on the Tablet of the Heart: Origins of Scripture and Literature.* Oxford, UK: Oxford UP, 1950.

Charlesworth, James H. *The Old Testament Pseudepigrapha,* 2 vols. Garden City: Doubleday, 1983.

Foster, Benjamin R. *Before the Muses: An Anthology of Akkadian Literature,* 3rd ed. Bethesda, MD: CDL Press, 2005.

Foster, John L. *Ancient Egyptian Literature: An Anthology.* Austin: U of Texas P, 2001.

Freud, Sigmund. "Obsessive Actions and Religious Practices." 1907. Reprinted in *Readings in Ritual Studies.* Ed. Ronald L. Grimes. Upper Saddle River, NJ: Prentice Hall, 1996. 212-17.

Glassner, Jean-Jacques. *Mesopotamian Chronicles.* Writings from the Ancient World 19. Atlanta: SBL, 2004.

Grimes, Ronald. *Ritual Criticism: Case Studies in Its Practice, Essays on Its Theory.* Columbia: U of South Carolina P, 1990.

Hamilton, Edith and Huntington Cairns. *The Collected Dialogues of Plato.* Princeton: Princeton UP, 1961.

Hoffner, Harry A., Jr. *Hittite Myths*. Writings from the Ancient World 2. Atlanta: Scholars Press, 1990.

Levine, Baruch A. "The Descriptive Tabernacle Texts of the Pentateuch." *Journal of the American Oriental Society* 85 (1965): 307–318.

—. "The Descriptive Ritual Texts from Ugarit: Some Formal and Functional Features of the Genre." *The Word of the Lord Shall Go Forth: Essay in Honor of David Noel Freedman*. Ed. C. L. Meyers and M. O'Conner. Winona Lake, IN: Eisenbrauns, 1983. 467–75.

Lichtheim, Miriam. *Ancient Egyptian Literature*. 3 vols. Berkeley: U of California P, 1973, 1976. 1980.

Lipson, Carol. "Ancient Egyptian Medical Texts: A Rhetorical Analysis of Two of the Oldest Papyri." *Journal of Technical Writing and Communication* 20.4 (1990): 391–409.

Lorton, David. "The Theology of the Cult Statues in Ancient Egypt." *Born in Heaven, Made on Earth: The Making of the Cult Image in the Ancient Near East*. Ed. Michael Dick. Winona Lake, IN: Eisenbrauns, 1999. 123-210.

McKeon, Richard. *The Basic Works of Aristotle*. New York: Random House, 1941.

Meskell, Lynn. *Private Life in New Kingdom Egypt*. Princeton, NJ: Princeton UP, 2002

Metzger, Henri. *Fouilles de Xanthos, Tome VI: La stèle trilingue du Létôon*. Paris: Librairie C. Klincksieck, 1979.

Metzger, David. "Pentateuchal Rhetoric and the Voice of the Aaronides." *Rhetoric Before and Beyond the Greeks*. Ed. Carol Lipson and Roberta Binkley. Albany, NY: SUNY P, 2004. 165-81.

Murnane, William J. *Texts from the Amarna Period in Egypt*. Writings from the Ancient World 5. Atlanta: Scholars Press/SBL, 1995.

Níssínen, Marttí. *Prophets and Prophecy in the Ancient Near East*. Writings from the Ancient World 12. Atlanta: SBL, 2003

O'Banion, John D. *Reorienting Rhetoric: the Dialectic of List and Story*. University Park, PA: Pennsylvania State UP, 1992

Pardee, Dennis. *Ritual and Cult at Ugarit*. Writings from the Ancient World 10. Atlanta: SBL, 2002

Parker, Simon B. *Ugaritic Narrative Poetry*. Writings from the Ancient World 9. Atlanta: Scholars Press, 1997

Parmenter, Dorina Miller. The Iconic Book: The Image of the Bible in Early Christian Rituals. *Postscripts* 2 (2006): 160-89.

Pernot, Laurent. "The Rhetoric of Religion." *Rhetorica* 24.3 (2006): 235–54.

Rappaport, Roy. *Ritual and Religion in the Making of Humanity*. Cambridge: Cambridge UP, 1999.

Roth, Martha. *Law Collections from Mesopotamia and Asia Minor.* Writings from the Ancient World 6. Atlanta: Scholars Press, 1995.

Sallaberger, Walther. "Vom politischen Handeln zu rituellen Königtum." *Ritual and Politics in Ancient Mesopotamia.* Ed. Barbara Nevling Porter. New Haven, CT: American Oriental Society, 2005. 63-98.

Sarefield, Daniel. . "The Symbolics of Book Burning: The Establishment of a Christian Ritual of Persecution." *The Early Christian Book.* Ed. William E. Klingshirn and Linda Safran. Washington: Catholic U of America P, 2007. 159-73.

Schott, Siegfried. "Die Opferliste als Schrift der Thoth." *Zeitschrift für die Ägyptische Sprache* 90 (1963): 103–110.

Schott, Siegfried. "Thoth als Verfasser heiliger Schriften." *Zeitschrift für die Ägyptische Sprache* 99 (1972): 20–25.

Singer, Itamar. *Hittite Prayers.* Writings from the Ancient World 11. Atlanta: SBL, 2002

Smith, Jonathan Z. "The Domestication of Sacrifice." *Violent Origins.* Ed. R. G. Hamerton-Kelly. Stanford, CA: Stanford UP, 1987. 191-235.

Smith, Jonathan Z. *To Take Place: Toward Theory in Ritual.* Chicago: U of Chicago P, 1987.

Staal, Fritz. "The Meaninglessness of Ritual." *Numen* 26.1 (1979): 2–22.

Strudwick, Nigel C. *Texts from the Pyramid Age,* Writings from the Ancient World 16. Atlanta: SBL, 2005.

Talon, Phillippe. "Le rituel comme moyen de légitimation politique au 1er millénaire en Mésopotamie." *Ritual and Sacrifice in the Ancient Near East.* Ed. J. Quaegebeur. Leuven, Belgium: Peeters, 1993. 421-33.

Talon, Phillippe. "Cases of Deviation in Neo-Assyrian Annals and Foundation Documents." *Ritual and Politics in Ancient Mesopotamia.* Ed. Barbara Nevling Porter. New Haven, CT: American Oriental Society, 2005. 99-114.

Watts, James W. "Story-List-Sanction: A Cross-Cultural Strategy of Ancient Persuasion." *Rhetoric Before and Beyond the Greeks.* Ed. Carol Lipson and Roberta Binkley. Albany, NY: SUNY P, 2004. 197-212.

Watts, James W. "Ritual Legitimacy and Scriptural Authority." *Journal of Biblical Literature* 124.3 (2005): 401–417.

Watts, James W. *Ritual and Rhetoric in Leviticus: From Sacrifice to Scripture.* Cambridge: Cambridge UP, 2007.

Westbrook, Raymond. "What is the Covenant Code?" In *Theory and Method in Biblical and Cuneiform Law: Revision, Interpolation and Development,* edited by Bernard M. Levinson, 15–36. Journal for the Study of the Old Testament Supplement 181. Sheffield: Sheffield Academic Press. 1994.

Wyatt, N. *Religious Texts from Ugarit: The Words of Ilimilku and his Colleagues.* The Biblical Seminar 53. Sheffield: Sheffield Academic Press. 1998.

3 The Gendering of Prophetic Discourse: Women and Prophecy in the Ancient Near East

Roberta Binkley

In rhetorical historiography, ancient prophecy (speech inspired by divine initiation) has largely been ignored as an important rhetorical discourse. While biblical scholars have looked long and deeply into the traditional biblical prophets, a rhetorical discursive analysis that takes into account the pre-Greek and pre-Judaic Ancient Near Eastern tradition has, to my knowledge, not been attempted by anyone in the discipline of rhetoric. Perhaps this neglect occurs because of the emphasis on the rational/*logos* in the Athenian rhetorical canon, promulgated particularly by the works of Greeks such as Plato, Aristotle, and Isocrates. This intellectual part of the mainstream of the Western tradition ignores the cultural implications of the important formative tradition of ancient prophecy. Secondly, the part of the prophetic tradition that survived was taken up in ancient Israel within the tradition of Judaism. Ancient Near Eastern techniques were adapted, between the eighth century BCE and the fourth century CE, and used for different social/cultural functions, often misogynist; they came to underpin the religious forms within the Western cultural tradition.

Prophecy, omens (a portent of phenomenon or circumstance or place), and the technique of divination (or gaining insight from reading omens) also suffer from the stigma of superstition, which perhaps helps to explain why rhetoricians have not looked at these phenomena. However, these techniques can reveal much about a society's fears and desires expressed through the rhetorical forms developed according to cultural mores.

The discourses of prophecy provide a revealing mirror into cultural attitudes and values. Prophecy can be broadly viewed as an ancient Near Eastern cross-cultural phenomenon (Overholt, 1986; Grabbe, 2000; Sasson, 1983; Parapola, 1997; Huffmon, 1976; Nissenen, 2003)[1]. Because the early prophetic tradition (pre-biblical) was primarily oral—prophets were orators and not scribes—texts are difficult to find, and even more problematic to evaluate since their existence depends on chance archeological finds, as is the case for much of pre-Biblical ancient Near Eastern history. Of course, much of this archeological history is centered in present-day Iraq and the destruction and looting of 12,500 ancient sites has been largely uncontrollable since the American invasion in 2002.[2]

Not until later in the tradition of literacy were prophecies written, when, around two thousand years after the development of literacy, scribes began to create a record of prophecies as a secondary development of the genre. But even then, the question of what was actually said remains murky throughout this period, up to and including the biblical prophets. Since archeological discoveries beginning in the nineteenth century, the record has become augmented, although still dependent on the chance discoveries of specific sites.

Among the more interesting discoveries are the extensive archives of the ancient city-states of Mari in southern modern Syria, and Ninevah from ancient Assyria. The Mari archives, from excavations of the royal courts of Zimrî-Lîm (Mari ca. 1760 BCE), and the Assyrian archives of Esarhaddon (Ninevah seventh century BCE), show an interesting continuity of women prophets over more than a millennium time span. The Mari site at Tell Harîri was the center of the ancient kingdom of Mari during the reign of Zimrî-Lîm, while Ninevah, located in present-day Iraq, was the capital of the ancient neo-Assyrian empire of Esarhaddon (680–669 BCE). In both places, due to historical circumstances, thousands of written artifacts have been preserved, including some of the discourses of prophets, both women and men. These artifacts suggest a great deal about prophecy and its cultural milieu. The prophets were more often women than men, which raises some significant issues.

In what follows, I am concerned with three questions: 1) What the women prophets are reported to have said, 2) how these women prophets authorized themselves as speakers (their tradition of oratory), and 3) what were the performative aspects in their presentations of prophecies? I look at the written tradition of prophecy extending over two and a half millennia (from ca. 2350 BCE until the final formation of the canon of the New Testament around the fourth century CE), a period of roughly 2,700 years.

LOOKING BACK BEFORE THE GREEKS

Why look back further than the classical Greek period? Rhetoric positions itself firmly within the intellectual tradition of the humanities in Western civilization, beginning with classical Greece. Rhetorical historiography begins its history of the discipline with the Greeks, either from the classical period (fourth-fifth centuries BCE) or, as scholars such as Sharon Crowley, Susan C. Jarratt, John Poulakos, Victor Vitanza and others argue, from the prior tradition of the earlier sophists.

Aren't 2,500 years of history enough? The problem is that two and a half millennia is only midway through the whole of the written record of civilization, which extends back more than two millennia before the classical Greek period. Of course, writing privileges a particular kind of history and understanding of the past, but to begin Western civilization with the Greeks is to distort even more the written historical record while privileging certain voices, certain historical periods, and particular social arrangements. In terms of the discipline of rhetoric—one of the oldest studies—blind spots in the use of our own terminology and systems prevents us from envisioning other possibilities. This ultimately restricts our understanding not only of the past, but also of other ways of seeing, being, and making knowledge.

Why focus on prophecy? As already mentioned, prophecy functioned as a powerful ancient rhetorical discourse. The prophet speaks and often acts as a powerful voice, her authority cloaked in the luminosity of the deity, to re-enforce underlying cultural beliefs, positions and mores . . . or sometimes to challenge them. Tracing the roles and the performers of the discourse of prophecy in the ancient Near East illustrates how this rhetoric of power, with the prophet speaking for the divine, reinforced a particular interpretation of divinity. That interpretation of divinity sanctioned particular social arrangements, authorizing *who* could speak and *to whom* they spoke. While the history of prophecy appears not to have begun as misogynist—women *and* men transmitted the voices of goddesses and gods—in the western sacred traditions, the voices and roles of women became erased or ignored, and largely lost. Prophetic power and performance became limited to men, who were instrumental in molding the spiritual rules that also operated as the sanctions of civil society, subordinating women's roles to the primacy of men in sacred tradition and in society.

DEFINING PROPHECY AND ORACLES

One of the problems with understanding what prophecy is and how it operates is that specialists in ancient history, including Assyriologists, Egyptologists, Old and New Testament scholars, and classical scholars, present differing nuances and sometimes-differing understandings. Biblical scholars tend to emphasize the element of prediction and, of course, to view prophecy as biblical-centered (Aberbach, 1993; Roberts, 2002). Others, Assyriologists, for example, underplay the element of prediction in prophetic discourse (Malamat 154). Other scholars define prophecy as an element of divination. In fact, there is a growing tendency in present-day biblical and ancient Near East studies to consider prophecy as a subset of divination (Varderkam 2083). The oldest techniques of divination are based on the interpretation of dreams and on the observation of the entrails of slaughtered sheep or goats (Hallo and Simpson 158).

In addition to the fact that the concept of prophecy is far from clear, the terms "prophecy" and "oracle" are frequently interchanged. Maria de Jong Ellis, in her extensive discussion of Mesopotamian oracles and prophetic texts, found that these terms come "loaded with hidden assumptions derived from the cultural background of modern interpreters" (132). "Oracle" seems to be often used as the term for a prophetic text, a message from the gods, but it also is frequently used for collections of divinatory omens, especially in later Greece. In his book *The Oracles of the Ancient World,* Trevor Curnow defined an oracle as an institution located at a place such as Delphi. After visiting 300 oracular sites in Egypt, Greece and Turkey (which existed much later than the ancient sites of Mari, Assyria and Judea), he determined that an oracle was a place "where people go to make a special kind of contact with the supernatural" (1).

Since the focus of this essay is on the role of women as prophets in the ancient world, I will sometimes conflate the two terms of oracle and prophecy, calling the text of a prophecy an oracle, as when I discuss the role of the Oracle of Delphi. At Delphi, the prophetess delivered prophecies that were later intermediated and interpreted by priests such as Plutarch and referred to by the Greeks as oracles, hence the term oracular prophecy in relation to Greek usage.

Martti Nissinen, an Assyriologist, has argued for a meaning of prophecy as intermediation between the divine (a deity) and a person[3] (20). While quite broad and not without problems, this definition will be the umbrella under which I discuss the tradition of prophecy in the ancient Near East. Hence, I define prophecy as inspired speech at the initiative of a divine power. My intention with this definition is to locate the discourse of prophecy within a broad religious and socio-cultural context. Religion and social life are intimately intertwined in the ancient world. Religion has always been the continuation of politics by other means.

Prophecy, the "Evolution" of a Genre?

Prophecy in its many forms, including dream interpretation, has been with us as a species as long as we've been alive. Prophets and people with paranormal abilities have existed throughout human history and far back into prehistory[4]. Women are documented in the ancient Near East from the "Antediluvian" age (3100–2900 BCE) in positions of sacred power (Hallo 23). Through the time of the biblical patriarchs and beyond to the time of Paul of Tarsus, women filled the roles of prophets and diviners as frequently as did men, with more female than male prophets in ancient Mesopotamia (Parapola, XLVIII).

The earliest mention of a woman's role as a prophet/dream interpreter comes from the ancient priestess, poet, Enheduanna (ca. 2350 BCE), who wrote three hymns to the Goddess Inanna as well as an important theological collection, The Temple Hymns. Enheduanna briefly speaks of her role as prophetess from the beginning of written tradition—as the first known writer. In her long hymn to the goddess Inanna known as "The Exaltation," Enheduanna tells of being driven from the temple by a rebellion. Her father, Sargon of Akkad, in the process of creating the first empire conquered Lugalzagesi of Uruk but left him to govern the city. It is this Lugalzagsi whom Enheduanna mentions by name in her hymn, The Exaltation, who rebels and drives her from her positions in Ur and Uruk. She mourns the loss of her role interpreting the dreams of the goddess Ningal:

> I no longer lift my hands from the pure sacred bed
> I no longer unravel Ningal's gifts of dream

As a result of her banishment, the connection to cosmic forces and to
the voice of the goddess has been severed:

> without YOU is no fate fixed
> without YOU is no keen counsel arrived
> She implies that truth is eternal:
> The oracles uttered on your tongue
> Never change in heaven or earth[5]

Not only does Enheduanna experience this loss on a personal level, but
as a loss to her people. In her exile she cannot perform one of the most
important duties of her office, the prophetic role of unraveling the
goddess Ningal's gifts of dreams both to herself and to others, the role
of elucidating the underlying truths or oracles. No one knows what the
cost will be, what mistakes will be made, or the end result of ignorant
actions taken unmediated by divine counsel.

Clearly, the holy site of the temple, because it was consecrated and
the place inhabited by the goddess, seems to be necessary to the prophetic process for Enheduanna in her role as interpreter of the goddess
Ningal's dreams, dreams elicited and meant for prophetic guidance. It
was in this consecrated place that the goddess Ningal dwelt, and there
her priestess, Enheduanna, lived (Westenholz). This tradition of the
sacred location of prophetesses, part of the authorization of their discourse of power, continued throughout Mesopotamian history when
later prophetesses, situated as temple officials, spoke in the authorized
voice of the Goddess Inanna/Ishtar under her many names.

Embedded in this tradition, there also seems to be a strong performative aspect. Whether Enheduanna proclaimed her dream prophecies and messages to an audience is unclear. Her hymn mentions the
absence of her prophetic function because of her banishment; however,
her hymns do not seem to be overtly prophetic, but more a celebration
and description of the Goddess Inanna, her power and her qualities.
We do know, however, that she wrote her hymns to be sung to an audience, for she says:

> That which I created for you at midnight
> May the cult singers repeat at noon.

Thus, her hymn, *The Exaltation of Inanna,* foresees the response of an audience, most likely a temple audience.

THE MARI PROPHECIES

Roughly 600 years after Enheduanna, the royal archives of Mari attest to the continued prominence of women as prophets and their performative roles. The ancient city-state kingdom of Mari was the center of a significant political and economic power in the Near East. The kingdom, dating back to the third millennium, became a formidable power in the second half of the third millennium and the first half of the second millennium BCE (before and during the lives of Abraham, Isaac and Jacob). Most of the 20,000 tablets evacuated from the temples and palaces of Mari date from the time of the last kings of Mari (Yasmah-Addu ca. 1792–1775 BCE and Zimrî-Lîm ca. 1774–1760 BCE) before Mari's destruction by Hammurabi (ca. 1700 BCE).

The words of some prophets have been preserved in royal correspondence, and come only from archeological finds centered in palace archives. Although these finds are rich in artifacts, any discussion of Mari prophetic texts is thus based on a somewhat limited and insufficient picture. The letter writers refer to prophecies, but do not necessarily quote the message word-for-word; according to Nissinen, the letter writers "present their own interpretations of what they consider the essential point of the message" (15). Dream reports and prophetic messages seem to be fundamentally the same from the scattered evidence at Mari. What is interesting about the preserved fragments of royal correspondence from Mari, especially during the reign of Zimrî-Lîm, are the gendered issues visible in the prophecies, which constitute discourses of power in this culture.

Abraham Malamat notes that more than half of the prophetic documents from Mari involve laypersons, both as reporters and as prophets, and that a "large proportion of women" are represented (165). Also among the professional prophets, a considerable number of women were active. A third to a half of all the published prophecies involve dreams, a widespread phenomenon throughout the ancient Near East including ancient Israel, a phenomenon first evident in Enheduanna's texts.

Translations by Jack Sasson reveal the format in which such written dream prophecies were presented. The following example by Addu-Dūra (a woman prophet) comes from a letter sent directly to the king,

Zimrî-Lîm of Mari. The Mari archives also include two other letters in which Addu-Dūri reports dreams. In this particular letter to the king, she reports her dream as follows:

> Since the restoration/destruction of your father's house, I have never had such a dream as this. Previous portents of mine were as this pair.
>
> In my dream, I entered the chapel of the goddess Belett-ekallim: but Belett-ekallim was not in residence! Moreover, the statues before her were not there either. Upon seeing this I broke into uncontrollable weeping.
>
> This dream of mine occurred during the evening watch!
>
> I turned around and Dada, priest of the goddess Istar-pishra was standing at the door of Belet-idallim's chapel: but a hostile voice (apparently an undefined voice, perhaps a spirit, she hears) kept on uttering. "Return, O Dagan, Return, O Dagan!": is what it kept on uttering.
>
> More! A female ecstatic of the goddess Annunitum arose in the temple to announce (note here the prophetess speaks as the goddess): "Zimrî-Lîm! Do not go on a journey: stay in Mari, and I myself will be responsible (for you)."
>
> My lord, therefore, should not neglect his own protection. I have herewith sealed a lock of my hair and fringes of my garment, sending them to my lord.
>
> (Sasson, "Mari Dreams," 286)

Zimrî-Lîm was the last of his dynasty. Ten years after the prophecy, Hammurabi of Babylon sacked Mari. In one of the most calculated destructive actions in ancient history, Hammurabi removed the population, sent scribes to catalog everything and then spent two years completely leveling the city, after which he torched it. What happened to Zimrî- Lîm is uncertain.

This dream prophecy, Sasson notes, focuses not on the cultic aspect of the goddess's presence, but on the theological import of her disappearance. The Goddess, Bellett-ekallim, apparently is one of the deities charged with protecting the king during his ventures. Her voluntary exit is obviously serious ("Mari Dreams" 287). Throughout the Middle East from the time of Enheduanna (ca. 2350 BCE) to that of the early biblical prophets, the abandonment by deities of their temples meant the abandonment of the city and the loss of the protection of that deity. Cities were often attacked and destroyed as a result of this abandonment. In both Mesopotamian as well as Hebrew convention, gods leave their shrines when they decide to abandon a city to its enemies. In Mesopotamia, the numinous vital qualities of the deities were resident in their images.

Here, the prophetess Addu-Dūri appears to be attached to a cultic center, the temple of the Goddess Belett-ekallim. Her concern is not with her authority to speak; she takes that for granted. She tells us that she had a previous dream about the father of the king. Obviously, her voice has been heard in the past in an official capacity. Thus, her cultural and cultic role as a prophetess seems to be self-evident both to her and her audience. In Mari, specialized personnel were attached to both the temple and to the divinity for that temple. Addu-Dūri is obviously authorized, even expected to speak, because of her official social position as an *apiltum* (respondent). Gilda Hamel explains that an *apiltum* gave more elaborate proclamations than did ecstatic prophets, and could write to the king (2).

Addu-Dūri's concern is primarily with the veracity of her message: "I have herewith sealed a lock of my hair and the fringes of my garment, sending them to my lord." This, too, was common practice at Mari. All prophecies sent to the king were conveyed with a lock of hair and a small part of the prophet's garment. The diviners[6], usually through extispicy (the examination of sacrificed sheep livers), checked and verified the oracles, according to Nissinen, to exclude the "possible misinterpretations and other faults resulting from the vulnerability of the intermediary and the often tangled process of communication" (16).

One of the most common designations of a prophetess is the term *muhhum*. Nissenen explains that the word is derived from the root *mahu*, "'to become crazy, to go into a frenzy,' which refers to receiving and transmitting divine words in an altered state of mind" (6). In this particular case, Addu-dūri received her information from the goddess in the altered state of a dream. Her performance may have occurred in a cultic context during a sacrifice in the temple before it was transmitted to the king. There were people under the obligation to send such reports to the ruler. Jean-Marie Durand quotes a letter to Zîmri-Lîm:

> When my lord prepared himself to leave for war, he
> gave me these instructions: "You live in the god's city.
> Write me (any) prophecy that will happen in the god's
> temple and that you'll hear. (26).

Abbu-dūri as a prophet could have also spoken directly for the Goddess Belett-idallim, as did the female ecstatic that she quoted in her prophecy to Zîmri-Lîm.

The prophets did not always support the king. They were sometimes critical of the king for failing in his duties to various gods or temples. In one prophecy, translated by Herbert Huffman, the king is reminded of his duty to promote justice. The God Adad says to him in a prophecy: "When a woman or a man has suffered injustice appeals to you, answer their plea and do them justice" (173).

The record from Mari indicates a predominance of the women prophets, both lay and priestly, whose words, as preserved in the royal archives, were usually addressed to the king. Sometimes they were automatically authorized to speak, often as priestesses or temple personnel; at times, they were lay people who had received a message. Among lay people, the message itself seems to be their authorization (Nissinen 14). Diviners verified all messages, both those of the temple prophets and the lay people. At Mari, the preserved reports are addressed to the king, usually in the form of letters or messages, but a performance of the prophecies seems to have taken place in cultic centers. It appears that in Mari, prophecy was an oratorical ritual performed and then later reported, which helps to account for the lack of written texts outside of preserved palace archives (Nissinen 13–17).

THE ASSYRIAN PROPHECIES

The Assyrian prophecies, first published in 1875, have been preserved in a copy of an unusual cuneiform tablet in the British Museum. The tablet came from Nineveh during the reign of the Assyrian king Esarhaddon (660–669 BCE). Still, more than 125 years after their discovery, the prophecies remain little known. Biblical scholars seldom mention them despite the fact that they provide close parallels to Old Testament prophecy (Parapola, XIII; Nissinen, 4–5). Prophecy was a cross-cultural phenomenon throughout the millennia of history in the Middle East (Overhold, Grabbe).

One of the most systematic studies of the theology involved in the Assyrian prophecies and their overall connection with Mesopotamian and biblical prophecy involves the work of Finnish scholar, Simo Parapola, who spent twenty-five years studying the state archives of Assyria. The preserved prophecies relate primarily to the seventh century BCE period of Assurbanipal and Esarhaddon. As at Mari, many are characterized as reports to the king. For example, the prophecy quoted below offers words of encouragement to Assurbanipal, and appears to have been delivered in the middle of the Samas-samu-urking rebellion (April, 650 BCE) . The tone of the prophecy reflects the military situation. Six months previously, the Babylonian army had captured Cutha, which for the Assyrian king was extremely provocative. Within months, Assyria attacked Babylon.

The prophecy opens with an address to Assurbanipal giving his lineage as the son of Millissu (Istar). Interestingly, it's known that the kings Assurbanipal and Esarhaddon shortly after their birth were separated from their birth parents and brought up in the temples of Istar of Nineveh and Arabela. They were nursed and educated by initiates in the sacred mysteries. (Parpola XL).

> O son (Assurbanipal) of Millissu, of the Lady of Arbela
> They are the strongest among the gods;

Then the prophetess, Dunnasa-amur of Arabella, speaks as the Goddess Istar of Arbela in the first person:

> I roam the desert desiring your life. I
> cross over rivers and oceans, I traverse mountains and
> mountain chains, I cross over all rivers.
> Droughts and showers consume me
> and affect my beautiful figure. I am worn out,
> my body is exhausted for your sake.
>
> I have ordained life for you in the
> Assembly of the gods. My arms are strong,

They shall not forsake you before the gods.
My shoulders are sturdy, they will keep carrying you.
I keep demanding life for you with my
words; . . . your life; you shall increase life

The prophecy closes in the last stanza with the voice of the prophet, continuing to speak as the goddess, blessing the king.

O favorite of Nabu, may your lips
Rejoice. I keep speaking good words about
You in the assembly of all the gods; I roam
the desert desiring your life.
In woe I will rise and slaughter
your enemy; [your . . .] will [. . .] and return to his
country.

Following a break, the prophetess then speaks as herself in a ritual conclusion:

May Mullissu and the Lady of Arabela
keep Ashurbanipal, the creation of their
hands, alive for ever.

By the mouth of the woman Dunnaša-amur
of Arabela (40–41)

How did this prophetess draw the self-confidence which enabled her to speak, as did all the prophets, not *for* but *as* the Goddess Ishtar? Part of the answer lies in the conception of the goddess. Parapola explains that Ištar is conceived as divine power working in particular humans and thus bridging the gulf between human and the divine. He says, "she is the emotion (*libbu*) moving through the prophet, the breath (*šāru*) that comes from her "heart," and the voice (*rigmu*) and words *(dibbī)* that emerge from the prophets mouth" (XXVI). Ištar, then, corresponds to the biblical holy spirit.

Based on lexical analysis, Parapola believes that "while any individual (and especially any devotee of Ištar) could have a vision or a dream and report it, only a few special individuals could qualify as prophets, to speak with the mouth of the Goddess." These individuals, he believes, were members of the temple community (XLVII). The Neo-Assyrian term for "prophet" was *raggīmu* (fem. *Raggintu*, "prophetess"), which literary means "shouter/proclaimer." The verb (*ragāmu*) implies that prophetic oracles were generally delivered in a loud voice—"shouted"—and hence, addressed masses of people rather than a single individual (XLV). These prophets, then, were orators. The character of the prophecy remained ecstatic in character: "The possession of the prophet by the Goddess, involved a change in consciousness, purposely triggered by ascetic techniques such as weeping and wailing. In addition to oral prophecy, these techniques also produced visions and dreams" (Parapola, XLVI).

After years of analysis and wide reading, Parapola linked the Assyrian prophetic tradition with "close ties to Ancient Near East prophecy in general and to the cult of Ishtar under her many names (Inanna, Istar of Arabela, Mullissu, Banitu, and Ukittu)" (XVI). By the time of the Assyrian prophecies, 1,700 years after Enheduanna, the strong tradition of women prophets continued to exist as a documented, wide cultural phenomenon. Similar to the case in Mari a thousand years earlier, women remained actively involved in prophetic roles in Assyria. In his close textual analysis of the texts, Parapola found that the authorship of the twenty eight oracles of the corpus could be assigned to fifteen different prophets; four were male and nine were female, with two apparently bisexual or asexual. He also found that the comparatively high number of women paralleled the prominence of prophetesses and female ecstatics in Mari, as well as in later Gnosticism, which includes the tradition of the Gospel of Mary Magdalene (Parapola XLVIII). In his summary, he states that Assyrian prophecy provides an example of the close ties of ancient Near East prophecy in general to the cult of the "mother goddess" and its esoteric doctrines of salvation. The cult of Ištar as a cross-cultural phenomenon, in light of comparative evidence, not only preceded, but also exerted a deep influence on the "mystery cults" of classical antiquity including Gnosticism, Jewish mysticism and Neoplatonism (XVII). It deeply influenced Greek sacred traditions, where Istar/Inanna and her myths have been shown to be the core of Greek mythology (Penglase 237–245).

Thus, it appears that from the time of Enheduanna near the beginning of writing, and likely long before, there existed traditions of esoteric knowledge, the application of which involved women in various roles as high priestesses, as prophets, as temple servers, and even as lay

prophecy and oratory

people, who occasionally donned the prophetic mantle. They generally spoke for a female deity, a goddess, usually Inanna/Istar. Their authority came from cultic position and long tradition, and they acted in the role of orators, often speaking to a large and elite audience.

What happened to this tradition? Evolutionary progress, the narrative of progress of civilization and religion, grew out of the invention of European imperialism, as "a way of constructing history in its own image and claiming precedence for Western culture" (Bahrani 10). This progress, defined as evolution, has worked to erase women's voices, even their presence, through its rhetorical control of powerful discourses such as prophecy. The Oracle of Delphi provides a clear example of just how this "evolution" took place.

THE ORACLE OF DELPHI

Even among the ancient Athenian Greeks, notorious for their misogyny, the most famous and influential person in the ancient Greek world was a woman, the Oracle of Delphi. Based on archeological evidence, the origins of Delphi go back to Minoan times before 2000 BCE. Recent research has come to see how deeply indebted Greek myths and sacred stories were to Mesopotamian influence.[7] Delphi had been, for many centuries, a sanctuary of the great earth goddess Ga or Gaia (Penglase 209; Walsh 58).

The oldest version of the myth, *The Homeric Hymn to the Pythian Appollo* (sixth century BCE), tells of the Greek-speaking Dorians invading the pre-Greek world toward the end of the second millennium BCE. As conquerors do, they took over the great sanctuaries, changed their character, while at the same time adapting the underlying function. Apollo replaced Gaia. Her cult image, the snake, was smashed, but the role of prophetic ecstasy performed by the priestess continued as long as Delphi existed, only the interpretation of the Phythia's words became the role of male priests, a classic example of the "evolution" of power. However, remnants of the tradition before Apollo remained. The far more ancient tradition of women speaking can still be seen from the fact that the *Phythia*, women priestesses, remained the primary voices. We know a lot about Delphi from the writing of Plutarch, who served as a high priest of Apollo. He dedicated several of his books to Clea, a high priestess of Delphi.

Lynda Walsh, in her examination of the Oracle of Delphi argues that "the oracle calls into question traditional dichotomies in Greek rhetoric and philosophy. . . . the binary distinctions of *muthos/logos*, *techne/tuche*, Self/Other" (56). In her study, she explained that understanding the function of the oracles in the Athenian polis, and their interaction with Athenian rhetoric, "requires an account of their production and reception that must consider social facts such as gender, ethnicity, political alignments, economics, literacy and religion." (57) The oracle, she claims, continually frustrated attempts to form an Athenian identity based on the logical dichotomies of *techne/tuche*, cosmos/consciousness, and *muthos/logos*. I would add that the oracle's central cultural function also frustrated Athenian attempts to completely erase living women from sacred traditions, despite female cultural representations of deity.

The tradition of the classics came to have as one of its primary *topoi* the opposition of *logos* (rationality) and *muthos* (irrational myth/ religious thinking) as David Hoffman explains. He claims that this opposition was staged in the context of a narrative of socio-political progress that told the story of how Athens was able to shake off the fetters of its mytho-religious tradition and build itself into a rational and democratic society (40). Thus, "the liberal tradition constituted the opposition between *muthos* and *logos* in the service of its narrative of socio-political progress" (44). Among those scholars who have challenged that particular progress narrative, Susan Jarratt demonstrates that logical thought continued to take place within the "mythic condition" (32–39).

Delphic oracles challenged *logos* with enigmatic pronouncements bringing into play the unconscious, and thereby opening up other interpretations. Pilgrims had to complete the oracle through their own thought, their own clarifications of feeling, and their own action. The holy words were only the beginning of a story. Roger Lipsey claims that "this characteristic incompleteness and ambiguity, and the call to intellectual and moral effort they implied, form a large part of the abiding appeal of Delphi" (xvii). For example, Croesus of Lydia donated a fortune to the oracle to find out if he should attack the Persian empire. The oracle told him, "If you go to war you will cause the destruction of a great empire." He went to war and ended up not only defeated but captured. He sent word to the oracle asking why he was misled. The word came back that he wasn't misled; he had been told that there would be the destruction of a great empire. It was his.

OLD TESTAMENT PROPHECY

Prophecy had its roots in Mesopotamia as a role primarily of priestesses. The Delphic oracles were spoken by women and later interpreted by priests, but in the Old Testament, prophecy became primarily a man's job. Symbolic vestiges of women's involvement remained, but only seven prophetesses are mentioned: Miriam, Sarah, Deborah, Hannah, Abigail, Huldah, and Esther. Forty eight male prophets are named in the Old Testament, with some quoted at length (Aune 338).

Old Testament prophecy traditionally is the work of scribes, writing redactions of redactions to tell the story of the prophets. In the Judaic prophetic tradition, the problem seems to be whose voice speaks and how close to the source are the stories of prophets in the final canonical version. These stories nevertheless—whatever the amalgam of truth and added fiction—have become canonized. The voices treated at any length are those of men. For women living in Western cultures deeply influenced by Jewish and Christian traditions, the Hebrew Bible is a central cultural document, a compilation of materials spanning approximately one thousand years of human experience, which often defines their sexuality and their way of life. As Drorah Setel notes, "examination of biblical texts shows an interesting congruence between ancient and modern depictions of female sexuality"; she adds that this is particularly evident in the writings of the second part of the division of Prophets in the Hebrew Bible that " . . . develop a specific use of female imagery that does not occur in previous periods. They seem to be the first to use objectified female sexuality as a symbol of evil" (86). The personification of the female as evil, worked out through metaphors of marriage (a property relationship) between Yahweh and Israel, has been examined by feminist biblical scholars (Bob Becking and Meindert Dijkstra, Athalya Brenner, Esther Fuchs, Margaret Miles, and Fokkelien Van Dijk-Hemmes) who specifically discuss the pornographic use of the metaphoric image of harlotry in these prophets.[8]

For example, the Book of Hosea begins with Yahweh telling Hosea "Go, take yourself a wife of harlotry/ and have children of harlotry" (Hosea 1:2). This results in the use of a speech act of verbal violence, the threat of an attack on Gomer, the wife, who is identified with the land as well as the people of Israel: "Let her put away her harlotries from her face/and her adulteries from between her breast/ lest I strip her naked/ (Hosea 2:4)." Public humiliation, part of the sadomasochism mechanism of pornography, also appears in Jeremiah and Ezekiel.

In Jeremiah, as in the Books of Hosea and Ezekiel, Israel again becomes the faithless wife, the harlot, but the description is extended to animalization. This animalization of the metaphorical woman is one of the most striking features of Jeremiah 2. Brenner calls it "an innovation an original contribution to biblical pornographic lore" (183). Thus, the role of women prophets disappears, their voices are no longer heard, and the rhetoric of prophecy becomes one that negatively characterizes women.

While women prophets are mentioned in the Old Testament, they are seldom given a voice. Miriam, mentioned in Exodus, is the first woman to be given the title of prophet in the Old Testament. As the sister of Moses, she is noted for her prophecies and her leadership role, but during the Exodus, she challenges Moses:

> "Has the Lord indeed spoken only by Moses? Has He
> not spoken through us also?" (Numbers 12:2).

Clearly, with this challenge to authority, she crosses the patriarchal boundary. Her punishment is immediate. Once these words are spoken, the deity strikes her with leprosy. While Moses graciously heals her, he also exiles her for seven days. Her example, even today, is held up to women as a warning against challenging male authority.

Women and Prophecy in the New Testament

In the Gnostic Gospel of Mary Magdalene—discovered in Egypt in 1896 and part of the topic of the best-selling mystery, *The DaVinci Code*—after Jesus's death, Mary Magdalene tells the disciples that Jesus's spirit and his grace are with them to protect them. She then goes on to relate a prophetic vision that she had the same day. Unfortunately, the papyrus texts breaks off, and so—as with most all women's prophecies—that vision is lost.

When the text resumes, the disciples make their doubt clear. Andrew challenges her, and Peter says that the savior did not speak with a woman and tell her things he did not tell the other apostles. Peter accuses her of saying untrue things, things she has made up. Her vision is not the authorized one, according to Peter, nor does it become part of the Biblical canon.

By the time of Paul, women prophets were becoming increasingly frowned upon. Scholar Antoinette Clark Wire analyzes Paul's first letter to the Corinthians in a brilliant social-historical reconstruction, *The Corinthian Women Prophets: A Reconstruction Through Paul's Rhetoric*. She attempts to hear the voices of the Corinthian women prophets through Paul's rhetoric in 1 Corinthians. Because there are no records of the women's' prophecies, Wire's reconstruction is an attempt to present as accurate a picture as possible of the women prophets in the church of first-century Corinth. To this end she employs rhetorical analysis to uncover the social world of the women by analyzing Paul's rhetorical techniques. Paul was clearly trying to persuade the Corinthian Christians in his rhetorical arguments. His opposition to the women prophets emerges in his discussion of the role of women in the community.

Paul used several arguments, both to counter the women's understanding of the gospel, and to nullify their claims of wisdom, freedom, *and* leadership in the church. He seems careful not to directly refute their interpretations. Instead, he sets up laws and structures that make it impossible for their equal participation. For example, he argues that the women who are married should not abstain from sexual relations with their husbands in order to be ecstatic prophets, and he encourages unmarried women to marry because it is necessary to preserve the morality of the men in the community. Thus, women have freedom to decide neither their roles, nor how they fulfill those roles.

When Paul admonishes the women to cover their heads, he offers the explanation that clearly signifies their subordination:

> For a man ought not to have his head veiled since he
> is the image and glory of God; but the woman is the
> glory of man. Man, you see, is not from woman but
> woman from man: for indeed man was not created for
> the sake of the woman but woman for the sake of the
> man. (Anchor Bible 11.2–16)

The practice of women letting their hair flow loose and uncovered was associated with ecstatic rituals in a number of pagan communities. Corinth was a major center for Isis, and possibly some of the women had once worshiped her. It was also well known that during the worship of Dionysus, god of wine and revelry, women let their hair loose like the mythic Maenads, the ancient ecstatic female worshipers of Dionysus.

This interpretation of gender relations clearly encourages the eventual invisibility of women in Christian sacred tradition. But Paul doesn't stop here; he goes even further, taking away women's voices:

> Just as it is in all the churches of the saints, let the wives be silent in the churches; for they are not permitted to talk. Then let them continue to be subordinate just as the law also says. If they want to learn anything, let them ask their husbands at home; for it is disgraceful for a wife to talk in church. (Anchor Bible 14:33b-36)

Paul's motivation emerges as enforcing gender differences while trying to distance Christianity from pagan practices with their emphasis on the Goddess and the feminine. As Wire points out, the activities of the women prophets jeopardized Paul's own gospel. Their interpretations endangered his leadership with its emphasis on the cross and sacrifice, his version of Christianity (184).

Yet ironically, the most famous part of I Corinthians, the section most often quoted from the pulpit, is about love:

> Love is patient, love is kind. It is not Jealous; it does not brag; it is not puffed with pride. It does not behave unpresentably; it does not calculate evil. It does not rejoice at injustice but rejoices over truth. It keeps all confidences, maintains all faithfulness, all hope, all steadfastness (Anchor Bible 12:31b-14:1a)

And that Pauline doctrine resembles far more ancient teachings. Socrates explains that he learned about love from the priestess Diotima. These teachings were part of the Mystery Religions and derived from the worship of ancient goddesses (Parapola XVI)

However, in the next stanza, after Paul talks about love, he immediately sets up love as an antithesis to prophecy, tongues, and the understanding of mysteries:

> Love never fails; but if there are gifts of prophecy, they will be nullified; if there are tongues, they will cease; if there is knowledge it will be nullified. For we know

partially, and we prophesy partially; . . . (Anchor Bible
12:31b-14:1a)

With this final move, Paul, takes away any authority that the Corinthian women prophets might have had. Instead, he reinforces the
authority and hierarchy of the church and the dogma of scriptures
while annulling the power of prophecy and women's leadership that
existed from far more ancient times.

John, the author of Revelations, provides another example of
the conflict between early Christianity and the authority of women
prophets. He launches a diatribe against a woman he labels as "Jezebel." The original Jezebel, mentioned in Kings 16, a pagan whom
Jeroboam married, was allegedly responsible for killing the prophets
of Yahweh. John terms the woman he calls "Jezebel" the false prophetess of Thyatira (Rev. 2:20–24). He accuses her of inciting Christians
to practice immorality and sanctioning the eating of meat previously
consecrated to pagan idols (a common and widespread practice in the
ancient world). John's tirade reflects a conflict of authority, his own
versus that of "Jezebel"; Jezebel may well have opposed John as a false
prophet of a "new" cult.

Jezebel's side of the story has not survived, and the ancient prophetic tradition of priestesses almost disappeared. The attitudes of Moses,
Paul, and John demonstrate the deeply embedded Judeo-Christian tradition of fear of the role of women prophets and women's leadership.
Esther Fuchs explains that "Prophecy entails a rhetorical and numinous activity, symptomatic of a close relationship between a messenger
and a divine source. The biblical text, both narrative and poetic, stren-
uously suppresses such a possibility in the context of female prophecy"
(68). The gradual patriarchalization of the church in the second and
third centuries, as Elisabeth Shüssler Fiorenza reminds us, ". . . not
only engendered the exclusion of all women from ecclesiastical leadership but also eliminated the freedoms that slave women had gained
by joining the Christian movement" (134). With the institutionaliza-
tion of Christianity and the rationalization of its authority structures,
prophecy became redundant as well as dysfunctional: "The much-dis-
cussed problem of the decline of prophecy in early Christianity must
be viewed as a social rather than a theological issue. . . . the earlier role
of the prophets as articulators of the norms, values, and decisions of
the invisible head of the church was taken over by the visible figures
of the teacher, preacher, theologian, and church leader" (Aune 338).

Throughout this "evolution" in tradition, female voices became progressively stifled and finally silenced altogether.

CONCLUSION

Yet, the tantalizing traces of women are also an indication of the strength and longevity of the female oratorical tradition that was first recorded by Enheduanna and continued as a strong, viable tradition within cultic roles for the next 2,700 years. The rhetorical condemnations of women, their voices and words in canonical scripture also demonstrate their lingering power and continuing challenge to patriarchal authority. No record exists of Enheduanna's specific prophecies beyond her poetry. Nor does it exist for the other women, including Miriam, who spoke in the Old Testament, nor for the Corinthian women prophets. Only indirectly, a few of the oracles pronounced at Delphi and some of the Mari and Assyrian prophecies were preserved. But Paul's need to erase the women's prophetic voices at Corinth and the Old Testament's glancing mention of powerful women prophets nevertheless indicate traces of that strong ancient tradition. Preserved texts from Mari and from Assyria provide insight into the continuity of the leadership role of women in the spiritual life of the ancient Near East that continued during the time of the patriarchs and the biblical prophets 600 years before Paul.

In the ancient world, prophecy operated in the area between human and deity (often a goddess). It was in this in-between realm of the conscious and subconscious that a rich exchange took place. Diotima describes the process to Socrates in the *Symposium,* as the welding together of two worlds. The first prophet, Enheduanna, writes of allowing the spirit of the goddess Ningal (the mother of the goddess Inanna) to come through her, bringing the words, wisdom and images of the feminine divine to the material world. The palace libraries of ancient Mari and Assyria testify to this continuing tradition of prophetesses and priestesses.

Throughout the ancient world, long before the male-monotheistic religions became the controlling expression of spiritual life, women and goddesses were an integral part of spirituality. The feminine was celebrated as part of the Indo-European stock of ideas. Part of this celebration included women's prophetic voices. In those ancient societies, women assumed important leadership and prophetic roles, their oratory and cultic roles authorized by tradition.

These are all
traditions for
meaning for
Western
thought?

Reading the tradition of prophecy diachronically through a critical rhetorical lens, documenting women who spoke and performed as orators, shows the "evolution" of prophecy as a rhetoric of power in the Western cultural and spiritual traditions. The role of prophet became exclusively a male role frequently exploited to disenfranchise, to denigrate and finally eliminate the feminine and women's voices from sacred and social tradition. Women's voices, their oratory, disappeared from the Western sacred and cultural tradition, replaced by the rhetoric of male-dominated monotheistic religions that offered the social justification for continued suppression, silence and social disenfranchisement of women.

NOTES

1. Martti Nissinen, in his intensive study of Ancient Near Eastern prophecy, explains that among prophetic texts in Egypt, as he defines prophecy—the process of intermediation between a deity and the prophet—only the Report of Wenamon qualifies as a prophetic text.

2. Dr. Donny George Youkhanna, chief administrator of the Iraqi Museum in Baghdad until forced to flee in 2006, in a speech, March 2, 2007 at Arizona State University, explained that throughout the country there are 12,500 sites that looters have been mining, moving from site to site. Unfortunately, lacking cars and guns, only 1,400 police are allocated to the protection of these sites. The museum in Baghdad was permanently sealed in 2004 because of drive-by shootings of guards. The major part of the collection remaining, after the looting of the museum, is now hidden. Of the 15,000 objects stolen, 3,709 have been returned.

3. A wide spectrum of ancient Near Eastern sources exist that either reflect the prophetic process of communication or mention a prophetic designation. At present, the updated list of documents that meet these requirements constitutes a group of some 140 individual texts, consisting basically of two kinds: oracles of deities in written form, and references in documents of different kinds—letters, inscriptions, administrative records and religious texts—that mention prophets, quote their sayings, or speak of their activities. Martti Nissinen has divided this material into four groups:

> (1) The largest corpus comes from eighteenth-century Mari, comprising fifty letters with prophetic quotations. In addition, the Mari corpus includes a handful of documents other than letters that mention prophets: two ritual texts, several administrative documents, a report of crimes and a yet unpublished literary text, the so-called "Epic of Zimri-Lin" (25).

(2) The prophetic activity of the Old Babylonian period was not restricted to Mari. This is demonstrated by two oracles of the goddess Kititum (Istar) to Ibalpiel II, a contemporary of Zimri-Lîm and the ruler of the Kingdom of Esunna located northeast of Babylonia.(26)

(3) The second largest corpus of ancient Near Eastern prophecy derives from seventh-century Nineveh. This Neo-Assyrian corpus comprises eleven clay tablets, including twenty nine individual prophetic oracles addressed to Kings Esarhaddon (681–669 BCE) and Assurbanipal (668–627 BCE), who ruled the Assyrian empire during the time Manasseh and Josiah were kings of Judah in Jerusalem; hence, the Neo-Assyrian prophets roughly coincide with the 'classical" prophets of the Hebrew Bible.

Apart from the oracles, there are more than twenty Neo-Assyrian texts—inscriptions, letters, administrative documents, cultic texts and a treat—alluding in one way or another to prophets or their sayings (26).

(4) This Mesopotamian documentation of prophecy is supplemented by a random collection of individual texts from different ages and different geographical areas classified as prophecy because of reference to a human intermediary transmitting divine messages, or because the texts include prophetic designations. The temporal and geographic distribution of these odd pieces of prophecy is surprisingly wide, ranging from the twenty-first to second centuries BCE, a period of almost two millennia, and covering considerable parts of the ancient Near East. The texts represent different genres, including letters, administrative texts, a literary text, a ritual, lexical lists and omens (26–27).

4. The oldest known shaman's grave dated during the Upper Paleolithic Era (60,000 years ago), excavated in the Pavlov Hills of the Czech Republic, is that of a woman. Anthropologist Barbara Tedlock, who has spent her life investigating the roles of women and shamanism argues that "Despite the proof of language and artifacts, despite pictorial representations, ethnographic narratives, and eyewitness accounts, the importance—no, the primacy—of women in shamanic traditions has been obscured and denied" (4). Tedlock sees shamanism as a universal phenomenon, but elaborated differently by individuals and cultures. She believes that at the heart of shamanic practice is the active pursuit of knowledge and that the transcendent role of women prophets is a dimension of shamanism. Still another attestation to the ancient roots of the practice of prophecy is Michael Winkelman's book, *Shamanism: The Neural Ecology of Consciousness and Healing;* he examines the psychobiological and psychocognitive foundations of shamanism and related universal traditions. The perspective articulated "is a neurophenomenological approach that links neurological structures and processes with cultural

practices and personal experience" (xii). In short, as a species, humans have always been wired with abilities to enter altered states of consciousness.

5. These translations are primarily based on Betty DeShong Meador's careful translations and excellent discussion of the three hymns of Enheduanna in her book, *Inanna, Lady of Largest Heart: Poems of the Sumerian High Priestess Enheduanna*. Austin: U of Texas P, 2000. I have also consulted William W. Hallo and J.J.A. Van Dijk's 1968 translation, *The Exhaltation of Inanna*. New Haven, CT: Yale UP, 1968.

6. Divination in Mesopotamia not only reflected the official worldview of the court and temple but also the popular beliefs of the masses: "Beginning with scattered allusions in Sumerian sources, it developed into the largest single category of Akkadian literature in terms of sheer numbers of texts" according to Hallo and Simpson (157). Divination became a scholarly pursuit with exhaustive handbooks. Also, " . . . biblical prophets derided the arts of the Mesopotamian diviners for, alone among cuneiform literary genes, the literature of divination had no precise parallels in biblical or other Near Eastern writings . . ." (Hallo and Simpson 157). Eventually, the omens became the Mesopotamian variety of historiography when the Babylonians and Assyrians abstracted the historical omens into special collections.

7. W. G. Lambert and P. Walcot, "A New Babylonian Theogony and Hesiod," *Kadmos* 4 (1965) 64–72; P. Walcot, *Hesiod and the Near East*. Cardiff: Wales, 1966. M.L. West, ed., *Hesiod Theogony*, Oxford, Clarendon Press, 1966; G.S. Kirk, *The Nature of Greek Myths*. Harmondsworth: Penguin Books, 1974; Friedrich Solmsen, "The Two Near Eastern Sources of Hesiod," *Hermes* 117 (1989) 413–22; Walter Burkert, *Greek Religion*, Cambridge, MA: Harvard UP, and London, 1985; Walter Burkert, *The Orientalizing Revolution: Near Eastern Influence on Greek Culture in the Early Archaic Age*, Cambridge, MA: Harvard UP, 1992.

8. According to T. Drorah Setel, the emphasis on harlotry, of central significance for Hosea (the first prophetic writing using the image of marriage between God and Israel) and other literary prophets, is indicated by the frequency of the forms of the verb *zanah* (to act like a harlot"), used eighty-four times in the whole Hebrew Bible. Fifty-one of these instances occur in the latter prophets. Hosea, for example, used forms of zanah twenty times (91).

WORKS CITED

Aberback, David. *Imperialism and Biblical Prophecy 750—500 BCE*. London: Routledge, 1993.

Anchor Bible. 44 vols. Garden City, NY: Doubleday, 1964. 44 vols.

Aune, David. E. *Prophecy in Early Christianity and the Ancient Mediterranean World*. Grand Rapids, MI.: William B. Eerdmans Publishing Company, 1983.

Bahrani, Zainab. "Conjuring Mesopotamia: Imaginative Geography and World Past." *Archaeology Under Fire: Nationalism, Politics and Heritage in the Eastern Mediterranean and Middle East.* Ed. Lynn Meskell. London: Routledge, 1998. 159-74.

Becking, Bob, and Meindert Dijkstra. *On Reading Prophetic Texts: Gender-Specific and Related Studies in Memory of Fokkelien van Dijk-Hemes.* Leiden, Netherlands: E. J. Brill, 1996.

Berchman, Robert M. *Mediators of the Divine: Horizons of Prophecy, Divination, Dreams, and Theurgy in Mediterranean Antiquity.* Atlanta: Scholars Press, 1998.

Beyerlin, Walter in collaboration with Hellmut Brunner . . . (et. al.) Trans. by John Bowden. *Near Eastern Religious Texts Relating to the Old Testament.* Philadelphia: Westminister Press, 1978.

Brenner, Athalya and Fokkelien Van Dij-Hemmes. *On Gendering Texts: Female and Male Voices in the Hebrew Bible.* Leiden, Netherlands: E. J. Brill, 1993.

Crowley, Sharon. "Let Me Get This Straight," *Writing Histories of Rhetoric.* Ed. Victor Vitanza. Carbondale: Southern Illinois UP, 1994. 1–19.

Curnow, Trevor. *The Oracles of the Ancient World.* Duckworth, 2004.

Ellis, Maria de Jong. "Observations on Mesopotamian Oracles and Prophetic Texts: Literary and Historiographic Considerations" *Journal of Cuneiform Studies.* 41.2 (Autumn 1989): 127–86.

Enheduanna. *The Exhaltation of Inanna.* Trans. William W. Hallo and J.J. A. Van Dijk. New Haven: Yale UP, 1968.

Fuchs, Esther. "Prophecy and the Construction of Women: Inscription and Erasure. *Prophets and Daniel: A Feminist Companion to the Bible* (Second Series). Ed. Athalya Brenner. London: Sheffield Academic Press, 2001. 54-69.

Grabbe, Lester L. *Priests, Prophets, Diviners, Sages: A Socio Historical Study of Religious Specialists in Ancient Israel.* Valley Forge, PA: Trinity Press International, 1995.

Hallo, William W. "Women of Sumer." *The Legacy of Sumer: Invited Lectures on the Middle East at the University of Texas at Austin.* Ed. Denise Schmandt-Besserat. Malibu, CA: Undena Publications, 1976. 23–139.

Hallo, William W. and William Kelly Simpson. *The Ancient Near East: A History.* 2nd edition. New York: Harcourt Brace, 1998.

Hamel, Gildas. "Comparing Mari, Neo-Assyrian, Aramaean, and Biblical Prophetic Texts." 2004. 20 Oct. 2004 <http://humweb.ucsc.edu/gweltaz/courses/prophets/ANEprophets.html>.

Hoffman, David. "*Logos* as Composition." *Rhetoric Society Quarterly.* 33.3 (Summer 2003): 27–53.

Huffman, Herbert B. "The Origins of Prophecy in *Magnalia Dei. The Mighty Acts of God: Essays on the Bible and Archaeology in Memory of G. Ernest*

Wright. Ed. F. M. Cross, W. E. Lemke, and P. D. Miller. Garden City, NY: Doubleday, 1976. 171–86.

Jarratt, Susan. *Rereading the Sophists: Classical Rhetoric Refigured.* Carbondale, IL: Southern Illinois UP, 1998.

Lipsey, Roger. *Have You Been to Delphi? Tales of the Ancient Oracle for Modern Minds.* Albany: SUNY P, 2001.

Luck, Georg. *Arcana Mundi: Magic and the Occult in the Greek and Roman Worlds: A Collection of Ancient Texts.* 2nd ed. Ed. and trans. George Luck. Baltimore: Johns Hopkins UP, 2006

Malamat, Abraham. "Forerunner of Biblical Prophecy: The Mari Documents." Frederick E. Greenspahn, Ed. *Essential Papers on Israel and the Ancient Near East.* New York: New York UP, 1991. 153–175.

Meador, Betty DeShong. *Inanna, Lady of Largest Heart: Poems of the Sumerian High Priestess Enheduanna.* Austin: U of Texas P, 2000.

Miles, Margaret R. "Mapping Feminist Histories of Religious Traditions." Introduction to a Roundtable Discussion on Feminist Religious History. *Journal of Feminist Studies in Religion.* 22.1 (2006): 45–74.

Nissinen, Martti. "What is Prophecy? An Ancient Near Eastern Perspective. John Kaltner and Louis Stulman, eds. *Inspired Speech: Prophecy in the Ancient Near East Essays in Honor of Herbert B. Huffmon.* New York: T & T Clark International Pub., 2004. 17-37.

—. *Prophets and Prophecy in the Ancient Near East.* Atlanta: Society of Biblical Literature, 2003.

Overhold, Thomaas W. *Prophecy in a Cross-Cultural Perspective: A Sourcebook for Biblical Research.* SBLBS. Atlanta: Scholars Press, 1986.

Pagels, Elaine. *The Gnostic Gospels.* New York: Random House, 1979.

Parapola, Simo. *Assyrian Prophecies.* State Archives of Assyria, Vol. IX. Helsinki: Helsinki UP, 1997.

Penglase, Charles. *Greek Myths and Mesopotamia: Parallels and Influence in the Homeric Hymns and Hesiod.* London and New York: Routledge, 1994.

Poulakos, John. *Sophistical Rhetoric in Classical Greece.* Columbia: U of South Carolina P, 1995.

Roberts, J.J.M. *The Bible and the Ancient Near East: Collected Essays.* Winona Lake, IN: Eisenbrauns, 2002.

Sasson, Jack M. "Thoughts of Zimrî-Lîm." *The Biblical Archeologist* 47.2 (June 1984): 110–120.

—. "Mari Dreams." *Journal of the American Oriental Society* 103.1 (1983): 183–293.

Schüssler Fiorenza, Elisabeth. "The Will to Choose or to Reject: Continuing Our Critical Work." Letty M. Russell, ed. *Feminist Interpretation of the Bible.* Philadelphia: Westminster Press, 1985. 125-36.

Setel, T. Drorah. "Prophets and Pornography: Female Sexual Imagery in Hosea." Letty M. Russell, ed. *Feminist Interpretation of the Bible*. Philadelphia: Westminster Press, 1985. 86-95.

Tedlock, Barbara. *The Woman in the Shaman's Body: Reclaiming the Feminine in Religion and Medicine*. New York: Bantam Dell, 2006.

Vanderkam, James C. "Prophecy and Apocalyptics in the Ancient Near East." *Civilizations of the Ancient Near East*. Vol. III. Ed. Jack M. Sasson. New York: Charles Scribner's Sons, 1995. 2083-2094.

Van Der Toorn, Karel. "From the Mouth of the Prophet: The Literary Fixation of Jeremiah's Prophecies in the Context of the Ancient Near East." *Inspired Speech: Essays in honor of Herbert B. Huffmon*. Ed. John Kaltner and Louis Stulman. New York: Continuum, T & T Clark International Pub: 2004. 191-202.

Van Dijk-Hemmes, Fokkelien. "The Metaphorization of Women in Prophetic Speech: An Analysis of Ezekiel 23." *On Gendering Texts: Female and Male Voices in the Hebrew Bible*. Ed. Athalya Brenner and Fokkelien Van Dijk-Hemmes. Leiden, Netherlands: E. J. Brill, 1993. 167-76.

Vitanza, Victor. *Negation, Subjectivity, and the History of Rhetoric*. Albany: SUNY P, 1997.

Walsh, Lynda. "The Rhetoric of Oracles." *Rhetoric Society Quarterly*. 33.3 (Summer 2003): 53–78.

Westenholz, Joan Goodnick. "Enheduanna, En-Priestess, Hen of Nanna, Souse of Nanna," *DUMU-E$_2$-DUB-BA-A: Studies in Honor of Ake W. Sjoberg*. Philadelphia: Occasional Publications of the Samuel Noah Kramer Fund. II (1989): 539-56.

Winkelman, Michael. *Shamanism: The Neural Ecology of Consciousness and Healing*. Westport, CT; London: Bergin & Garvey, 2000.

Wire, Antoinette Clark. *The Corinthian Women Prophets: A Reconstruction Through Paul's Rhetoric*. Minneapolis: Fortress Press, 1990.

Works Consulted

Bloom, Harold. *Omens of Millennium: The Gnosis of Angels, Dreams, and Resurrection*. New York: Riverhead Books, 1996.

Broad, William J. *The Oracle: The Lost Secrets and Hidden Message of Ancient Delphi*. New York: Penguin Press, 2006.

Johnson, Sarah Illes. Ed. *Religions of the Ancient World: A Guide*. Cambridge, MA: Belknap Press of Harvard UP, 2004.

Murphy, Cullen. "Women and the Bible," *Atlantic Monthly* (August 1993): 39-64.

Yee, Gale A. *Poor Banished Children of Eve: Woman as Evil in the Hebrew Bible*. Minneapolis: Fortress Press, 2003.

4 Rhetoric and Identity: A Study of Ancient Egyptian Non-Royal Tombs and Tomb Autobiographies

Carol S. Lipson

THE RHETORICAL PROJECT OF THE ANCIENT EGYPTIAN TOMB, THE TOMB AUTOBIOGRAPHY, AND RELATED TOMB ELEMENTS

Wayne Booth, in his 2004 book entitled *The Rhetoric of Rhetoric: The Quest for Effective Communication,* defined rhetoric as "the entire range of resources that human beings share for producing effects on one another" (xi). Though in ancient Egypt, audiences for texts often included the gods, as well as human beings, I am going to use this definition of rhetoric in analyzing one of the most well known aspects of ancient Egyptian culture—the devotion of huge resources to create tombs. While the enormous pyramids of the early dynasties of kings are well known, these are in fact not characteristic of tomb construction over the 3,000 years of the tradition (Baines 2001, 10). I will instead examine a more common form of tomb—those created for non-royal members of the elite, specifically during the eighteenth dynasty of kings (approximately 1540 to 1290 BCE), in what is termed the New Kingdom period.[1]

Scholars of Egyptology have long studied ancient Egyptian tombs, along with the texts, art, and objects they contain, as representing a major focus of attention in the culture. Much of the consideration has involved a search for the meaning of the tomb texts, the objects, the spaces, and the artwork as these may have been understood by ancient Egyptian religion and culture. Since hieroglyphs have been deciphered only for a century and a half, much effort has been devoted to translating and "fixing" the texts and to understanding their pur-

port. In addition, typically the art and architecture have been studied as somewhat separate specialties from the study of texts, and the
material objects without textual or artistic value have often gained
little attention.[2] Referring to a study examining eighteenth dynasty
tomb painting (Hodel-Hoenes 2000), Melinda Hartwig deplores the
book's lack of attention to the communicative aspect of tomb painting. Her observation is true for studies of other historical periods as
well. Hartwig's own study, while admirable, focuses only on the flat
paintings in New Kingdom tombs before the Amarna age. That is, she
examines the communicative aspects of the paintings in selected New
Kingdom tombs at Thebes, without close attention to the texts and
other objects in the tombs. In this essay, I am interested in extending
a rhetorical gaze to the entire experience of the tomb, specifically the
tomb chapel—including the texts and the material surroundings; I
view these as a complex of resources working together to produce effects on human visitors to the tombs.

Our society is familiar with the concept of the Egyptian tomb as
more than a burial place. Many studies in Egyptology present the
tomb as a home for the dead, a house for the afterlife that includes all
the things both valuable and necessary in this world—from jewelry
and cosmetics to furniture and food (Hodel-Hoenes 2). Indeed, the
Egyptian name for tomb, *per djet,* literally means house of eternity
(Taylor 21). However, the field of Egyptology has developed a far more
complex understanding of the function of the tomb. As currently understood, "the tomb was mainly a point of transition from one world
to another," though everything in it was needed for existence in the
next world (Baines 2001, 16, 26). Significantly, scholars argue that
ancient Egyptian society viewed the tomb as creating material forms
of the deceased's identity, material modes of the deceased's self (Baines
2001; Hartwig 2004; Meskell 1999; Taylor 2001). In the tomb, the
owner created and presented a performance of the self in visual, textual, and material form. The stylized performance presented the best
self, not the full reality, but the version of self one would want to live
as forever. Visually, it's a perfect self, young and attractive, and it had
to be a self that would be deemed worthy, by its actions in society,
to warrant permanent existence in the afterlife (Hartwig 5–7). That
is, in presenting a personal identity, the tomb's project was to justify
the individual in terms that reflected and reinforced the values of the
cultural identity. Thus, the tomb existed to perpetuate the individual

identity by relating it to, and preserving, the collective identity (Assmann 1996, 12–14; 2002). In ancient Egypt, this collective identity was inexorably tied to the Pharaoh and the state; all tombs were acquired through the authorization of the king and his officials. Only the elite acquired and built tombs, and in most periods, the elite were all affiliated with the state.

One of the chief textual elements in the tombs designed to contribute to the overall tomb project involved what is called the tomb autobiography. Notably, these texts did not appear in tombs of kings, but did in non-royal tombs. While there is some disagreement among Egyptologists about what to call them, generally they are referred to as autobiographies. The texts do show two of the chief attributes of autobiography: they offer a description of a particular human life, and they are presented in the first person, as voiced by the individual being described. The term autobiography is a quite recent one, appearing late in the eighteenth century (Misch 5). It was developed to name certain kinds of texts, and carried implicit values in its application: particularly inquiry by the writer into the life, and a consciousness of self. Without such self-revelation or self-awareness, scholars of autobiography judge such texts as "superficial or intellectually attenuated," and as lacking. Georg Misch, in his *History of Autobiography in Antiquity* notes the predominance of autobiographical inscriptions in ancient Egypt, and characterizes their motive as a desire for self-glorification or self-justification, with the self-praise being guided by a ruling cultural ideal of morality (28). He terms the texts monotonous, and implies that the Egyptian genre never reached a mature level (8, 20–33). Misch is not alone in his judgment of one culture's practices by the standards, practices, and values of his own culture.

Even scholars of Egyptology have at times also condemned the autobiographies as formulaic, bombastic, self-glorifying, and too standardized (Donadoni 128; Dunand 179–80). These texts are then easily dismissed as primitive and uninteresting. Miriam Lichtheim, who published extensively on the autobiographies and termed them one of the foremost of the literary genres of the period, criticized "their self awareness [as] more elementary and naive than the modern varieties" (1988). However, it seems imperative to attempt to reconstruct the Egyptians' local understanding of the self-representation in these autobiographies, which form prominent parts of their tombs. Just as it seems problematic to consider the Greco-Roman understanding of rhetoric as the only rhetoric, it is equally troubling to consider the Greek understanding of autobiography as the only valid approach. Egyptologists have struggled with this issue. Jan Assmann proposed auto-thematizations as a better description (See for instance Assmann 1996, 55). Ludwig Morenz has proposed using the term self presentations, or presentations of self. Some of the concern has involved the fact that since we don't know that the tomb owner actually wrote the biographies, as opposed to the scribe or a descendant, the term autobiography might be inaccurate. Baines thus uses the term biography rather than autobiography (1999, 23). There has been concern also that the biographies don't always present narrative, and generally don't present any description of change in the individual (Morenz 184–186). However, since they are most commonly referred to as autobiographies, are most often written in the first person, are intended to describe a human life, and—as Baines notes—look "back upon and present . . . a life as something in the past" (1999, 23), I will refer to them as autobiographies here.

The tomb autobiography and the setting it existed in—the tomb itself and all other elements of the tomb—shared a mutual function of representing a deceased individual's identity. As Naguib points out, the personal identity and the social identity were always combined in these texts; they demonstrate the individual's behavior according to the principles of *Maat*, the foundational values of the culture. Notably, the Egyptian culture did not see the tomb and its many artistic, architectural, and textual components as sufficient for the afterlife of the deceased. The central focus of Egyptian religious belief involved the need for repeated cult performances. Such was true for the king and for the gods, whose existence and well-being were governed by regular repetition of cultic rituals. This was true, as well, for any deceased official. Thus, one of the main purposes in the design and construction of the tomb involved persuading and enticing visitors—living Egyptians—to perform the necessary rituals. Thus, as a whole, the tomb served a highly rhetorical, fundamentally persuasive purpose: to convince living Egyptians to fulfill the conditions necessary for the deceased's sustained individual existence (Roth 245). The persuasive approach will be described below.

The Ancient Egyptian Concept of Personal Identity

The ancient Egyptians had a complex notion of identity, in which an individual consisted of a composite involving many components, both material and nonmaterial. Each component was crucial to a person's identity, and together these *kheperu* or aspects constituted a united integral individual. It was fundamental to Egyptian religious belief that a discrete individual identity had the possibility of surviving after death. In particular, five components could continue after death: the body, the name *(ren)*, the *ka,* the *ba,* and the shadow. The body had to be mummified and preserved to form a constituent part of the individual identity after death. The name identified the person, bearing the individuality. It remained essential in preserving identity after death, but to do so, it had to be recalled and pronounced with some frequency. The other parts can only be addressed briefly here; in any case, the precise meaning of each remains somewhat unclear. The *ka,* considered a double of the self, was thought to have been created by the god Khnum on his potter's wheel when he created the person. According to Assmann, "the *ka* was soul, protective spirit, and doppelganger, all rolled into one" (2005, 97). After death, the *ka* remained in the tomb; it united with the deceased, but "it was not body and soul that were united, it was the deceased himself and his alter ego" (92). The *ka* could inhabit the body after death, or even a statue of the deceased. In life, the *ba* was considered as attached to the physical body, though it was separated from the body at death. It was necessary for it to "remember" and return to the corpse, to maintain the identity of the individual. Depicted as a bird, it had freedom of movement in the daytime, moving between the earthly realm and the next realm; it spent the days in the spheres of the gods and the sun, but it had to return to the corpse at night (92).

While the body, the name, the *ba* and the *ka* existed together with the corporeal body in life, death was understood to have severed the connections. For the individual to attain status eventually as an *akh*—a transfigured spirit in the afterlife—the connections of the parts needed to first be re-established. The *akh* was understood to have the ability to exert influence on the living. A number of surviving letters attest to the practice in which living Egyptians addressed the *akh* of a deceased individual in writing, with requests or complaints. The ultimate goal in death was not just to enter the divine world, but also to remain embedded and integrated within the community of the living (Assmann 2005, 12–13). For this to happen, relatives, colleagues, employees, and at times priests were responsible for providing food and beverage offerings necessary for the *ba* (Assmann 2005, 330–31); in addition, the standard formula for such offerings stated that the recipient for the offerings was the *ka* of the deceased.

Another component of post-death identity formed part of the belief system. As Thomas Hare points out, from the Middle Kingdom on, the central myth of Egyptian religion involved the deceased integrating with and becoming the god Osiris; in death, upon being deemed worthy in the judgment process, the deceased individual would be named Osiris. Yet, the distinctive individual identity was considered as preserved even while merging with Osiris (Hare 33,131). The individual gained a multiplicity of modes of being in death that together were understood to preserve the unity of identity.

Because ancient Egyptian society considered it so important to guarantee continuance of the self ever after, the culture developed approaches to the design of the tombs with this need in mind. The deceased's name was carved repeatedly in the tomb, in order to help sustain this aspect of the deceased's individual identity. A named statue could also preserve the name while providing a "body" for the *ka* to inhabit. In fact, the term for sculptor meant "he who keeps alive" (Meskell 2004, 112). Visual representations could serve as important repositories of the deceased's identity by illustrating important aspects of the deceased's professional and personal life on earth. And the biographical texts, too, presented the identity, by reciting the life project and worthiness of the deceased. Together, all of these representations formed a collage of identity. But it was not enough to carve names, to carve statues, or to paint representations of the deceased in the tomb. The repeated participation of living Egyptians was required to perform ritual actions in the tomb that would enable the religious and magical functions of these elements in preserving the identity.

THE DESIGN AND CRAFTING OF NON-ROYAL TOMBS IN THE EIGHTEENTH DYNASTY

In considering the rhetorical function of the tomb for its audience, it's important to understand that non-royal tombs were not inaccessible to the public or to visitors (Hartwig 8–9). Quite the opposite is true. They tended to be built with courtyards and chapels large enough to accommodate groups of family and professional colleagues on the many festivals that featured visits to the dead (Hartwig 11–13). Such festivals could involve all-night commemorative celebrations, with feasts including sacrificing and cooking of animals. Combined with the effects of beer and wine, incense and music, as well as the narcotic properties of lotus perfume, such occasions could well blur the boundaries between life and death, and generally maintain the integration of the deceased within the society of the living (Hartwig 99–101; Hare 31). As Baines points out, the family visitors would include not only elite male relatives, but also women, servants, and children (2001, 12). Biographies would have been spoken orally at funerals and by tomb visitors in a kind of ceremonial performance (Baines 1999, 36; 2007, 151, 153). Baines notes the oral construction and performative character of the biographies. In addition, scribes, craftsmen, and officials would visit tombs as we today might go house hunting, or as we might visit the annual Parade of Homes in our respective communities—to get ideas, to see different approaches, to see what's new or what grabs our fancy, as we think about our own house-renovation and building projects. Such tomb tourism was quite common, and a multitude of graffiti attest to such visits (Hartwig 13–15; 43–45). While the actual burial chamber would not be accessible, the courtyard, tomb chapels, and hallway rooms leading to these would be open for visitation.

According to Baines, the non-royal tombs generally were arranged for and begun at the height of an official's career, when he had proven himself to rulers and higher state administrators as worthy (2001, 10). Scholarship indicates the likelihood that design books existed with standard scenes, structures, and text, though none have surfaced (Hartwig 19). Those who crafted the tomb—painters and sculptors— were part of state or temple workshops (23). Some of the elite had to pay fully for the tombs, though they also depended on royal patronage to be allowed to build them at all. Others were given statues and grave goods. Tomb owners would regularly consult with the tomb makers, and could individualize approaches to some extent. Within limits, owners could develop a layout, select appropriate scenes, and select an approach to the biographical discussion (see Vischak 257). While no two tombs are identical, convention was a strong force (Bolshakov 37, 60).

As shown by Hartwig, the non-royal tombs of the eighteenth dynasty in the Thebes area tended to be built in an inverted T design, at times incorporating multiple T's (15). Generally, the areas close to the entrance presented scenes illustrating the earthly life of the deceased, while less accessible inner areas showed the transition to the next world. The scenes showing the deceased's existence on earth were often presented in image vignettes, which tell a story of what the deceased did in his career. These vignettes can be especially beautiful and lively, at times presenting a narrative with amusing dialogue by individuals portrayed, often using visually intriguing details. Such images are meant to show how important an individual the deceased was, conveying visually his prestige, status, and professional duties. These pictorial vignettes tended to fill the walls that visitors would see upon entering the tomb, serving to engage, to impress, and to draw people farther into the tomb.

Hartwig's study shows that in the location and period she studied, the main texts of the tomb appeared deeper into the structure. The main such text involved the autobiography, which tended to focus on two elements: the career path and/or the moral behavior of the deceased (Lichtheim 1988). While the autobiographies are presented in the first person, the tomb owner would normally not have written them, but would more likely have given ideas to a scribe to work into standard presentations. The early versions, dating from the fifth and sixth dynasties, are quite short, but by the time of the eighteenth dynasty, these texts had expanded considerably.

Other texts existed in close proximity to the autobiographies. These include prayers requesting food and beverage offerings, often immediately preceding the autobiographies, as well as appeals to the living to recite the offering formula; these appeals often appear right after the autobiographical statements (10). The term for offering, *peret-kheru*, translates as 'going forth at the sound of the voice,' indicating the necessity for the offering formula to be recited aloud in order that the *ba* can emerge and receive the offering, and the *ka* can benefit (Taylor 96; Assmann 2005, 330). The autobiographical genre was designed to present an individual identity as worthy of being sustained in the afterlife. If it did so convincingly, and the reader continued reading, the appeal would ask the visitor to "read," "recall my name," and as enticement, would promise that the visitor's god would then favor him and his children; the appeal would often offer persuasion and even threats designed to convince the visitor to recite the offering prayer for the deceased. Such texts thus all constitute and at times overtly include persuasive appeals to the living tomb visitors. Reading of these texts—a very elite (and male) activity in ancient Egypt—was considered to have magical and religious powers. The enticing and impressive scenes on the walls leading to the areas that displayed these texts were meant to draw visitors in so that they would reach the texts, and to sufficiently impress and entertain the visitors that they would be willing to recite an offering prayer, even if they chose not to, or could not, read the full text. Thus, Hartwig's analysis shows that the general design of the Thebes eighteenth dynasty non-royal tombs seemed to employ the artwork as a hook to draw the visitors to the offering place deeper in the tomb (17, 51, 123).

ANALYSIS OF EIGHTEENTH DYNASTY EL KAB TOMBS

Sigrid Hodel-Hoenes and Melinda Hartwig both examined eighteenth dynasty non-royal tombs from the Thebes area, the central seat of power. However, in ancient Egypt, areas at some distance from the center of power tend not to be studied quite as intensively, though they are of considerable interest. As Deborah Vischak points out in a study of tombs from an earlier period, important differences existed in provincial contexts, with stronger local ties that could lead to some changes in traditions (268–69). I will closely examine one particular example arising from the eighteenth dynasty of the New Kingdom period in Egypt, the same general period as in Hartwig and Hodel-Hoenes' analyses, and then look briefly at the three other tombs in the same area from the eighteenth dynasty. All four of these tombs are found in El Kab, once called Nekheb, a capital of one of Egypt's powerful divisions. El Kab is located on the east bank of the Nile, about 90 km from the locus of power in Thebes. The town seemed to have played an important role in the early eighteenth dynasty.

The Tomb of Paheri

In his tomb, Paheri gives his main title as scribe of the accounts of the corn, "superintendent of the corn-land of the south district, the one who satisfied the desire of his master from Per-Hathor as far as Neckeb" (Tylor, 1894). He was thus responsible for grain in a substantial sector of the country. His other titles include being tutor for a prince, chief of priests for his city's goddess named Nekhbet, and mayor of two prominent towns. He must have had a lot more titles, given other non-royal tombs (Tylor 1894, 5–6); Rekhmire, for instance, includes approximately 100 titles (Davies). Paheri has presented a limited and restricted selection of titles. Titles function in conjunction with the name to identify an individual professionally, but Paheri's tomb relies heavily on a large number of vignettes to show his professional functions.

The tomb chapel is laid out in a rectangular fashion, with longer sides than ends, as shown in Figure 1. The dimensions are approximately 25 feet by 11 and a half feet (Tylor 1894, 1). Visitors enter the tomb at the south end, where the façade has been eroded and largely destroyed. On the right façade, a representation of Paheri is still visible, dressed simply, as he kneels and offers prayers to the local goddess Nekhbet. An inscription presents prayers on the right. The doorway once was flanked by inscriptions offering prayers for the *ka* of Paheri, now mainly destroyed. Immediately on entering, on the right inner south wall beside the doorway, the visitor would see a large figure of Paheri, dressed more formally, holding a staff of office, seemingly about to walk out the doorway of the tomb. Whatever was displayed on the left inner wall beside the entrance has been destroyed. The long west wall, on the left of the entrance, has been planned in three major sections, with the nearest and largest one showing Paheri performing his scribal and mayoral functions outdoors, primarily involving agriculture. The middle section shows Paheri as a private individual. The third and farther section shows a range of funerary rituals.

Similarly, the long east wall has been divided into major sections, and also consists mostly of visuals. Here, there are two major scenes, both involving indoor activities. The group of scenes closest to the entrance displays a banquet attended by deceased ancestors, along with Paheri's parents, relatives, and colleagues. The scene farther from the entrance displays funerary and worship scenes. A later addition—a doorway—disrupts the second set of scenes, for the tomb was later taken over by others and extended by adding additional rooms off the east side. The arched ceiling is decorated in a diamond design along the whole length of the chapel room.

J. J. Tylor, in 1894, suggested that the designer—perhaps Paheri himself—may have intended the viewer to move all the way to the back wall of the tomb first, to honor the offering shrine and statues there, and then to move to the east wall with the banquet, finally viewing the west wall with the professional, private, and funerary scenes (10). Tylor suggested that the visitor was intended then to read the prayers on the ceiling. However, the study by Hartwig and my own

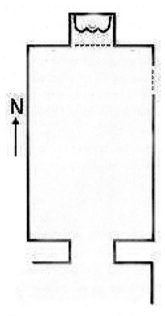

Figure 1. Plan of Paheri's tomb. Excerpted and modified
by C. Lipson with permission of Thierry Benderitter. ©
Thierry Benderitter/www.osirisnet.net.

study both suggest a different pathway. Family and colleagues may
have been most interested in the east side banquet immediately on
their right when they entered the tomb chapel. They may have been
eager to see who was depicted and named, in what order, and who was
shown carrying out what functions in the funerary scenes. On the
other hand, strangers and other elite may well have gravitated first to
the west wall, on their left upon entering the tomb. Both of these long
walls consist primarily of visuals, brightly painted and finely executed.
The back wall, facing the visitor upon entering the tomb, is especially
dense with text; non-family visitors would not have needed to go there
to discover whose tomb this is, since the identification was available
on the outer façade. The west wall, with the scenes addressing Paheri's
professional responsibilities, is the most original, and combines many
textual captions alongside the many visual vignettes. One can imagine
that it would have been more common for non-family visitors to approach that wall first.

Egyptologists have been particularly interested in the west wall
scenes, largely for the information they provide on life and work in

Egypt. However, the audience for these scenes consisted of ancient Egyptians, for whom the information value was not such a crucial factor. Figures 2 and 3 present the largest scene on the west wall—the first the visitor would encounter on that side. In Figure 2, the original hieroglyphics have been preserved. In Figure 3, the hieroglyphics accompanying the small vignettes have been translated into English. Paheri presides over these vignettes as a large figure, dressed simply but with the scepter of power visible in his hands. He is accompanied by much smaller assistants. The scenes right beside Paheri deal with planting and harvesting grain, and the accompanying hieroglyphic inscriptions indicate that he is scribe of the grain, inspecting the fields throughout the three seasons of the Egyptian year. The peasants are given dialogue as they work. One peasant describes the day as beautiful, while one urges others to work quickly so they may finish soon and because they are being watched. One declares that he will do no more than is required of him. Later scenes show the harvest, and again display light-hearted banter among the workers. The dialogue praises the beauty of the day and the joy of being out in the sun. Finally the men are shown collecting the grain, having it recorded by scribes, and having the many bags of grain loaded on boats—all under Paheri's direction. Paheri presides over the counting of livestock, and over the recording of weights of gold delivered by miners, to be transported to the King. Paheri is also shown supervising fishing and the hunting of birds from the banks of the Nile, as well as the making of wine from grapes.

All of these scenes include details of considerable interest value. For instance, as Paheri supervises the counting of livestock, some oxen are shown lying down, shackled, about to be branded and one man in this vignette is being beaten, presumably for faults in his work or behavior. In the nearby scene in which Paheri and his brother record the weights of gold brought from the desert, another beating is shown, perhaps here for a problem in the quantity brought. In the scenes showing birds being caught in nets, some of the birds escape the nets. In a scene showing the process of making linen, an older man boasts to a younger one bringing him a container of flax to be combed, claiming that if the young man brings him 11,000 sheaves, he will comb them all. The younger worker responds with a reprimand, basically telling his co-worker to keep working and stop talking, calling him an old braggart. In a scene showing corn being reaped, a woman with a heavy load on

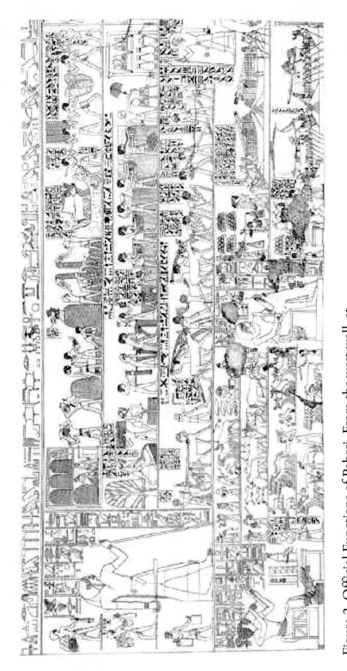

Figure 2. Official Functions of Paheri. From the west wall, at the south end. Excerpted from Osirisnet.net with permission; © Thierry Benderitter/www.osirisnet.net

Figure 3. Official Functions of Paheri, with hieroglyphic captions translated into English. From Hans Gumbrecht and K. Ludwig Pfeiffer, editors, *Materialities of Communication.* © 1994 by the Board of Trustees of the Leland Stanford University.

her back and a child carrying provisions are shown behind the reapers, gleaning. A shelter is shown nearby with jars of liquid for their benefit, as well as for Paheri's benefit when he arrives to inspect the work. In the dialogue, one individual admonishes another not to repeat the mean behavior of the prior day. In a scene showing boats being loaded to transport grain and materials to the government granaries, the dialogue presents the workers complaining that the boats are too full, and the granaries as well, so that corn is falling out, but Paheri insists that they keep at it, which they are doing.

Thus, there is much here on the west wall, within the primarily visual presentation accompanied by verbal dialogue, that would maintain the interest level of visitors. Though the reproductions are presented here in black and white, the scenes were actually painted colorfully and drawn beautifully, providing myriad points of interest.

The mid portion of the west wall shows Paheri in his private life, sitting with his wife under a canopy. Six individuals bring food and drink to the couple. The wife's parents and her brother are shown as named figures, as are other relatives. Notably in ancient Egyptian art, none of the representatives would show any features particular to any elite individual's appearance. So relatives would not approach these scenes as our generation would examine photos or paintings in which we appear, to see what has been made of individual's personal characteristics. The Egyptian art displays the ideal portrayal of an elite figure. But relatives would certainly be extremely interested to see if they were included and named, and in what scenes and capacities.

A second scene in this mid portion of the west wall displays a large representation of Paheri seated, with his arms around a small elite male child on his lap. The child is identified as Prince Uadjemes, and Paheri is identified as the guardian or tutor of this youngster. Additional virtually destroyed scenes show adults and children bringing offerings to Paheri, with the text identifying these as "his children and grandchildren," though the names, if given, are lost.

The third and farthest section on the west wall shows a funerary procession for Paheri, with various ritual ceremonies and offering scenes at chapels along the path of the procession. At the top, porters transport the mummy. The words of the accompanying two nobles are given. This scene seems to depict the presentation of the mummy of Paheri to the different gods, with offerings presented to the gods at their respective temples.

The lower register immediately below shows two men dancing behind the casket, with two small mourners under the casket. This small scene is unusual in showing the dancers facing each other, virtually touching. Thus far, Paheri's tomb constitutes the first appearance of such a depiction of the traditional *muu* funeral dancers, now understood as boatmen entrusted to ferry the deceased to the afterlife (Reeder). Also in this scene, several priests bring a chest, presumably with the viscera of Paheri removed from the mummy, and one holds a papyrus. In the lower section, Paheri is shown before the god Osiris, who is seated on a throne. Paheri kneels in worship, dedicating offerings to the god. Beyond this scene, mourning *muu* dancers wear tall crowns, and Osiris stands under a canopy. Finally, two men are shown facing two other men, all without arms. In another tomb of the New Kingdom, that of the vizier Rekhmire, such figures are specifically described as gods guarding the gates to the afterlife.

If the visitor now turns to the opposite wall—the east wall—at the north end, the scenes here show life-size representations of Paheri and his wife, seated. Beneath their chair, a small monkey is chained, eating fruit from a basket. Paheri and his wife face a table of offerings, presented by their son Amenmes. The inscription voiced by Amenmes states that he is presenting a funeral offering for their *kas*. Beneath this scene, many non-elite bring items—papyrus sandals, a staff, a stool. Guests at a banquet appear behind the son (Figure 4). Beside each guest, the family connection to Paheri is noted. Servants are given text that encourages guests to drink until intoxicated, as befits a holiday. One female guest requests 18 bowls of wine, saying she enjoys drinking until intoxicated. A male guest indicates that it is owed to the lord Paheri to drink and not to spoil the fun.

In the south-most part of the east wall closest to the tomb entrance, two large standing figures are shown—Paheri and his wife; they make offerings to several named gods, including the local god Nekhbet. Three of their children stand behind them, shown as smaller figures. The inscription in front of Paheri expresses his desire to become a perfect spirit in the afterworld, whose *ba* can leave the tomb and go forth ("walk out"). Underneath the offering scene, butchers carve oxen, which seem to be alive. Drinks, breads, and flowers, are also shown, as are a goose, wine, and flowers. If viewed after the banquet scene, this would appear to be a continuation of the banquet scene; if viewed before the banquet scene, this would appear as preparatory to the banquet scene, but also as connected to sacrifices in the offering scene.

Above the wall scenes appear lines of text in which the King makes offerings—to Osiris on one wall, and to the local god Nekhbet on the other—dedicated to the *ka* of Paheri, in order to transform him into a living *ba*. It's common for the offering prayer to be inscribed frequently in the tomb—on walls in different locations, as well as on stelae and objects (Taylor, 96).

Having encountered and enjoyed the lively visual scenes and the humorous dialogue—the latter more densely situated on the west wall than on the east—the visitor would then likely move to the back wall of the tomb (see Figure 5). This back wall contains a niche in the center with three statues—of the deceased Paheri, surrounded by his wife and mother. This wall is filled with text, more so than is usually provided. Here the visitor will find the prayer requesting offerings for Paheri, the autobiography, and Paheri's appeal to the living to recite the offering formula in order to provide for his *ka*. This is indeed the goal of the tomb: to preserve Paheri's identity in the afterlife and to provide for his afterlife. The positive experience of enjoyment of the enticing colorful scenes, with their intriguing detail and dialogue, may have made it all the more likely that literate visitors would be willing to read the offering prayer, as well as the biography on the dense back wall of text. That biography focuses not on Paheri's career or life events, but on his moral nature and behavior. The prayer for offerings is much more extended and elaborated than in most versions (Lichtheim 1976, 15). In addition, Paheri presents a quite unusual text—a lengthy hymn describing his imagined life in the afterworld, where he sees himself as eating bread with a god, being welcomed by the gods, walking among the gods, plowing in the fields of the afterlife, being rewarded for the rich harvest he reaped on earth, and living eternally in joy, fully provisioned.

But since Paheri has to be sure that the provisions needed for his afterlife will be offered by those on earth who visit his tomb, the general description of his moral conduct is designed to help accomplish this. His version of an autobiography does not recite any career events or offer any narrative of progress in a career. Instead, it presents Paheri as deserving in his conduct. It begins as follows (Lichtheim 1976, 18-19):

He says:

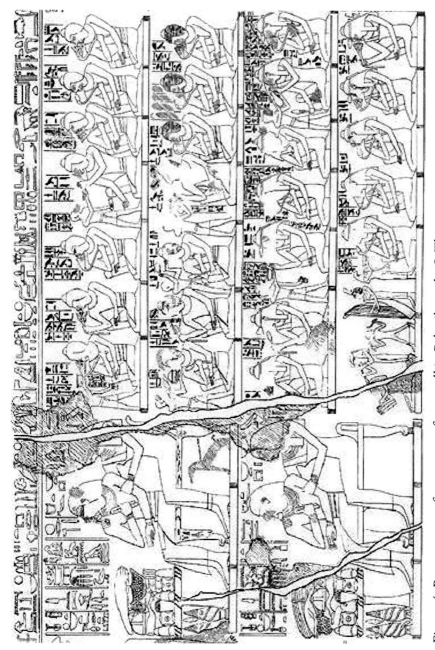

Figure 4. Banquet scene from center of east wall in Paheri's tomb. © Thierry Benderitter/www.osirisnet.net. Used with permission of Thierry Benderitter

I am a noble who served his lord,
One skilled and free of negligence.

. . .

I reckoned the limits in the books,
The boundaries of the king's concerns,
All things that pertained to the palace,

. . .

My mouth was firm in serving the lord,
I was fearful of deficiency;
I did not neglect making payment in full,
I did not take a slice of the expense.

. . .

On the road of those praised by the king.
My pen of reed made me renowned,

Figure 5. Back wall of Paheri's tomb, with statues in offering niche.
© Thierry Benderitter/www.osirisnet.net. Used with permission of
Thierry Benderitter.

It gave me right in the council;
It made my nature, I surpassed the nobles.

My good character raised me high,
I was summoned as one who is blameless.
. . .
I did the tasks as they were ordered,
I did not confuse the report with the reporter,
I did not speak with low-class words,
I did not talk to worthless people.
I was a model of kindliness, . . .

Thus, Paheri announces that he served his lord skillfully and without negligence or deficiencies, paid his superiors all that was owed, acted blamelessly, surpassed nobles with his fine character, told no lies, did tasks as ordered, exhibited kindliness, and never spoke "low-class words." He was a model official serving the King, having displayed positive behaviors and avoided negative ones. In the second of the two sections of the autobiography, he announces that when he will be placed on the scales of justice, presumably in the judgment ceremony before Osiris that determines the deceased's deservedness for the afterlife by weighing the heart, "I would come out complete, whole, sound" (Lichtheim 1976, 19).

Immediately following this moral autobiography, Paheri goes on to directly address the living:

He says,

Listen, all who now have being,
I speak to you without deceit;
You who live, who have existence,
Nobles, people, upon earth;
Servants of god, priests, attendants,
Every scribe who holds the palette,
Who is skilled in words of god;
Whosoever is good to his subjects,
Whosoever excels in his task:
Re, everlasting, will commend you,
Also Nekhbet, the White one of Neckhen,
And whoever guides your task.

You will bequeath to your children,
If you say, "An offering, given by the King,"
In the form in which it is written;
"An invocation-offering," as said by the fathers,
And as it comes from the mouth of god.
Whosoever will bend his arm,
He'll be on the path of truth,
To act as befits, as forms to the rules. . . .

I say to you, I let you know:
It is a recital without expense,
It does not make poor, it makes no trouble;
. . .

There is no strain, no fatigue in it,
It is good for you when you do it,
You will find in it [profit] and praise.
While I was in the land of the living,
No sin against god was reproached me.
. . .

I shall not fail to respond.
The dead is father to him who acts for him, . . .

(20)

Thus, Paheri appeals to the visitors to recite the standard offering
prayer—whether these visitors are nobles, priests, attendants, scribes,
or any people on earth who do tasks well. He therefore covers a wide
range of possible visitors. This appeal promises the visitors that the
gods Re and Nekhbet will commend and reward them. He points out
the ease of the task—there's no cost, no strain, no unpleasantness. In
fact, he portrays the recital as an uplifting duty, which will bring profit
and praise. Paheri then goes on to remind the reader that he is deserving, having never been reproached with sin, and in death he is now in
a position to help the living who act for him. The last two lines clinch
this persuasive strand:

He forgets not him who libates for him,
It is good for you to listen!

(20)

The text ends with a concluding sentence that served as a formulaic ending to letters: "May your hearing of this be pleasant."

As seen here, the crowded back wall presents first lengthy prayers of offerings, then an innovative hymn imagining the joys of the afterlife, followed by a biography and then an appeal to the living. This wall is architecturally innovative, for the entire wall has been constructed to resemble a round-topped stela common in mortuary settings. To get to that back wall, the visitors would have been drawn in by the beautiful, enticing scenes on the east and west walls, containing the humorous dialogic interchanges among laborers and the engaging visual details. The positive experience of enjoyment may have made it all the more likely that literate visitors would be willing to read the dense text on the back wall. Paheri's tomb suggests that the artwork and small portions of text on the side walls were designed to draw the visitor to the moral biography and the offering place, in the niche occupied by the statues, on the back wall. We can see that the moral biography does not exist on its own as a text on this wall or in the tomb. It is embedded within a larger array of visual and dense textual surroundings.

The Other Eighteenth Dynasty Tombs in El Kab: Ahmose of Abana, Renni, and Ahmose Pennekhbet

Other tombs in El Kab show different approaches, but still show powerful rhetorical consideration. The grandfather of Paheri, named Ahmose son of Abana, presents a very event-laden biography detailing his career as military commander under more than one 18th dynasty king. An inscription in Ahmose's tomb explains that Paheri had it engraved; scholars have often linked this Paheri to the Paheri whose tomb has just been examined (Lichtheim 1976, 11), though one fairly recent published note claims that Paheri's brother—also named Paheri—was actually the one responsible and referred to (Whale 5). In any case, Ahmose was indeed the grandfather of the Paheri already discussed. And Ahmose's tomb presents a very different rhetorical approach to its design and a very different identity than does Paheri's.

Ahmose's tomb also has the entrance at the south end; it, too, has a rectangular shape, with the east and west walls longer than the back north wall.[3] Here the west and north walls show many scenes of family: Ahmose with numerous named descendants, with his parents, with each of two wives, and before a table of food offerings dedicated by his grandson Paheri to various deities. Ahmose's children and grandchildren are shown a number of times. Family is given great emphasis in these quite traditional visuals. On the west wall, in the upper portion, Ahmose is displayed with his descendants and parents in front of him. His grandson Paheri dedicates a table replete with food offerings to several gods; the Egyptian offering ritual system understood offerings to the gods to then transfer the benefit of offerings for the deceased. The lower scene on the west wall presents a smaller version of a table of offerings for Ahmose, with Ahmose's children shown behind Paheri.

The north wall contains two main horizontal divisions, unlike Paheri's tomb where the sections were divided vertically; horizontal subsections appear within each main section of Ahmose's north wall. In the back of Ahmose's tomb, a couple sits before each of these two scenes, the couple in each case involving Ahmose with a different wife. In each case, two generations of Ahmose's family are shown alongside an offering table. The quite traditional offering-table motif is thus repeated numerous times in this tomb—with Ahmose's large immediate family given much attention in the depictions and named in the inscriptions.

The east wall of Ahmose's tomb is dense with hieroglyphic text, with few images. An entrance created for access to the burial chamber has destroyed the left part of this wall. Beyond that, a life-sized image of Ahmose appears, with a small image of Paheri in front of it. Above Paheri's image appears his dedication text. The rest of the wall is taken up with the first part of a long autobiography of Ahmose; this text is continued on the adjacent south wall, to the right of the entrance.

Contrary to his grandson, Ahmose offered a career-focused autobiography, reciting the battles he was involved in and the rewards he gained. The autobiography begins with the traditional "he says" opening, going on to address the visitor:

> I speak to you, all people. I let you know what favors came to me. I have been rewarded with gold seven times in the sight of the whole land, with male and female slaves as well. I have been endowed with very many fields. The name of the brave man is in that which he has done; it will not perish in the land forever. (Lichtheim, 1976, 12)

Ahmose then begins to tell his story of growing up in Nekheb, taking his father's position as a soldier on a ship, then being assigned to another ship "because I was brave" (12). Twice, he cut off an enemy hand and brought it back to the king, earning the gold of valor award each time, along with some slaves. He sailed with the king to Avaris, Nubia, and Syria, earning more spoil, more gold, land, and more slaves (men and women). He served two other Kings beyond the first. Several times, Ahmose praises himself directly: "I was taken to the ship 'Northern,' because I was brave"; "I fought really well [in Nubia under King Amenhotep I]. His majesty saw my valor (13)," and later in Nubia under King Thutmose I, "I was brave in his presence in the bad water, in the towing of the ship over the cataract. Thereupon I was made crew commander" (14). In Syria under Thutmose I again, "I was in the van of our troops, and his majesty saw my valor. I brought a chariot, its horse, and him who was on it as a living captive [to the King]" (14). Ahmose ends, "I have grown old; I have reached old age. Favored as before, and loved [by my lord], I [rest] in the tomb that I myself made" (14).

This autobiography illustrates the type that presents a list of praiseworthy actions, career titles, service to the King, and rewards received from the King. It is organized according to a list of military campaigns that Ahmose participated in, starting with a battle under King Ahmose against the Hyksos, then battles against the Nubians under Kings Amenhotep I and Thutmose I, and finally campaigns against the Syrians under King Thutmose I. The following indicates the no-nonsense list-like style of the presentation:

> I brought his majesty back to Egypt in two days from
> "Upper Well," and was rewarded with gold. I brought
> back two female slaves as booty, apart from those I had
> presented to his majesty. Then they made me a "War-
> rior of the Ruler." (Lichtheim, 1976, 13–14)

Ahmose's tomb, in comparison with that of his grandson Paheri, is text heavy, with far less liveliness or innovation in the visuals. For visitors who are not family, the force of persuasion in this tomb relies on the career biography, showing bravery in many battles with many of the country's enemies. The various campaigns all succeeded, and left Egyptian sovereignty intact. In this tomb, readers would have been persuaded to recite the offering formula based on the accomplishments of this military man rather than based on the enticements of the visuals.

In Ahmose's tomb design, the visitor cannot begin the visit by immediately turning to the right and attending to the inner east wall on the entrance side or the long east side wall next to the entrance, since these locations present the latter portion of the autobiography. The direction of hieroglyphs would offer clues to the visitor as to the direction for reading. In this tomb, the visitor would more logically begin with the west or north walls, or the northern end of the east wall. The location of the offering place is not clear, but in the New Kingdom period, offering stelae were generally located near the entrance/exit, or in the open court preceding the tomb-chapel entrance (Lesko 1771). Because much of the tomb art and text is no longer visible, there is no comprehensive publication devoted to this tomb, though the autobiography itself is excerpted frequently.

These two examples—from tombs of Paheri and his grandfather Ahmose—offer two extremes in several ways. One gives solely the moral narrative and the other a career narrative. They differ in the approach to using visuals, as well as in tying success and worthiness to the king's favor. They show similarities as well. Both present the best version of the identity they portray. They offer no introspection, no analysis of experience, and no admission of missteps. Both present the identities as admirable, and as widely recognized. Both present ideal visual versions of ancient Egyptians. The two tombs represent very different identities. If seen alone, Paheri's moral biographical text presents a rather solemn, wordy individual, perhaps sanctimonious. The moral autobiography, in fact, depends greatly on what Egyptologists call a negative confession, reciting the bad things the tomb owner did not do. In his moral autobiography, Paheri comes across as reliable, careful, avoiding mistakes, but unimaginative. However, the context within the tomb—including the innovative hymn and the visuals, the joking and light-hearted banter, the lack of lengthy recitation of titles, and the willingness to let the images speak for his career responsibilities—frames the moral biography and the long appeal to visitors, suggesting an identity that involves a sense of fun, a sense of modesty, a sense of imagination, and the vision and courage to break new ground. Ahmose, presented as brave and courageous in the autobiography, shows himself in more conventional and traditional fashion in the rest of his tomb, primarily as a family man.

Two other El Kab tombs date to the eighteenth dynasty period. Another early tomb of this dynasty, belonging to a warrior named

Ahmose Pennekhbet, presents the biographical text on an inner wall around the doorjambs at the entrance/exit of the tomb. The visuals in the tomb have all been destroyed. The placement of the autobiography resembles that of the later tomb belonging to Ahmose, son of Abana, except that Ahmose's autobiography starts at the far end of the long east side wall, extending to the immediately adjacent side of the inner entrance wall. A tomb of Renni, an eighteenth dynasty mayor of Nekhbet preceding Paheri, offers a design plan quite similar to that of Paheri's tomb, though Renni's tomb is less refined in execution. Renni's tomb too incorporates multiple instances of engaging visual details, such as monkeys on tables nibbling on the food offerings provided for the benefit of Renni.[4] Thus, on the whole, the eighteenth dynasty tombs in the El Kab provincial area seem to exhibit two different design models—one involving a plan that leads and entices visitors to the back wall of the tomb, where autobiographies, offering formulae, and appeals are found. The other model leads visitors via the west wall to the autobiography on the east and south walls; the autobiography ends or exists wholly by the entrance/exit to the tomb. In this model, seen in the tombs of Ahmose son of Abana and Ahmose Pennekhbet, visitors would then presumably find the offering prayers and offering place near the chapel door. Every tomb chapel would contain an offering stela and an offering table, either built into a niche in the wall or free standing (Taylor 155). Since the tombs examined here had been vandalized and such free-standing objects had been removed or destroyed, it's not known precisely where these would have been located.

Discussion

As evidenced here, the ancient Egyptian non-royal tomb of the eighteenth dynasty is a profoundly rhetorical project, enacted differently in different cases. Two provincial tombs at El Kab, ninety kilometers from the center of power at Thebes, do seem to follow somewhat similar patterns to those at Thebes, though some substantial innovations do occur. For example, the innovations involve Paheri's hymn imagining his afterlife, as well as Paheri's new approach to showing the *muu* dancers; he also shows and names five full generations of family, which is quite unusual. The El Kab eighteenth dynasty tombs, of which only four in varying states were available for study, all arise from an earlier period than do the thirty tombs involved in Hartwig's study, which concentrates on non-royal tombs in Thebes during two reigns: that of Amenhotep III and Thutmose IV. Paheri and Renni, whose tomb designs most closely resemble those in Hartwig's study, served under Thutmose I (~1493) and Amenhotep I (~1514 to 1493 BCE) respectively; Paheri's service possibly extended to the reign of Hatschepsut (1473 to 1458 BCE), before Thutmose III (~1479 BCE). The owners of the other eighteenth dynasty El Kab tombs—Ahmose Pennekhbet and Ahmose, son of Abana—began service under King Ahmose, the first king of the eighteenth dynasty (~1540 to 1514 BCE). Ahmose Pennekhbet continued to serve into the reign of Thutmose III (~1479 to 1425 BCE); Ahmose, son of Abana, served under two pharaohs following King Ahmose: Amenhotep I and Thutmose I (~1493 BCE). Thus, Ahmose Pennekhbet's tomb seems to be the latest of the four to be constructed, closer to the time period of Hartwig's Theban study, which covered 1419 to 1372 BCE, but its pattern seems quite different from the later Theban models, which Paheri's and Renni's tombs resemble. Notably, the two Ahmoses, whose tomb designs seem to share considerable resemblance, were both military figures. Renni and Paheri were both state officials and mayors. The close professional affiliations may have influenced the tomb designs.

One notable difference between these provincial El Kab tombs and the central Theban tombs studied by Hartwig is worth noting. Hartwig points out that in the tombs she examined, those of state officials mainly show colleagues and anonymous participants in their banquet scenes (130, n. 47), and focus primarily on official scenes. On the contrary, the El Kab eighteenth dynasty tombs, arising from a somewhat earlier period than the Theban tombs analyzed by Hartwig, focus much more heavily on family in the banquet and private scenes. As Deborah Vischak points out in studying an earlier period, "the provincial elite likely would have felt tied more closely to their local community, including to each other, as crucial sources of stability and tradition" (269). The provincial elite indeed would have depended more heavily for cult offerings on family and other local elite in their communities than on the king. In Thebes, where the king was located, it's more likely that he would have set up a fund for continued priestly offerings. In the provincial El Kab setting, the tombs communicate the high value they place on their families and the other elite members of their communities more than do the tombs near the central seat of government. The El Kab tomb designs reflect and convey this aspect of their local culture, while adhering to the basic conventions of the traditional central approaches.

However, in all cases during this period—in Thebes and in El Kab—as well as in Old Kingdom tombs studied by Vischak, Ann Macy Roth, and Andrey O. Bolshakov, the ancient Egyptian tombs are meant to fulfill similar functions: to communicate an identity as an elite, impressive, and worthy individual in the Egyptian social order; to preserve the identity of the tomb owner; and to encourage the likelihood that visitors to the tomb would be willing to perform the ritual acts necessary for the preservation of identity. As Lynn Meskell observes, the tombs create a materialization of the self, a material biography involving multiple media (2004, p. 10). The textual biographies present information that cannot readily be conveyed in images. Visuals, text, and architecture were combined in a united presentation to accomplish these goals. Such persuasion to influence attitudes and actions is fundamentally rhetorical. Based on this analysis, I would argue that rhetorical study of early cultures such as ancient Egypt should not ignore the material dimensions, the visual dimensions, or the oral dimensions, only to concentrate on text taken out of the total performative experience and examined in a false isolation.

NOTES

1. I use the chronology found in *The Cultural Atlas of Ancient Egypt* by Baines and Malik (2000).

2. Notable exceptions include the following: Assmann, Baines, Meskell, and Hartwig.

3. Photos from the tomb of Ahmose of Abana are available online at http://www.osirisnet.net/tombes/el_kab/ahmes/e_ahmes.htm

4. Photos from the tomb of Renni are available online at http://www.osirisnet.net/tombes/el_kab/renni/e_renni_01.htm

See also http://www.egyptsites.co.uk/upper/edfu/elkab.html for photos of Renni's tomb and for a brief description of the tomb of Ahmose Pennekhbet. The osiris.net site has been established and maintained by Thierry Benderitter.

Works Cited

Assmann, Jan. "Ancient Egypt and the Materiality of the Sign." *Materialities of Communication*. Ed. Hans Gumbrecht and K. Pfeiffer. Stanford, CA: Stanford UP, 1994, 15-31.

—. *Death and Salvation in Ancient Egypt*. Trans. David Lorton. Ithaca, NY: Cornell UP, 2005.

—. "Preservation and Presentation of Self in Ancient Egyptian Portraiture." *Studies in Honor of William Kelly Simpson*. Ed. Peter der Manuelian. Boston: Museum of Fine Arts, Department of Ancient Egyptian, Nubian, and Near Eastern Art, 1996, 55-81.

—. *The Mind of Egypt: History and Meaning in the Time of the Pharaohs*. Trans. by Andrew Jenkins. New York: Metropolitan Books: Henry Holt and Company, 2002.

Baines, John. "Contextualizing Egyptian Representations of Society and Ethnicity." *The Study of the Ancient near East in the 21st Century*. Ed. Jerrold Cooper and G. Schwartz, 339–84. Winona Lake, IN: Eisenbrauns, 1996.

—. "Forerunners of Narrative Biographies." *Studies on Ancient Egypt in Honour of H.S. Smith*. Ed. Anthony Leahy and John Tait. London: Egypt Exploration Society, 1999, 23-37.

—. "On the Composition and Inscriptions of the Vatican Statue of Udjahorresne." *Studies in Honor of William Kelly Simpson*. Ed. Peter der Manuelian. Boston: Museum of Fine Arts, Department of Ancient Egyptian, Nubian, and Near Eastern Art, 1996, 83-92.

—. *Visual and Written Culture in Ancient Egypt*. New York; Oxford UP, 2007.

Baines, John, and P. Lacovara. "Burial and the Dead in Ancient Egyptian Society: Respect, Formalism, Neglect." *Journal of Social Archaeology* 2.1 (2001): 5–36.

Baines, John, and J. Malik. *Cultural Atlas of Ancient Egypt*. New York: Checkmark Books, Facts on File, 2000.

Benderitter, Thierry. The site of El Kab. 8 Dec. 2007 <http://www.osirisnet.net/tombes/el_kab/e_el_kab.htm>

Bolshakov, Andrey O. "Arrangement of Murals as a Principle of Old Kingdom Tomb Decoration." *Dekorierte Grabanlagen Im Alten Reich: Methodik Und Interpretation*. Ed. Martin Fitzenreiter and Michael Herb. London: Golden House Publications, 2006, 37-60.

Booth, Wayne. *The Rhetoric of Rhetoric: The Quest for Effective Communication*. Malden, MA: Blackwell Books, 2004.

Davies, Norman de Garis. *The Tomb of Rekh-Mi-Re at Thebes*. Vol. I and II, *Metropolitan Museum of Art Egyptian Expedition*. New York: Arno Press, 1973.

Donadoni, Sergio, ed. *The Egyptians.* Trans. Anna Lisa Crone Robert Bianchi, Charles Lambert, and Thomas Ritter. Chicago: U of Chicago P, 1997.

Dunand, Francoise, and Christiane Zivie-Coche. *Gods and Men in Egypt: 3000 BCE to 395 CE.* Trans David Lorton. Ithaca, NY: Cornell UP, 2004.

Fitzenreiter, Martin, and Michael Herb. *Dekorierte Grabanlagen Im Alten Reich, Methodik Und Interpretation.* Vol. VI, *Ibaes—Studies from the Internet on Egyptology and Sudanarchaeology.* London: Golden House Publications, 2006.

Hare, Tom. *Remembering Osiris: Number, Gender and the Word in Ancient Egyptian Representational Systems.* Stanford, CA: Stanford UP, 1999.

Hartwig, Melinda. *Tomb Painting and Identity in Ancient Thebes: 1419–1372 BCE., Monumenta Aegyptiaca X, Serie Imago No. 2.* Brussels: Fondation Egyptologique Rine Elisabeth, 2004.

Hodel-Hoenes, Sigrid. *Life and Death in Ancient Egypt: Scenes from Private Tombs in New Kingdom Thebes.* Translated by David Warburton. Ithaca, NY: Cornell UP, 2000.

Lesko, Leonard. "Death and the Afterlife in Ancient Egyptian Thought." *Civilizations of the Ancient Near East.* Ed. Jack Sasson. Peabody, MA: Hendrickson Pub., 1995, 1763-64.

Lichtheim, Miriam. *Ancient Egyptian Autobiographies Chiefly of the Middle Kingdom.* Freiburg, Germany: Freiburg University Verlag, 1988.

—. *Ancient Egyptian Literature.* Vol. II: The New Kingdom. Berkeley, CA: U of California P, 1976.

Meskell, Lynn. *Archaeologies of Social Life.* Oxford, UK: Blackwell, 1999.

—. *Object Worlds in Ancient Egypt: Material Biographies Past and Present.* New York: Berg, 2004.

—. *Private Life in New Kingdom Egypt.* Princeton, NJ: Princeton UP, 2002.

—. "The Egyptian Ways of Death." *Archeological Papers of the American Anthropological Association* 10.1 (2001): 27–40.

Misch, George. *A History of Autobiography in Antiquity.* 2 vols. Vol. I. Cambridge, MA: Harvard UP, 1951.

Morenz, Ludwig. "Tomb Inscriptions: The Case of the I Versus Autobiography in Ancient Egypt." *Human Affairs* 13 (2003): 179–96.

Naguib, Saphinaz-Amal. "Interpreting Abstract Concepts: Towards an Attempt to Classify the Ancient Egyptian Notion of Person." *Discussions in Egyptology* 29 (1994): 99–124.

—. "Memoire De Soi: Autobiographie Et Identity En Ancienne Egypte." *Alif: Journal of Comparative Poetics* 1 (2002): 216–25.

Reeder, Greg. "The Mysterious Muu and the Dance They Do." *KMT: A Modern Journal of Ancient Egypt* 6.3 (1995). Available online at http://www.egyptology.com/reeder/muu/.

Roth, Ann Macy. "Multiple Meanings in Carrying Chair Scenes." *Dekorierte Grabanlagen Im Alten Reich: Methodik Und Interpretation*. Ed. Martin Fitzenreiter and Michael Herb. London: Golden House Publications, 2006, 243-53.

Sasson, Jack. *Civilizations of the Ancient near East*. 4 vols. Peabody, MA: Hendrickson Pub., 1995.

Taylor, John H. *Death and the Afterlife in Ancient Egypt*. Chicago: U of Chicago P, 2001.

Tylor, J. J. and F. Griffith. *The Tomb of Paheri at El Kab*. Vol. 11, *The Egypt Exploration Fund*. London: Kegan Paul, 1894.

Vischak, Deborah. "Agency in Old Kingdom Elite Tomb Programs: Traditions, Locations, and Variable Meanings." *Dekorierte Grabanlagenim Alten Reich: Methodik Und Interpretation*. Ed. Martin Fitzenreiter and Michael Herb. London: Golden House Publications, 2006, 255-75.

Whale, Sheila. "Pahery, the Supervisor of Works in the Tomb of Ahmose Son of Ibana." *The Rundle Foundation for Egyptian Archaeology Newsletter* 28 (March 1989): 3–5.

5 The Hebrew Bible as Another, Jewish Sophistic: A Genesis of Absence and Desire in Ancient Rhetoric

Steven B. Katz

In previous work (1995; 2003; 2004), I have examined the mystical view of the Hebrew alphabet, and the underling philosophy seen in the later ancient Jewish writings of midrash and the kabbalah[1]; these essays discuss the *alefbet* as the embodiment of an ancient Hebrew theory of rhetoric, a rhetoric that both shapes and reflects important but relatively unrecognized epistemological and ontological assumptions, as well as religious beliefs. I have argued that this ancient rhetorical theory appears to be positioned, philosophically if not chronologically, between Platonic and sophistic philosophies of knowledge—between a belief in Ideal Forms as essence apprehended by rational intellect and the basis of certain knowledge, versus a skepticism of the Ideal Forms and a belief in the sensuosity of rhetorical style as the grounds of necessarily uncertain knowledge. The ancient rhetorical theory in Jewish mysticism that I have been examining appears to philosophically fall between and subsume these positions: it seems to assume that essence is embodied in the sensuous substance of language itself, in the material shapes, sounds, numerical equivalents, positions, and permutations of the Hebrew letters, which is apprehended through a hermeneutics of textual production and interpretation. In this philosophy (or as a result of it), language and the endless interpretation of language become the ontological basis of reality itself.

In this article, I will focus primarily on the possible origins of this alternate philosophy of rhetoric in the Hebrew Bible itself. I will begin

125

to show how this ancient Jewish rhetorical philosophy, understood not only as a response to acute crises in Jewish history, but also to a 'linguistic existentialism' of absence and desire, may *signify* (in the fullest sense—not only to represent but also to materially embody) a compensatory rhetorical theory of uncertainty that stands in counter-distinction to the Greek and Roman (and Christian) traditions from which it differs in some remarkable although little noted ways.[2] Further, I will suggest that beginning in the Hebrew Bible, known in Hebrew as the Tanakh (which includes the Torah—the Five Books of Moses [the Pentateuch, or Law]—as well as the Prophets and the Writings)[3], this rhetorical theory (as well as the Jewish hermeneutic tradition of commentary found in Talmud and midrash and kabbalah that descend from it and that stretches over five millennia to the present day) may be conceived of as another, "Jewish sophistic."

Given that this Jewish rhetorical tradition extant in writing starts with Genesis, in this article I am "writing backward" from my prior work on the later rhetoric of Jewish esotericism and mysticism, to finally begin at the beginning. The reasons—historical, philosophical, cultural, and religious—for the lack of recognition or understanding of the Hebrew Bible as a rhetorical theory are manifold. However, we can identify four major obstacles based on traditional assumptions and interpretations of the Hebrew Bible: 1) the Christian concept of God in the Judeo-Christian tradition; 2) the hegemonic Greek concept of rhetoric as persuasion; 3) the question of the authorship of the Bible; and 4) the hidden rhetorical dimensions of the Hebrew language itself. This essay will explore each of these obstacles to understand how the Hebrew Bible might not only contain but perhaps constitute a rhetorical theory, and *how* this ancient Hebrew rhetorical theory might be considered a 'Jewish sophistic.'

God Speaks Creation, and a Rhetoric of Uncertainty Is Born

At the basic level of the Bible (what in Jewish hermeneutics might be called *peschat,* or "plain" reading of the text[4]) is the "storyline" of the Tanakh: God created the universe and everything in it. One of the major obstacles to understanding the Tanakh as a rhetoric, and the Tanakh rhetoric as a kind of sophistic, is the seeming omnipresence and thus foundationalism of God in the Judeo-Christian religion. This foundationalism is based on the Bible as received in the

Judeo-Christian tradition, from Genesis to Revelation, which depicts God as an almighty, determining presence, continually evolving, and intimately involved with human history, the apex of which is with the birth of his son on earth and his life, death, and resurrection. Generally speaking, other than the lack of acceptance of Jesus as the Messiah and as the Son of God (no small matter, of course), the Judeo-Christian heritage and its Bible are commonly perceived as a culturally mono-lithic and philosophically undifferentiated tradition, even within rhet-oric (e.g., see Kennedy, who like countless other rhetorical and biblical scholars makes little distinction between Jewish and Judeo-Christian rhetoric). Unlike the Christian tradition, in which the Word becomes flesh and so introduces the surety of the visible ("a *physical* image of God" [Handelman 1992, 17]), in Judaism God's words remain text, and God remains invisible and uncertain.

There are some fundamental differences between the Hebrew and Christian versions of the Tanakh/Old Testament—and of God—when the Tanakh is placed in its own rightful historical and cultural context, as Jack Miles does in *God: A Biography*. As Miles makes clear, one of the most salient differences between the Hebrew Tanakh and the Christian Old Testament is the reversal of the last two portions of the Tanakh, the Prophets and the Writings, so that the last section of Prophets in the Old Testament predicts and prepares for the coming of Christ in the New Testament. Most significant for my argument is Miles's central thesis that the order of the Tanakh (as opposed to the Christian Old Testament) narratively reflects God's character as a voice that progresses from speech to silence (Miles 1995, 16–19)—an important progression that is disrupted by the reordering of all Greek and Christian versions of the Septuagint, "the Old Testament"! (Miles 1995, 416).[5] As Miles states, "Well short of the halfway point in the text, the narrative breaks off. What then follows are, first, speeches spoken by God; second, speeches spoken either to or, in some degree, about God; third, a protracted silence; and, last, a brief resumption of the narrative before a closing coda. . . . After action yields to speech in the Hebrew Bible . . . speech yields in its turn to silence" (Miles 1995, 11).

In the Hebrew canonical order, as the Tanakh unfolds the course of (Biblical) Jewish history, God gradually grows distant and increasingly removed from the human world. In the oldest part of the Tanakh, the Torah, God (or God's divine emissaries, the angels) talks to Abraham,

From speech ⟶ silence

wrestles with Jacob, appears before Moses as a burning bush and a moving back, a hovering pillar of cloud in the desert over the tents of the Israelites by day and a pillar of fire by night. But even in this first part of the Tanakh, despite this direct presence, so uncertain is the covenant between God and Jewish people—perhaps also symbolized by Moses smashing the first set of Ten Commandments—so tenuous their relationship, that God has to write "the basic principles" down for the Israelites—twice! (Exod. 24:12; 31:12–18; and 34:1). God has to *write*—and so begins the slow process of God's removal from the immediacy of the human life world. By the end of the Torah, as the Hebrews are about to cross the Jordan into the Promised Land, God is already in retreat—later in the Jewish history of the Tanakh to fulminate only through Prophets, and later still, in the Writings, to fall absolutely silent. Locating the Biblical "moment," the end of the Book of Job, when God goes silent, Miles observes:

> God's last words are those he speaks to Job, the human being who dares to challenge not his physical power but his moral authority. Within the Book of Job itself, God's climatic and overwhelming reply seems to silence Job. But reading from the end of the Book of Job onward, we see that it is Job who has somehow silenced God. God never speaks again, and he is decreasingly spoken of. . . . What is the meaning of the long twilight of the Hebrew Bible, its ten closing books of silence? The twilight is not followed by darkness: God does not die. But he never again intervenes in human affairs. . . . (1995, 11)

The logic of the structure of the narrative suggests the literal withdrawal not only of God's voice in the Tanakh, but of God in the Tanakh. The referent—the "Final Signified"—of the words who had existed for the ancient Hebrews in voice and act, a flux of fire and cloud, appears, and disappears, over and over, until only words and their interpretation as the basis of meaning and ethical authority are left. In fact (at the second hermeneutic level, *resh,* or "allegorical" reading), perhaps rhetoric—the act of speaking and writing in the Bible, the written Torah, the language of the Tanakh itself—in the context of Jewish history comes to stand in for God.[6] As Miles points out, discussing the later book of Ezra in which the Torah is read publicly and probably for the first time: "The books of Ezra and Nehemiah present, in effect, both an objectification and a functional incarnation of the Lord God. The mind of God is objectified in his law, which is now written down in multiple copies and interpreted and translated, as may be necessary, for every Jew. . . . The divine scroll contains all that God needs to say. He need not speak again and he does not" (1995, 388–89).

This substitution of the language in the Tanakh for the voice of God represents an important development in the rhetoric of the Hebrew Bible, and an essential dimension of the Hebrew Bible as a rhetorical theory. (This substitution can be seen, for instance, in Ps. 119, where "*love* of 'torah' replaces love of God" [Berlin and Brettler 2004, 1423].) In a "real" as well as rhetorical sense, the Tanakh itself becomes an uncertain "trace" of the absent God in Judaism, and therefore one basis for understanding the Hebrew Bible as a Jewish sophistic. The Tanakh becomes a rhetorical simulacrum—a copy without an original—that compensates for divine silence that is also a source of eternal uncertainty, the genesis of "endlessly vigilant anxiety" that we also see in the Tanakh (Miles 1995, 338). Rather than certainty, "[d]iffuse anxiety . . . is the more characteristic mood of the Tanakh: What will be may not be—it all depends on a frighteningly unpredictable God" (Miles 1995, 401).

Thus, at this level of interpretation, the rhetoric of the Tanakh suggests that the Tanakh itself speaks for God, replaces God as the basis of deliberative rhetoric and moral life. Speaking of the book of Daniel, in which the archangel Gabriel makes his first appearance, Miles writes: "scripture as written and consulted has now a divinatory importance matching that of dreams or visions and that, again and still, God himself is inactive and silent. God's Bible is replacing the Bible's God" (1995, 369). As the unknown point of origin beyond time and space grows ever more distant in an endless expansion of the universe, all we really have is the smoking residue of creation, and the somewhat ambiguous if not contradictory language of the Tanakh (materially as well as figuratively, for even the parsing of the words themselves are open to interpretation because Biblical Hebrew has no vowels). Thus, the words of the Tanakh, as signifiers of presence and absence, become keen figures of uncertainty, tropes of desire, "as the absent presence becomes a present absence" (Miles 1995, 344).

VOICE, UNCERTAINTY, AND LANGUAGE IN
THE ANCIENT HEBREW RHETORIC

The withdrawal of God's voice in the Hebrew Bible, and the profound absence that follows, is essential for understanding the Tanakh as a rhetorical theory, and that rhetorical theory as a form of sophistic rhetoric. But the withdrawal of God's voice that we witness in the evolution of the Hebrew scriptures is not the only source of uncertainty in the Bible. The contradictions even in the story line, to say nothing of the contradictions in God's character which Miles's book explores so thoroughly, remain latent, hidden in unconscious acceptance, Biblical convention, or theological reinterpretation that normalizes the contradictions and/or renders them meaningful. For example, take the two different versions of creation (Gen. 1.1–2.3, and 2.4–25 which is primarily focused around Adam and Eve).[7] As the *Jewish Study Bible* discusses, "The classical Jewish tradition tends to harmonize the discrepancies by intertwining the stories, using the details of one to fill in the details of the other. Even on the source-critical reading, however, the contrast and interaction of the two creation accounts offer a richer understanding of the relationship of God to humankind than we would have if the accounts were read in isolation from each other" (Berlin and Brettler 2004, 15n.). However, for those who take the Bible as a literal, foundational document—perhaps even written by God—these contradictions themselves can become foundational, become alternate versions not only of textual material, but of reality itself.[8] For many Jews, ancient as well as modern, the contradictions in the stories, in the text, and in God's character, may raise questions and doubts, but pose no real problem. For not only is the belief in God fundamental, but also the ambiguity. Beginning in the Bible, in the Jewish tradition it is almost a commandment that every Jew discuss, argue, debate, and reinterpret the Tanakh—God's words—and even argue with God, as we see in so many of the stories in the Bible, from Abraham to Moses to Job to David.[9]

In fact, we see this tendency to argue and interpret and debate the meaning of the written Bible not only in the later rabbinic treaties; as Benjamin D. Sommer states: "The interpretation of the Bible begins in the Bible itself" (2004, 1829). In "Inner-biblical Interpretation," Sommer discusses the various "forms that inner-biblical revision take and the effects of those revisions at the level of ideas," going so far as to label this process in the Bible "the rhetoric of reuse and rereading"

A shift to textual analysis and production [handwritten]

(2004, 1829). Thus, Sommer concludes, "It is often stated that post-biblical Judaism is a religion of the Book, and that interpretation and debate are quintessentially rabbinic activities. In light of the phenomenon of inner-biblical exegesis and allusion, it becomes evident that these characteristics of Jewish creativity did not begin with the Rabbis" (2004, 1835). Although less inclined to grant that a fundamental polysemy exists in the Bible, David Stern suggests that "The origins of midrash lie in biblical tradition itself where many biblical passages self-consciously look back upon earlier passages and, in one way or another, reinterpret their meaning" (2004, 1864), and that "the Bible [is] essentially a cryptic document" (2004, 1866).[10]

One of the most important points for understanding of the Tanakh as a Jewish sophistic rhetoric is that for Jews, God was, is, and always will be ultimately beyond all human comprehension, beyond all language, hidden. In the Hebrew Bible, as distinct from the Septuagint or the Christian Bible in which the Word becomes flesh, even God's name (one of many), the Tetragrammaton, which is commonly pronounced Jehovah or Yahweh, remains literally unsayable in Hebrew—and thus unknowable even in its material form![11] Perhaps at a fundamental level that can never be ascertained, for many Jews, to paraphrase Gorgias' dictum, God may or may not exist; if God does exist, we can't understand; if we understand, we can't communicate. "All" we have are faith in the words, the "Final Signified," or what the kabbalists later call the *Ein-Sof* ("the infinite," "the Nothingness" [see Ariel 1988, 58–63; Scholem 1941, 11–14, who also refers to God as *Deus Absconditus*]).

And yet, despite this essential uncertainty, and the fact that the Jews in the Bible are "a stiff-necked people" (e.g., Exod. 33:3–5), God in absence—and perhaps in part because of absence—is both doubted and loved, feared and revered. God becomes not only the source of absence and despair, but also of a source of longing and hope. God is the obscure object of desire. Thus an equally important point to the incomprehensibility of God is that the journey over the infinite abyss of doubts and contradictions, of our finiteness and ignorance—the attempt to know anything of an omnipotent and omniscient and utterly unknowable holy God—must transpire wholly and only in and through language: "According to the outlook of Psalms, the main religious function of human beings is to offer praise to God. . . . God is called upon to hear prayers and respond; this is one of His attributes. Worst of all is when He 'hides His face' and refuses to pay attention to

Jewish sophistic as challenging to Judeo-christian old testament [handwritten]

the psalmist, because this puts into question the efficacy of prayer. If there is one primary underlying assumption of the book of Psalms, it is the potential efficacy of prayer" (Berlin and Brettler 2004, 1284).[12]

This point about the possible inadequacy but absolute necessity and centrality of language is crucial in understanding the Tanakh as a Jewish sophistic. Despite the inscrutability of God, and the problem of communicating incommunicable experience, we find a profound love of and reverence for God throughout the Tanakh, and throughout Judaism—a love that perhaps at least in part results from the existential and exilic condition of uncertainty, the absence of and desire for a definitive reality, a Final Signified and Signifier, the owner of the "Blessed Name." "What even the Jewish mystic desires," according to scholars such as Gershom Scholem (1941, 8), "'is to taste and see that the Lord is good'" (Ps. 34:8). In fact, Judaism, beginning with the Tanakh, does not just merely celebrate language and the delight of the limited senses, but also rejoices and exults in them. For if God withdraws from the human world and leaves the cosmic void of the universe in the wake, we have sacred text—language—and a god-like mind, senses, and spirit to experience it.

A further parallel with the Greek sophists, then, is the belief in the physicality of language, the sensuousity of style, as a necessary aspect of meaning. The materiality and beauty of language is a locus of the Book, just as the materiality of the physical world is the location of any kingdom come in Judaism. According to Miles, in the chronology of the Hebrew Tanakh, this is the function of the Book of Psalms (which follows the agony and promise of the Prophets and opens the Writings) and later, the Song of Songs (which follows the wrenching Book of Job, and doesn't mention God at all)—to make divine fruit of language physical in a celebration of the delight of the senses and of earthly love. We don't have God and can't know God, but Halleluiah! We have a physical text, the Tanakh itself—the Tree of Life (Prov. 3.17–18), which in Judaism became a synonym for the Torah—its poetry and music and words. Like Mario Untersteiner (1954) in regard to the Greek sophists (e.g., xvi), Miles therefore argues that the dwindling dialogue between God and humanity in the Tanakh (even in the Book of Job, where God refused to answer Job's questions) is not a tragedy (at least, he argues, not in the Greek sense) but rather "a refusal of tragedy": "Tragedy has clarity and finality. The refusal of tragedy has neither. The Tanakh refuses tragedy and ends, as a result, in its

The centrality of text and language

own kind of muddle, but its protagonist ends alive, not dead. Taken as a whole, the Tanakh is a divine comedy, but one that barely escapes tragedy" (Miles 1995, 404).

This existential absence leads not only to uncertainty, but also to a developing rhetorical theory that we find throughout Judaism, in which language, each word, every letter, embodies something of the divine that is eternally hidden from us: "Each configuration of the letters in [Torah], whether it makes sense in human speech or not, symbolizes some aspect of God's creative power which is active in the universe" (Scholem 1941, 14).[13] Situated in and growing out of both historical *and* existential conditions that create not only cultural but metaphysical abysses, the Tanakh, with its longing for the ecstasy of the possibility of reaching beyond the limits of transcendental igno-rance, its exultation of the ambiguity and power of language within a framework of mystical uncertainty, its celebration of the senses in the finiteness of the material world, can therefore be understood to constitute a kind of sophistic philosophy of rhetoric—certainly not Greek or Roman sophistry, to be sure, since the rhetoric of the Bible is constituted primarily in narrative and legal forms. But it is a sophistic philosophy nonetheless, one that "the contemporary sophism" of post-structuralism can and has been understood to grow out of.[14] Indeed, the whole Jewish tradition, beginning with the Tanakh, is concerned with the hermeneutics of the production and interpretation of physical and moral reality as a material text (see Handelman 1992, esp. 27–50). The result is both ethical and relative, a faith in God and a belief in the final albeit uncertain reality of language.

The Tanakh as Alternate Rhetorical *Theory?*

If the rhetoric of the Tanakh appears to parallel and share certain af-finities with sophistic philosophies of rhetoric, is it a sophistic *theory* of rhetoric? Given the fact that much of the rhetoric of the Tanakh seems to takes place in the form of narratives and their inner-reinter-pretations, where is the *theory?* Remembering that the ancient Greek sophists themselves did not leave us much that is highly theorized but rather embodied theory in practice, how does the Tanakh as a rhetori-cal theory work? The ancient Hebrew Scriptures are not "only" a his-torical document (which Miles argues is highly questionable [e.g., 21]), a magnificent literary production (as Miles demonstrates [e.g., 4]), or even divine revelation (although as Miles discusses [e.g., 5–6], they

are foundational documents for over three world religions). Rather, I
suggest that the Scriptures also represent a rhetorical theory, one that is
quite different from the Greek and Roman theories we have inherited,
and so not obvious or well known. The basic *telos* of Greek rhetoric—
whether Platonic, Aristotelian, or sophistic—is persuasion. Indeed,
the second major obstacle to understanding the Tanakh as a rhetorical
theory is the hegemonic Greek and Roman concept(s) of rhetoric *as
persuasion.* Other studies, including those in this volume, have recognized that ancient rhetorics that preceded or co-existed with the
Greeks' are different, and that persuasion is not always central to them
(e.g., Chinese, Egyptian, and Mesopotamian rhetorics). To further understand the Tanakh itself as a rhetorical theory requires a somewhat
radical shift away from Greek and Roman perspectives concerning the
nature and purpose of rhetoric, as well as a deeper understanding of
the Hebrew Scriptures *as distinct from* Christian scriptures. The reinterpretation of the Tanakh as an alternate rhetorical theory also entails
some questioning not only of the Tanakh (based on the third level of
Jewish hermeneutics, *drash,* "digging," "study," "interpretation"), but
also of Western rhetorical theory generally.

   In *Greek Rhetorical Origins of Christian Faith,* the late James Kinneavy points out that while there are beautiful demonstrations of rhetorical knowledge, skill, and persuasion in parts of the Old Testament,
such as in the Prophets, there is no word in the Torah that corresponds
to the Greek words for "persuade," "persuasive," or "convinced," and
thus that there "is no reflective *concept* of persuading or convincing in
the Hebrew tongue" (1987, 54).[15] In one sense, Kinneavy appears to
be right: The overt, full-fledged acts of interpretation, argumentation,
debate, and persuasion that we find in the written commentary on the
Tanakh did not begin until the Rabbinic period, roughly 400 BCE-
200 CE, in the Talmud (the "Oral Torah") and the midrash (moral
parables and stories)—after "the period of Greek influence," and in
fact, under Roman occupation. But in another sense Kinneavy is reading from a perspective that tends to obscure if not occlude what may
be unique to ancient Hebrew rhetoric, an alternative philosophy of
language and knowledge begun in the Tanakh, continued in the Rabbinic Aramaic writings, and developed in the mystical kabbalah of the
Middle Ages. Indeed, there is no word for "persuasion" in the Tanakh,
if that is what one is looking for—if one is looking for rhetorical concepts that resemble those of the Greeks or Romans.

I would suggest that there is a conscious theory of rhetoric embedded in the Tanakh, one that entails not only a different perspective on and methodology of rhetoric, but a different epistemology and ontology as well. While the rhetoric of the Bible is certainly persuasive, the *telos* of the Tanakh as a rhetorical theory is not persuasion but the creation of reality, and its manifestation and interpretation in the language of the material text. In the very first verse of Genesis, known in Hebrew as *Bereshith,* ("in the beginning"), we read: "God created the heaven and the earth . . . And God said: 'let there be light,' and there was light.'" Is this foundational story of the creation of the world 'merely' the tenet of three plus major world religions? Or is it also the beginning of a powerful rhetorical theory that has become invisible to us? As Joseph Dan, one of the world's foremost contemporary scholars on Jewish mysticism, states:

> [That] God created the world using language can be read in two radically different ways. One emphasizes God's creation of the world by the use of language, but His arbitrary decision to use language as a tool is insignificant. . . . so that the linguistic aspect of creation is meaningless for us. Most theologians throughout history have understood the narrative in Genesis 1 in this way, drawing no conclusions concerning the nature of language from this primordial divine enterprise. . . . The same statement can also be understood as saying that creation was the direct result of language; it was employed by God, but the power of creation actually resides in language. When understood this way, the story of the creation and the nature of language are united in one concept. (Dan 1998, 129–30)

The first interpretation is so commonplace in the thinking of the West that we don't stop to wonder about the rhetorical significance of the speech act described in the opening of Genesis, or the epistemology and ontology presumed by the use of language demonstrated in it. In fact, we don't even think of it as *a use of language.* (Perhaps God only had to pre-linguistically think "Let there be light" for it to be so; yet our knowledge and understanding of the act takes place in language.) But in the second interpretation (based on the first of the two accounts of creation in Genesis), God, the master rhetorician, creates the world by speaking. God speaks reality into existence. What does this mean? How does it work? That has been *the* subject of interpretation by rabbis and mystics throughout the ages. In the rhetorical theory of the Tanakh, language creates reality, a belief and assumption that eventually led to the complex hermeneutic principles employed in Talmud, midrash, and kabbalah as the primary method of investigating and arguing not merely "text," but the physical, legal, and moral reality of God. While the creation of the world via language is not new in world religions, and is a part of Greek mythology as well (but ridiculed by Plato in the *Cratylus*), it is fundamental in Judaism (see Katz 2003). This is the power that God gave Adam (Gen. 2:19–20), and that humans "lost"—to name the *essence* of things—via an original rhetorical sin that leads directly to the tragedy of linguistic representation/signification, to an existential position of eternal uncertainty, to an essentialist rhetoric of absence. Is this "original rhetoric" not only a rhetoric, but the ultimate rhetoric, the ideal rhetoric, beyond the wildest ethical Ciceronian dream of the unity for form and matter in eloquence, and compared to which all others are paltry "imitators"—a rhetoric not of consubstantiality but of "substance" to which, as Kenneth Burke suggests in *A Rhetoric of Motives* (1950), all other (Western) rhetorics can be seen to strive? And fail to achieve?

Within our rhetorical diaspora—our exile from the reality of language—the rhetorical theory of the Tanakh is so different from any rhetorical tradition that we know in our daily lives that it is very hard for us to understand, never mind use. As Dan states, "It is very difficult for us to fathom a system in which language completely loses its standing as an intermediary, and becomes the thing itself. One way or another, we always assume that beyond language there is something nonlinguistic. To perceive reality the other way around, that is, that language is ultimate reality, and everything else is derived from it—and signifies it—is very difficult to accept" (1998, 152). Given God, the master rhetorician who creates all reality contained in the Hebrew Bible, and by extension, *olam* ("world," "universe," "forever"), all of space and time—and who speaks *to* Patriarchs and later *through* the Prophets, perhaps it doesn't make sense to talk about persuasion in Tanakh at all.

The Tanakh as a *Written* Sophistic Rhetoric?

The conception of language as the basis of reality announced in the opening verses of *Bereshith* is contained there, but also appears to be central, if not necessarily discussed, not only in the later Talmud, midrash, and kabbalah up to the present day where it underlies Jewish liturgy and sermons. It also appears elsewhere in the Tanakh itself. Many of the stories, prayers, rituals, and customs that emerge in the course of the Tanakh in one way or another have to do with inscribing: e.g., Adam naming essences (Gen. 2:19–20); the writing of the "Ten Principles" (the Decalogue, the Ten Words, or Commandments) and the Book of the Covenant, which are both spoken and written by Moses and by God in the Torah (Exod. 19–24; 31:12–18; 32:15–16; 34:1–28); the invocation to recite God's words at home and when away, when lying down and rising, to bind them as a sign on the hand and as a symbol on the forehead, to inscribe them on doorpost, gate, and impress them on the heart (Deut. 6:4–9, 11:13, 11:18–20); all the incidents and examples where God speaks and events, usually of salvation or destruction follow, or where humans speak to God or to other humans, and words or events follow; the narratives and images and metaphors of the divine (such as those found in the Prophets, Psalms, Song of Songs). Indeed, this self-reflexive, self-consciousness act of writing is reflected in the many deliberate manipulations of the materials of the text to create meaning, including in addition to those already mentioned, formatting (e.g., the splitting of the written text of the song sung during the parting of the Red Sea—the only place in the Tanakh that such a split occurs [Exod. 15]); the use of different sizes of certain letters in what became the central prayer in Judaism, the Shema (Deut. 6.4–9; see Katz 2004); the use of the alphabet as acrostics in many of the Psalms (Ps. 25, 34, 37, 111, 112, 119 ["comprised of an eight-fold alphabetic acrostic" with "eight main words used for 'torah' . . . corresponding to the eight-fold acrostic" (Berlin and Brettler 2004, 1415), and 145]); and many other distinct features of the physical text that later became the subject of intense Rabbinic and kabbalistic scrutiny and interpretation—all consistently preserved across time and space from handwritten scroll to handwritten scroll up to the present day.[16]

Given the omnipresence of this awareness of language in the Tanakh, it would seem that the Tanakh represents an alternate philosophy of language that is realized at least indirectly, if not conceptualized and set forth as theory. Indeed, some might say that because it does not conceptualize and describe itself as theory, the Tanakh is not a theory of rhetoric. And they would be correct, since like the "idea" (from the Greek *eidos*, "image"), the word Greek word *theoria* (from Greek *thea*, "a view," and *horan*, "to see") reflects the Greek drive to visualize ideas and abstractions, including God, and leave the word behind (Handelman 1992, esp. 17). As Erich Auerbach pointed out, because the Hebrew God is bodiless, spatial-less, invisible, and only to be apprehended in voice (1953, 8–9; cf. Deut. 4:15), the Hebrew Bible does not conceptualize reality in the same way that Homer—or Plato or Aristotle—do.[17] But from its earliest parts, the Tanakh, even if multi-authored, when taken as a whole is a carefully composed, crafted, integrated, symbolized, written document![18] The content of these stories, as well as the deliberate act of shaping of text, would seem to suggest a level of awareness of language as a symbolic and material object that may belie claims of simple narrative or "unconscious" principles, and in fact go well beyond our normal, pre-post-modern, a-theoretical non-recognition of stylistic features that remain transparent and so invisible. This consciousness of writing, like the sweep of the Bible as a literary epic (Miles 1995, 5), is impressive, especially considering the dates of this "treatise" (the earliest material may be from about 1200 BCE, with the redaction of Genesis by J from about 1000—900 BCE!—more or less contemporaneous with Homer [circa 1500–1200 BCE], and final redaction in Babylonian exile in the sixth century BCE, long before the sophists spoke or Platonists wrote.

The perspective of the Tanakh as a rhetorical "theory" is closely related to the fact that it is a written document. In *Writing Systems of the World*, linguist Peter Daniels states that "the Bible is silent on the institution of writing" (1996, 6). This is ironic because not only is the *Tanakh* as a whole one of the earliest written epic narratives, but it also reflects a conscious and very explicit awareness of writing as a rhetorically special and specific act (as when God tells Moses to "[i]nscribe this in a document as a reminder, and read it aloud to Joshua" [Exod. 17:14]). Such description certainly reflects a degree of literacy, a consciousness of the practical function of writing (which Plato rejected in the *Phaedrus*). But more than that, although not theorized or conceptualized in Greco-philosophical terms, the Tanakh as we have just seen also reflects a philosophy of writing as a fundamental act of creation. Thus, the question of whether the Tanakh represents a rhetorical "theory" is intimately related to the question: who wrote the Hebrew Bible, or more specifically in Judaism, the Five Books of Moses? Within and without Judaism, there are basically three positions on the authorship of the Torah, or parts of it: First, many orthodox Jews believe that God wrote the Torah and gave it to Moses on Mt. Sinai (most Jewish mystics believe that God wrote the Torah as a blueprint of the universe before ever beginning creation) or that God dictated the Torah on Mt. Sinai to Moses who wrote it down. Second, many religious Jews and non-Jews alike believe that Moses himself wrote the Torah. Third, according to the "Documentary Hypothesis," the Torah was written by at least four authors (J, E, P, and D) beginning in the period of David and Solomon in the tenth century BCE.

The first two positions, and the ambiguity and tension between them, are supported by the Torah itself (Exod. 31:18; 34:1–7, 31:28; see Berlin and Brettler 2004, 145); the third position is supported by science. But no matter which position we grant, if we also accede that literacy creates and/or reflects linguistic consciousness, which Kinneavy does,[19] the repeated descriptions of the use of language to create reality by the writers of the Hebrew Bible—whoever they are—may be a testament (pun intended) to the fact that the ancient Hebrews were philosophically aware of their rhetorical position, repeatedly referencing the act of writing as connected with divine creation. (The concept of God as author of the world is embedded deeply in Judaism.) Even in the Tanakh itself, the act of God speaking or writing is not pre-theory in need of theory, nor beyond all theory, but a sophistic theory of the inscription of ambiguity.

For example, because the people will sin, and God's countenance will remain hidden, he enjoins Moses to "write down this poem and teach it to the people of Israel; put it in their mouths, in order that this poem may be My witness against the people of Israel" (Deut. 31:19); that is, this poem, to be placed in the Ark beside the Book of the Covenant along with the Decalogue (Deut. 31: 26), itself will bear witness (cf. Josh. 24:25)–something we see the Hebrew letters of the Torah do later in Lamentations XXIV of the *Midrash Rabbah* (Cohen 1983, 45). The words of the Torah, in this case Moses,' bring things to life: "Give ear, O heavens, let me speak;/Let the earth hear the words I utter!/May my discourse come down as the rain,/My speech distill as the dew,/Like shower on young growth,/Like droplets on the grass./For the name of the Lord I proclaim;/Give Glory to our God" (Deut.

32:1–3). Here, as in so much of the Tanakh, "theory" is expressed in narrative arrangement, in the sensuous style of metaphor and image.

It would seem that the Tanakh is a kind of written sophistic rhetorical theory after all. Certainly the centrality of interpretation and concomitant development of a complex and possibly unique system of hermeneutic principles that focus on the text—not only content, but also on words, letters, textual marks as integral not only to meaning but to reality, and the production of commentary itself as an essential activity in Judaism—is directly related to the Torah as a written document. But more than that is the love for that "written document" in Judaism, seen, for example, in the story about Ezra holding up the scroll. But the fact that these "People of the Book" carried the Torah around in a heavy, awkward Ark through the desert for forty years (and out of the burning buildings and hostility of history) would appear to be a witness to their reverence not only for God, but for the Book.

"A Rhetoric of Grammar"

It could be argued that previous discussion probably reflects later culture and consciousness more than Biblical culture (the times described in the Bible and/or the times the Bible was written). There is no doubt that the kind of self-reflexive, interpretive theory of the grammatical, such as the elaboration of the structure of language in relation to the structure of the cosmos in the first-century *Sefer Yetsirah,* came later in history (see Dan 1998, 137). But perhaps its presence later in history should make us suspect an earlier inception, suggesting that at some level the writer(s) of the Torah and the Tanakh as a whole were aware of the meaning of their grammar and style as a textual reality to be interpreted (the inner-interpretations of the Bible bear this out). Indeed, regardless of who wrote the Hebrew Bible, there is another level of meaning and interpretation in the Tanakh as a written sophistic rhetorical theory (perhaps at the hermeneutic level of *sod,* "secret")—an alternate epistemology and ontology embedded and reflected in the Hebrew language itself! The fourth major obstacle to understanding the *Tanakh* as a theory of rhetoric, then, and that rhetoric as sophistic, is understanding Biblical Hebrew grammar. For in addition to Hebrew being a foreign language in a different alphabet, our understanding of Hebrew, like our understanding of the Tanakh and Judaism generally, is very much conditioned and colored by Greek and Christian conceptions of language and knowledge. In prior research, I have explored this hermeneutic level by examining the rhetoric of the Hebrew alefbet in midrash and kabbalah. In this article, I will focus on Hebrew diction and syntax. I will have space to offer one example—the Hebrew noun *d'var.*

At a simple level, if *logos* in Greek denotes "word" and "idea," in Hebrew *d'var* denotes "word" *and* "matter/thing." As Thorlief Boman discusses in an excellent and controversial little volume called *Hebrew Thought Compared with Greek* (1960), the difference is significant, for while Greek culture focused on ideal forms as the transcendental basis of truth, the ancient Hebrews focused on language as the *material* basis of the world. Thus, the connection between speaking/writing and reality is also revealed in biblical and modern Hebrew grammar and syntax itself. Further, "The basic meaning [the verb form of *d'var*— *dahbar,* "to speak"] is 'to be behind and drive forward,' says Boman, "or even better, 'to drive forward that which is behind'"; thus the noun *d'var* "means not only 'word' but also 'deed.' . . . 'Word' and 'deed' are thus not two different meanings of *dahbar,* but the 'deed' is the consequence of the basic meaning inhering in *dahbar*" (Boman 1960, 65). Word and deed—action in the physical world—are contained in the same word in Hebrew. And just as Kinneavy points out that there is no word for persuasion, Boman points out that there is no Hebrew word for "thing" either. It therefore would seem that both "persuasion" ("deed") and "thing" are subsumed under the verb *dahbar,* to speak. If there is no separation between word and thing (the reference to be bridged), and no separation between word and deed (the action to be accomplished), there is no need to persuade. For persuasion assumes a separation between words and things, or words and action, differences and distances that always have to be bridged by reference to real world objects (ostension) or by the social process of consensus (nominal reference). It appears that, as for Boman, at a fundamental grammatical level language reflects not only thought, but also deed. Language, thing, and deed are all instantiated not only in the act of speaking (*dahbar*), but also in the word itself (*d'var*). For the ancient Jews, as for the modern, language was not something theoretical, not just "symbolic action"; it was physical action in the material and moral world. A sophistic rhetoric, indeed.

If there is no biblical Hebrew word for convincing or persuading, one reason may very well be that the biblical conception of speaking and of persuasion, of speaking and of acting/behaving, are substantial—one in the same—as revealed in the equation of teaching and learning (Torah), of deeds and doing, throughout the Tanakh. Beyond the fact that most Hebrew words are derived from three letter root verbs, a grammatical analysis of the form of the verb *dahbar* also reveals that it is not a *pa-al* verb, which communicates simple action, but rather a *pe-el* verb form which communicates intensification or repetition of simple action. As S. R. Driver discusses in *A Treatise on the Use of the Tenses in Hebrew and Some Other Syntactical Questions,* the form of Hebrew verbs (there are only two tenses that are not really tenses, but rather modalities) communicates rhetorical intention, including the Biblical Hebrew of the Tanakh. And as the *Jewish Study Bible* states, the intention is to teach—not just through the laws, but also through every part and element of the text (Berlin and Brettler 2004, 2).[20] These complex, hidden rhetorical dimensions of the Hebrew verb are not picked up or communicated in translations into any other non-Semitic language. As Boman remarks, "Thus, [*d'var*]—'the word in spoken form,' hence 'efficacious fact,' is for the Semites the great reality of existence . . . When the Hebrews represent *dahbar* as the great reality of existence, they show their dynamic conception of reality" (1960, 184).

Thus, Boman demonstrates not only that there is a difference in epistemology between the ancient Hebrews and Greeks, but also a difference in ontology. Based on his analysis of Hebrew and Greek that I can merely hint at here, he concludes that the Greek conception of reality was primarily static-spatial, and the Hebrew dynamic-temporal. In talking about persuasion, theory, even consciousness, this is essential. For what Boman's analysis reveals (and explores in depth) is that the ancient Hebrews possessed a more temporal than spatial consciousness! According to Auerbach (1953), Susan Handelman (1992) and others, Plato and Aristotle did not. Perhaps the sophistic "theory" of rhetoric in the Tanakh, and of "persuasion" if we still insist on that category, is mostly invisible to the Western mind because its "theory" operates in dynamic time rather than contemplative space right from the beginning.

In the End Is Genesis

In subsequent Jewish religio-rhetorical history, prolific interpretations and extensions of the Tanakh in Talmud, midrash, and kabbalah[21] by prophets and rabbis and mystics reveal that the language of the Tanakh is both foundational and ambiguous. At the heart of the Tanakh as a rhetorical theory is the fundamental uncertainty about God, an uncertainty that, as with the Greek sophists, renders language—and the connection between word, thing, and act—central and the only means of understanding. In *Major Trends in Jewish Mysticism*, Scholem, the foremost scholar in the twentieth century of Jewish mysticism, points out that mysticism begins precisely where religion ends: at the edge of the abyss. "Religion's supreme function," he states, "is to destroy the dream-harmony of Man, Universe, and God . . . For in its classical form, religion signifies the creation of a vast abyss, conceived as absolute, between God, the infinite and transcendental Being, and Man, the finite creature" (1941, 7). At the end of religious reflection, as the end of Tanakh, comes the vast abyss to be crossed by mysticism.

> Man becomes aware of the fundamental duality, of a vast gulf which can be crossed by nothing but the *voice:* the voice of God, directing and law-giving in His revelation, and the voice of man in prayer. Mysticism does not deny or overlook the abyss; on the contrary, it begins by realizing its existence, but from there it proceeds to a quest for the secret that will close it, the hidden path that will span it. (Scholem 1941, 7–8)

Scholem argues that the mystic quest—to journey over or bridge that abyss via language—is not entirely subjective (1941, 7). However, while Scholem indicates the more "metaphysically positive attitude [of Jewish mystics] toward [the Hebrew] language as God's own instrument" (1941, 15), he also does so within a discussion of the paradox of mystical experience and language—"one of the fundamental problems of mystical thought throughout the ages" (Scholem 1941, 14). As David Ariel points out, "mystical experiences are frequently ineffable and indescribable" (1988, 6). While these two positions may seem incompatible, they are really not, for they both point to the highly subjective, uncertain nature of mystical experience, and the difficulty of knowing it and of communicating it. As Scholem reports, although mystics "continuously and bitterly complain of the utter inadequacy of words to express their true feelings . . . they glory in them; they indulge in rhetoric and never weary of trying to express the inexpressible in words" (1941, 15). Though he would never use the word, Scholem is, in fact, describing the Jewish sophistic, in which the transcendental is shrouded in mystery, and hermeneutics of the text is the only method of knowing reality.

When God said: "Let there be light" in the Tanakh, 'the writer' of Genesis set in motion a chain of signification, a rhetoric of absence in Judaism that is still reverberating in the abyss of uncertainty to this day. In this abyss, in the Hebrew Bible in which God is the master rhetorician, the Final Signifier as well as the Final Signified forever concealed in absolute uncertainty, it is the world that is the physical representation of language—the first words spoken a true "rhetoric of substance," rather than the other way around. The Tanakh contains and constitutes an alternative temporal theory of rhetoric in written, sophistic form of stylistic indirection. For despite the divine silence that descends in the second half of the Tanakh, God's speaking is a major onto-orthographic act. And although the written letters are perhaps not so much essences as deconstructive "traces," this initial act gives language an epistemic power that social constructionists in the Greek/Roman tradition of rhetoric can only dream of.

Argumentation, in which each ambiguous/multi-faceted/"supercharged" word, every fervent letter, becomes the means and expression of the obscure object of desire, is the hallmark of Judaism. As a rabbi once told me, most Jews are essentially agnostic. Thus, the rhetorical position also philosophically seems to subsume the Platonic and sophistic elements. The essentialist but ambiguous ethical narratives and textual dynamics of the Tanakh, the Talmud's acts of erasure where prior arguments are left intact and new ones written around the edge of the text, the midrash's contrary opinions added to former opinions, the kabbalah's contradictory and ineffable if also neo-Platonic mystical systems of God and the universe—all reflect the endless interpretation and debate of the Tanakh that characterizes Jewish religion and culture. To which we say, Amen.

NOTES

1. The midrash (from the Hebrew *drash*, "to study," i.e., interpret, hence, "midrash," "from study," "interpretation"), is a vast and varied collection of stories and commentary on the Torah and other religious texts stretching from the Rabbinic period (approximately 400 BCE-200 CE), if not earlier, but really extending to the present day. Jewish kabbalah is another vast and varied collection of texts, mostly begun in the Middle Ages in Spain, Italy, and after the expulsion from Spain, Palestine. Like the earlier midrash,

kabbalah (which literally means "tradition,") constitutes a commentary on the Hebrew Bible; unlike the midrash, whose stories and commentary are allegorical and fanciful, the stories and commentary in kabbalah are also mysterious and hidden, and venture far from the Torah. Most kabbalistic texts present mystical systems that try to account for the nature of God, the act of divine creation, and other such questions.

2. There is considerable controversy and debate about the historical and cultural relations between ancient Greek and Jewish culture, and the direction of the arrow of influence. (For a review and sources of the debate, see Katz 2003 and the bibliography therein.) There is less debate about the historical and cultural relations between Judaism and Christianity, although there should be; this paper attempts to begin to redress this problem.

3. In typical Hebrew fashion, the word *Tanakh* is a "post-biblical acronym" (Miles 1995, 18) of its three parts: *Torah* (Law), *Nevi'im* (Prophets), and *Kethuvim* (Writing)—without vowels, *TNK*. As we will discuss shortly, this order, materially embodied in the Hebrew word itself, is crucial in understanding the Hebrew Bible as a rhetorical theory. (See Strack and Stemberger 1996, esp. 15–30, for a discussion of the hermeneutic principles, such as the one above, used in Talmud and midrash.)

4. In the exegesis of the Torah, four hermeneutic levels for interpreting the text were developed; these are: *peschat* (plain), *resh* (allegorical), *drash* (interpretative), and *sod* (secret), which together create the word PaRDeS—paradise. I discussed these in some detail in Katz 2003; in the present article, I will apply these hermeneutic levels loosely to explore the Tanakh as an ancient Hebrew rhetoric of uncertainty, and how absence and desire get re-enacted at several layers of the text.

5. This part of my argument is heavily indebted to Miles's in-depth, detailed, complex, provocative, and Pulitzer Prize winning analysis of the 'literary' character of God. What follows are just a few points from that book. Though different parts were written at different times by different authors, my analysis like Miles's will treat the Tanakh as a "unified" literary work.

6. As Miles explains, "The scroll is not an idol; but when Ezra shows it to them, the people do bow down before it as to the Lord . . . It is the sight of the holy scroll that brings this reaction" (1995, 389). And still does. This, the intensity of this reaction, the deep emotional relation of people to the Book and the genuine reverence and love for every part of it—the covers, the scrolls, the text, the words, the letters—is hard to convey. (See Katz 2003, 132–33, for a discussion of the phenomenon.)

7. In the first version of creation, God speaks the entire seven days into existence; in the second version, God creates the world around, and for, Adam and Eve. As the *Jewish Study Bible* notes, "Whereas [Gen.] 1–2.3

presented a majestic God-centered scenario of creation, [Gen.] 2.4–25 presents a very different but equally profound story of origins. This second account of creation is centered more on human beings and familiar human experiences, and even its deity is conceived in more anthropomorphic terms. Source critics attribute the two accounts to different documents (P and J, respectively), later combined into the Torah we have now" (2004, 15).

8. In an interesting Jewish gloss on the ambiguity of divine language, Sommer notes that "[t]he word of God is not like the word of a human; divine speech is infinitely more meaningful. When the human utters the consonants of the word . . . it means only one thing . . . but when God does so they have (at least) another layer of meaning, and thus they can be read twice in two different ways . . . Precisely the same *theory* of divine language as "supercharged" with meaning (as opposed to simply being misunderstood) underlies biblical interpretations found in postbiblical Jewish literature" (2004, 1832; *emphasis mine*). Here, Sommer is discussing Daniel's (Daniel 9.24) rereading of Jeremiah (2004, 29).

9. Perhaps nowhere is the difference between Judaism and Christianity more evident that in the religious injunction to argue about the holy words. This tradition is continued and especially apparent in the Rabbinic Talmud whose very pages are formatted to contain the layered commentary and debate of many sages, and midrash where prior, often contradictory arguments are preserved in the text. See Steinsaltz (1976) for a discussion of this dimension of Jewish argument. Also see Handelman (1992) for a discussion of the reality of the text and of hermeneutics in Jewish thinking and religious practice, and the profound differences between that tradition and the ancient Greek.

10. But for Stern, "its true meaning was . . . to be discovered in the text" (2004, 1866). Stern says that "Unlike their postmodern descendents, in which polysemy signifies an indeterminacy that reflects the fundamental instability of meaning, multiple interpretation as found in the midrash is actually a sign of its stability, the guarantee of a belief in Scripture as an inexhaustible font of meaningfulness" (2004, 1874). An argument could be made that the Tanakh is inexhaustible because it is ultimately indeterminate; its stability is the stability of ambiguity, an eternal source of interpretation.

11. But for Stern, "its true meaning was . . . to be discovered in the text" (2004, 1866). Stern says that "Unlike their postmodern descendents, in which polysemy signifies an indeterminacy that reflects the fundamental instability of meaning, multiple interpretation as found in the midrash is actually a sign of its stability, the guarantee of a belief in Scripture as an inexhaustible font of meaningfulness" (2004, 1874). An argument could be made that the Tanakh is inexhaustible because it is ultimately indeterminate; its stability is the stability of ambiguity, an eternal source of interpretation.

12. According to the *Jewish Study Bible*, "[M]ost *Psalms*, which "fall into three general categories . . . : hymns of praise; complaints or pleas for help (sometimes called laments); and thanksgiving psalms. . . . Praise is the quintessential nature of the psalms" (Berlin and Brettler 2004, 1283).

13. Scholem (1941, 15) and many other scholars within the field of Jewish mysticism, such as Dan (1998) or Steven T. Katz (1992) talk about this special feature of Judaism and Jewish texts, but few if any outside Jewish mysticism recognize or discuss it (Boman [1960] being one exception); even within the rituals and conventions of Judaism most even Jews do not recognize its uniqueness.

14. Handleman (1992), and Steven Fraade (2007) who questions and partially argues against the centrality of uncertainty in Rabbinic Judaism.

15. Scholem actually makes a similar point when he states that "Classical Judaism expressed itself: it did not reflect upon itself" (1941, 23). However, Scholem's whole book is an articulation of the different mode of philosophical apprehension underlying ancient Jewish mysticism that he dates back to the Tanakh, and its later oppositional relation to Jewish rationalism that developed in tandem with the Greek classical period. (These oppositional modes of apprehension can be seen to run through the neo-Platonism of Philo of Alexandria that overlapped with the Rabbinic period; the more *halachic* [legal] Talmud and more *haggadic* [allegorical] midrash of the rabbis themselves; the Aristotelian philosophy of the medieval Maimonides in opposition to mystical kabbalah; the reform and secular movements of Judaism in opposition to Chasidic and orthodox strains of the religion. For fuller and much more detailed expositions of some of the hermeneutic threads in Jewish history, see the excellent collection of essays in the *Jewish Study Bible* [Hindy Najman 2004; Yaacov Elmann 2004; Barry Walfish 2004; Edward Breuer 2004; S. David Sperling 2004].)

16. The consistency of textual features is more than less borne out by the oldest copies of the Tanakh, the Dead Sea Scrolls.

17. In fact, as already mentioned in the text, the theories of the sophists were in a Platonic-Aristotelian sense "pre-conceptualize," and best illustrated in practice. But Isocrates and Cicero, if not the earlier sophists, seemed to believe that the attempt to articulate eloquence directly—to separate and make its parts conceptually visible—would result in the reduction and destruction of the art, and the inherent indeterminacy of affect (Katz 1996).

18. For example, the *Jewish Study Bible* notes that in the first version of creation discussed earlier (1.1–2.3), the number seven, considered significant in the ancient Near East, "extends, in fact, beyond the obvious division of the acts of creation into a seven-day sequence. For example, the expression, *And God saw that* [something he made] *was good or very good* occurs seven times .

. . Similarly, the word "God" occurs exactly thirty-five times (i.e., five times seven) in our passage, and the section devoted to the seventh day (2.1–3) has exactly thirty five words in the Heb[rew]" (Berlin and Brettler 2004, 12). The *Jewish Study Bible* points out that the seven-day week cycle was by no means common at the time. As if to offer further proof of the application of a rhetorical consciousness of the Bible, and another difference with later/ Christian versions, the *Jewish Study Bible*, in discussing the commenting on the line that connects the two versions of creation (2.4), states that "The Jewish textual tradition places the major break between 2.3 and 2.4, rather in the middle of v.4, where many modern interpreters put it, and for good reason. If the latter verse, or even its first half (2.4a), is read with 1.1–2.3, then several of the multiples of seven in 1.1–2.3 . . . disappear" (Berlin and Brettler 2004, 15).

19. Note the epistemic power Kinneavy (1987) accords language in his equation of the presence or absence of the linguistic term "persuasion" with the existence or lack thereof of the self-reflexive category/concept.

20. As the *Jewish Study Bible* points out, the earliest Biblical term for the Torah is *torat moshe*—"the instructions of Moses": it is only later, in Ezra, Nehemiah, and Chronicles, that *"torat (ha)elohim/YHVH"*—the Torah as divine revelation—appears; "[i]n the Torah, the word torah never refers to the Torah" (Berlin and Brettler 2004, 2). An important point here is that historically, an awareness of the "theoretical" does appear in the Tanakh.

21. The laws contained in the Mishnah and commented on in the Gemara, which together constitute the Talmud, "the oral Torah," often don't bear any direct relation to the Tanakh the way midrash and kabbalah do; and kabbalah often interprets in ways that go far beyond the text.

WORKS CITED

Ariel, David S. *The Mystic Quest: An Introduction to Jewish Mysticism.* Northvale, NJ: Aronson, 1988.

Auerbach, Erich. *Mimesis: The Representation of Reality in Western Literature.* Trans. Willard R. Trask. Princeton, NJ: Princeton UP, 1953.

Berlin, Adele, and Marc Zvi Brettler, eds. *Jewish Study Bible.* New York: Oxford UP, 2004.

Boman, Thorleif. *Hebrew Thought Compared with Greek.* New York: Norton, 1960.

Breur, Edward. Post-medieval Jewish Interpretation. In *Jewish Study Bible,* ed. Berlin, Adele, and Marc Zvi Brettler, 1900–1908. New York: Oxford UP, 2004.

Burke, Kenneth. *A Rhetoric of Motives.* New York: Prentice Hall, 1950.

Cohen, A., trans. 1983. Lamentations. *Midrash Rabbah*. Ed. H. Freedman, and Maurice Simon. New York: Soncino, 1983, 189-245.

Dan, Joseph. *Jewish Mysticism: Late Antiquity*. Vol. 1. Northvale, NJ: Aronson, 1998.

Daniels, Peter T., and William Bright, eds. *The World's Writing Systems*. New York: Oxford UP, 1996.

Driver, S. R. *The Treatise on the Use of the Tenses in Hebrew and Some Other Syntactical Questions*. Grand Rapids, MI: Wm. B. Eerdmans, 1998.

Elman, Yaakov. Classical Rabbinic Interpretation. *Jewish Study Bible*. Ed. Adele Berlin and Marc Zvi Brettler. New York: Oxford UP, 2004, 1844-63.

Fraade, Steven D. Rabbinic Polysemy and Pluralism Revisited: Between Praxis and Thematization. *Association for Jewish Studies Review* 31:1 (2007):1–40.

Handelman, Susan. 1992. *The Slayers of Moses: The Emergence of Rabbinic Interpretation in Modern Literary Theory*. Albany, NY: SUNY P, 1992.

Kaplan, Aryeh. *Sefer Yeitzirah: The Book of Creation*. York Beach, ME: Samuel Weiser, 1990.

Katz, Steven B. The Alphabet as Ethics: A Basis for Moral Reality in Hebrew Letters, *Rhetorical Democracy: Discursive Practices of Civic Engagement*. Ed. Gerard A. Hauser and Amy Grim. Hillsdale, NJ: Lawrence Erlbaum, 2004, 195-204.

—. *The Epistemic Music of Rhetoric: Toward the Temporal Dimension of Reader Response and Writing*. Carbondale: Southern Illinois UP, 1996.

—. The Epistemology of the Kabbalah: Toward a Jewish Philosophy of Rhetoric. *Rhetoric Society Quarterly* 25 (1995):107–122.

—. Letter as Essence: The Rhetorical (Im)pulse of the Hebrew Alefbet. Special Issue on Jewish Rhetoric. Ed. David Franks. *Journal of Communication and Religion*. 26 (2003): 125–60.

Katz, Steven T. Mystical Speech and Mystical Meaning. *Mysticism and Language*. Ed. Steven T. Katz. New York: Oxford UP, 1992, 3-41.

Kennedy, George. Classical Rhetoric and its Christian and Secular Traditions from Ancient to Modern Times. Chapel Hill: U of North Carolina P, 1999.

Kinneavy, James L. *Greek Origins of Christian Faith: An Inquiry*. New York: Oxford UP, 1987.

Miles, Jack. 1995. *God: A Biography*. New York: Vintage, 1995.

Moskow, Michal Anne, and Steven B. Katz. Composing Identity in Cyberspace: A "Rhetorical Ethnography" of Writing on Jewish Discussion Lists in Germany and the United States. *Judaic Perspectives on Writing, Literacy, and Pedagogy: History, Politics, Culture, & Identity*. Ed. Andrea Greenbaum and Deborah H. Holdstein. Cresskill, NJ: Hampton Press, 2008, 87-110.

Najmen, Hindy. Early Nonrabbinic Interpretation. *Jewish Study Bible.* Eds. Berlin, Adele, and Marc Zvi Brettler. New York: Oxford UP, 2004, 1835-44.

Scholem, Gershom. *Major Trends in Jewish Mysticism.* New York: Schocken, 1941.

Sommer, Benjamin D. "Inner-biblical Interpretation". *Jewish Study Bible.* Ed. Adele Berlin and Marc Zvi Brettler. New York: Oxford UP, 2004, 1829-1835.

Sperling, S. David. 2004. Modern Jewish Interpretation. *Jewish Study Bible.* Ed. Adele Berlin and Marc Zvi Brettler. New York: Oxford UP, 2004, 1908-19.

Steinsaltz, Adin. *The Essential Talmud.* Trans. Chaya Galai. London: Weidenfeld and Nicolson, 1976.

Stern, David. Midrash and Midrashic Interpretation. *Jewish Study Bible.* Ed. Adele Berlin and Marc Zvi Brettler. New York: Oxford UP, 2004, 1863-75.

Strack, L. Hermann, and Günter Stemberger. 1996. *Introduction to the Talmud and Midrash. 2nd ed.* Trans. Markus Bockmuehl. Minneapolis: Fortress, 1996.

Untersteiner, Mario. *The Sophists.* Trans. Kathleen Freeman. Oxford, UK: Basil Blackwell, 1954.

Walfish, Barry D. Medieval Jewish Interpretation. *Jewish Study Bible.* Ed. Adele Berlin and Marc Zvi Brettler, 1876–1900. New York: Oxford UP, 2004, 1876-1900.

Rhetorical Studies of the Ancient Far East

6 Reading the Heavenly Mandate: Dong Zhongshu's Rhetoric of the Way (*Dao*)

Yichun Liu and Xiaoye You

Studies of Confucian rhetoric in the West have largely focused on Confucian figures in pre-imperial China.[1] The reasons for the enduring interest in this historical period, we suggest, are mainly two-fold. First, the hundreds of schools of thought during the Spring and Autumn period (770 BCE—476 BCE) and Warring States period (475 BCE—221 BCE) produced numerous philosophical texts that furnish a treasure trove for interested rhetoricians. Many existent texts have been translated into Western languages, offering Western rhetoricians, such as Robert Oliver and George Kennedy, direct access to classical Chinese thought and allowing them to compare classical Chinese and Greco-Roman rhetorics. Second, rhetoricians seem contented with knowledge of Confucius, Mencius, and Xunzhi, assuming that perspectives developed by these pre-imperial figures offer sufficient explanatory power for Confucians' rhetorical practices in imperial China, where Confucianism gained state patronage. These two major reasons have largely defined, and unwittingly circumscribed, the purview of Confucian rhetoric known in the West.

The complacency with the knowledge of pre-imperial figures is unwarranted. Changing socio-cultural factors in China, Confucian intellectuals' responses to new sociopolitical exigencies, and the discursive engagement between Confucian and less influential schools would necessarily lead to reformulations of Confucian rhetorical theories. Knowledge of several key figures dating from a period prior to imperial China will not suffice, if we hope to determine how Confucian rhetoric has metamorphosed in response to, and in interaction with, evolving Chinese feudal politics, or if we hope to determine the enduring ramifications of Confucian rhetoric in modern Chinese political discourse.

Once rhetoricians move into study of Confucianism in the imperial period, they will inevitably encounter daunting challenges. First, since so many Confucian schools and intellectuals prevailed in the two thousand years of Chinese imperial history, one can easily be overwhelmed by the task of selecting representative figures and texts. Second, most texts were written in classical Chinese, a language hard to penetrate even for Chinese scholars. Even worse, few texts have been translated into Western languages yet, which discourages interested Western scholars from delving into the primary texts. Despite these challenges, which we equally face, we will venture into the territory less trodden, hoping that our endeavor will inspire more scholars to join the expedition. In this chapter, we examine a Confucian erudite named Dong Zhongshu (195 BCE—115 BCE), who became an influential statesman three hundred years after Confucius's death. Dong is an opportune figure for our endeavor because, first, he developed his political thought by assimilating those of many other Confucian intellectuals of his age (Queen 23). His rhetorical theory, particularly his rhetorical understanding of Heaven, was representative of the then influential Gong-Yang exegetical school of Confucianism. Second, Dong played a pivotal role in establishing academic Confucianism in the Western Han Dynasty (206 BCE—24 A.D.). In the process, he had to reconfigure Confucian philosophical and rhetorical frames to suit the sociopolitical reality of his time, which creates an opportunity to examine Confucian rhetoric in early imperial China.

In this chapter, we first offer an overview of Confucian rhetoric in pre-imperial China, focusing on rhetorical frames and concepts developed by Confucius but later extended or revised by Dong Zhongshu. Then, we discuss Dong's rhetorical theory. In Dong's rhetorical reformulations, he underscored Heaven as a powerful interlocutor in the discourse of the Way (道 *dao*) and articulated a new historical *topos*. Dong's theory is most concerned about how human beings could understand Heaven, the arbitrator of both the natural and human realms, and how political leaders could communicate with Him in their execution of the Heavenly mandate on earth. Since Dong developed his rhetorical theory largely through interpreting and appropriating a

Confucian classic, the *Spring and Autumn Annals,* in the spirit of the Gong-Yang exegetical school,[2] we conclude with a brief discussion of Dong's hermeneutics. By charting some key components of Dong's rhetorical theory, we hope to show that Confucian rhetoric underwent a salient reformulation in the Western Han Dynasty, thus warranting further scholarly inquiries of the imperial period.

CONFUCIAN RHETORIC IN ITS PRE-IMPERIAL FORMULATIONS

Although scholars have devoted much attention to Confucian rhetoric over the last several decades, they have not settled on what Confucius's rhetorical framework truly is. They, in fact, represent a wide spectrum, from denying to affirming its existence. Those who deny its existence are not deconstructionists but scholars who have entertained Greco-Roman rhetorical precepts as their "terministic screens." For example, Kennedy has characterized Confucius (551 BCE-479 BCE), when compared with Socrates, as being less systematic with epistemology and dialecticism and as failing to develop a system of argumentation.

Moving away from Western precepts and embracing native terms such as *ming* (rational thinking, logic, and epistemology), *bian* (argumentation, discussion, and eloquence) and *yan* (language), Xing Lu has identified some "rhetorical perspectives" expressed by Confucius. For instance, Confucius emphasized the importance of rectifying names, i.e., assuring a truthful representation of reality, particularly a clear demarcation of individuals' social status and kinship identities, through the use of language. Such a rhetorical perspective implies that a clear prescription and maintenance of everyone's roles and functions in society will lead to social stability and harmony. Further, as Lu correctly observes, Confucius emphasized the appropriate use of language in communication, and he developed a set of terms to describe moralized language behaviors, such as virtuous speech, trustworthy speech, upright speech, cautious speech, and correct speech.

Departing from dependence on Western traditions, LuMing Mao also recognizes three components of Confucius's *Analects* that constitute what he calls "participatory discourse." The text embodies three key components of Confucius's teaching of rhetoric. First, Confucius associates truth with antiquity, and emphasizes his role in accumulating and transmitting ancient knowledge. Second, Confucius assigns a prominent orientation to others in one's self-cultivation and moral conduct. Even a privileged individual needs to treat others the same way as he expects others to treat him. Third, Confucius admonishes that one should act in accordance with rites to facilitate self-cultivation and to achieve both humaneness and social harmony. Together, these components "promote an open-ended interaction between antiquity and the present, and between the individual and an ever-expanding circle of human-relatedness" (515).

While we admire both Lu's and Mao's characterizations of Confucius's rhetoric, we understand Confucius's rhetoric as being a theory of the multimodality of ritual symbols, articulated to salvage the tumultuous Zhou Dynasty (ca. 1100 BCE to 221 BCE). It is a rhetorical theory on how to properly mobilize ritual symbols, including linguistic symbols, to restore a disintegrated, corrupted Chinese society to an ideal state (You). The ideal state is a perfect embodiment of *dao*. In metaphysical speculations of ancient China, the universe did not start from a clear distinction of different worlds, but rather from a chaotic mass. What most attracted the ancient Chinese was not something that would transcend this chaotic state, but the innermost essence of the chaos that remained hidden and mysterious. The answer to everything about this world that lay at the heart of the chaos is called *dao* (the Way). Among ancient Chinese philosophers, Confucius was particularly keen in seeking out *dao* in order to end the turmoil of the Zhou Dynasty. For him, *dao* offers not only the answer to how the natural world operates but, more importantly, the key to the moral-spiritual order and the prosperity of human society. Therefore, Confucius once said, "In the morning, hear the Way; in the evening, die content" (4.8). *Dao* is all one needs to know, thus the proper realm of Confucian ontology and epistemology.

In Confucius's teaching, he was most concerned about human society and refrained from entering the realm of the Spirits and Heaven. For him, the desirable knowledge or wisdom (知 *zi*) for an individual is the complete mastery of attributes of being good, or in practical terms, seventeen kinds of rites established in the early Zhou Dynasty, six centuries before Confucius. Being good involves concern about human affairs, rather than about any supernatural or metaphysical matters. A true gentleman shows respect to the Spirits but maintains a distance from them (6.20). Any further exploration into the Spirits is discouraged by Confucius, because a gentleman takes as his sole responsibility the attempt to exemplify the desirable attributes of being good to the multitude. Heaven is the dispenser of life and death, wealth and rank

(12.5). A gentleman must learn to know the will of Heaven (20.3) and submit to it patiently. However, Confucius is unwilling to discourse on "the ways of Heaven" (5.12; 9.1) with his students,[2] probably due to his conviction that his students were not ready for this subject. He confessed that he came to understand Heaven's will quite late in his own study: "At fifteen I set my heart upon learning . . . At fifty, I knew what were the biddings of Heaven. At sixty, I heard them with docile ear" (2.4).

Human history, as the evidence of *dao,* is what Confucius tuned in to "hear the Way." Confucius saw social rites (禮 *li*) as an indicator of *dao*'s status quo in the late Zhou society. Rites are a sophisticated complex of social codes that signify what was valued the most in the Zhou society. They embody the total spectrum of social norms, customs, and mores, covering increasingly complicated relationships and institutions. The appropriate acts prescribed by the rites not only oversee ceremonial occasions, but also govern daily human interactions. Confucius praised the social rites of the past, critiqued their practice in the present, and envisioned an ideal society of rites for the future. For example, when consulted about statesmanship, Confucius referred to ritualistic features of previous dynasties as ideal practices: "One would go by the seasons of Hsia (Xia); as state-coach for the ruler one would use that of Yin, and as head-gear of ceremony wear the Chou (Zhou) hat. For music, one would take as model the succession dance, and would do away altogether with the tunes of Cheng" (15.10). State calendars, the state coach, the headgear for ceremonies, and music are all key features of state rites. In Confucius's view, certain ritualistic features in antiquity perfectly embodied *dao.* Sound historical knowledge, thus, allows one to identify social rites that were practiced in alignment with *dao,* and to employ them for current state-making.

Due to the pivotal role that historical knowledge plays in practicing *dao,* Confucius served as cultural transmitter in his teaching and erudition. Allegedly, he edited several important classical documents, such as the *Book of Songs,* the *Book of History,* the *Book of Rites,* the *Book of Music,* and the *Spring and Autumn Annals.* These classics embody the knowledge of ancient Chinese history and tradition that Confucius believed a statesman should master. Thus, when one of his students quoted from the *Book of Songs* to elucidate the hardship of seeking out *dao,* Confucius remarked delightedly, "Now I can really begin to talk to you about the *Songs,* for when I allude to sayings of

the past, you see what bearing they have on what was to come after"
(1.15). In his remark, Confucius emphasized the historical bearing on
the present; that is, knowledge of the past can assist a statesman in
making wise decisions for the present and the future.

Confucius also believed that studying history was a process of cultivating a righteous individual, a process of building a gentleman for
leadership positions or for assisting rulers. Once, he recommended,
"Let a man be first incited by the *Songs,* then given a firm footing by
the study of ritual, and finally perfected by music" (8.8). By immersion in ancient songs, ritual, and music, one would gain a repertoire
of approaches to expand understanding and skill in using ritual symbols, and would easily identify with the spirit of *dao.* The rhetorical
power of the *Songs,* for example, in Confucius's words, "will help you
incite people's emotions, to observe their feelings, to keep company,
to express your grievances. They may be used at home in the service
of one's father, abroad, in the service of one's prince" (17.9). Through
conscientious study of historical practices of songs, ritual, and music,
an individual would be initiated into the culture of ritual symbols and
acquire new rhetorical agency.

While Confucius emphasized history for ritualizing gentlemen
and guiding state-making, he adopted history as, using an Aristotelian
term, an archetypical *topos* in his discursive activities. The *topos* works
in this way: The past informs and guides the present. What happened
in the past occurred because someone followed or did not follow the
appropriate ritual practices or the spirit of *dao.* Therefore, we need to
practice rituals in accordance with *dao,* and peace and social harmony
will arrive thereafter. Historical figures and events are mentioned or
implied numerous times in the *Analects.* On many occasions, Confucius only stated a historical figure or an event, without comment.
The premise that the past informs and guides the present and the
conclusion are both implied, because they are the cornerstones of his
teaching and familiar to his audiences, including both his students
and government officials. To quote two examples from the *Analects:*

> The Master said, Of T'ai Po it may indeed be said that
> he attained to the very highest pitch of moral power.
> No less than three times he renounced the sovereignty
> of all things under Heaven, without the people getting
> a chance to praise him for it. (8.1)

> The Master said, Duke Wen of Chin could rise to
> an emergency, but failed to carry out the plain dictates
> of ritual. Duke Huan of Ch'i carried out the dictates
> of ritual, but failed when it came to an emergency.
> (14.16)

On both occasions, Confucius brought up historical figures with-out stating his theses. For his students, or someone who has studied the *Analects* carefully, Confucius's intent is quite unambiguous. He wanted to say that T'ai Po, Duke Wen, and Duke Huan were histori-cal figures from whom we could learn about appropriate ritual prac-tices. T'ai Po, the oldest son of King Tang, gave up the throne to his younger brother because he wanted to travel afar to collect medicine for his ailing father. Giving up the throne constituted the highest ritu-alistic expression of filial piety. In the case of Duke Wen and Duke Huan, neither ancient nor modern scholars have agreed as to which particular events made Confucius denigrate them.[4] However, there is little doubt that Confucius intended to say that T'ai Po was a perfect example of a virtuous leader who performed in the spirit of *dao*, while Duke Wen and Duke Huan were imperfect as leaders for the state. Thus, Confucius encouraged his audience to emulate the great deeds of T'ai Po and avoid the weaknesses of Dukes Wen and Huan. As these two examples show, history was mobilized as an archetypical *topos* for Confucius to bolster his teaching. In the process, we contend, he in-stalled a particular line of reasoning in his audiences.

We end this synoptic discussion of Confucius's rhetoric by reiter-ating its several key elements. Siding with Daoists, Confucius looked up to *dao* as the highest world order that human beings must submit to. However, differing from Daoists, while respecting Heaven's will, he concerned himself chiefly with human affairs in his teaching, dis-tancing himself from natural and metaphysical matters. He believed that only through performance of rituals in alignment with *dao* would human society reach the ideal state of *dao*. He saw human history as offering individuals guidance in learning and practicing proper ritu-als; therefore, he compiled several important historical documents and offered his own interpretations in his teaching. He evoked history as an archetypical *topos* in his discourse with both his students and gov-ernment officials. As we are going to show, some of these components were later dismissed and some were revised by Dong Zhongshu three hundred years later.

Dong Zhongshu was remembered as a Confucian exegete who expanded Confucian thought through his close reading of the *Spring and Autumn Annals*. After the Western Han was established following the tumultuous Zhou Dynasty and the short-lived Qin Dynasty (221 BCE—206 BCE), the government took a Daoist laissez-faire approach to state-making. The Daoists emphasized non-action (无为 *wuwei*) in their philosophy. The Western Han government imposed lower tax rates on peasants and enforced lenient laws and regulations. The Daoist-style governance allowed the masses to gradually recuperate from the difficulties of the wars. Several decades later, Emperor Wu, who favored Confucian thought, came to the throne and saw the need to strengthen his imperial governance. Therefore, he invited Confucian intellectuals to discuss state matters with him in 134 BCE. One of those learned men was Dong Zhongshu, an adept of the *Spring and Autumn Annals* in the Gong-Yang interpretive lineage. In his three renowned responses to Emperor Wu's enquiries, he expounded political matters grounded in his exegesis of the *Spring and Autumn* text, thus offering his view of history and state-making. At the end of his third response, Dong suggested that only the Confucian school of thought be studied and other schools be eradicated in the imperial academy. Dong's forthright recommendations deeply impressed the emperor, who promoted Dong to serve as a regional administrator and later as a grand master of the palace. Our rendering of Dong Zhongshu's rhetorical perspectives will be based on his three responses and on a collection of his writings called *The Luxuriant Dew of the Spring and Autumn,* which offered an extended treatment of points made in his three responses.[5]

Modern Chinese rhetoricians have expressed keen interest in Dong Zhongshu's rhetoric. Quite unanimously, they concur that Dong offered important rhetorical perspectives in *The Luxuriant Dew*. For example, Dai Wanying highlights Dong's three rhetorical perspectives. First, like Confucius, Dong addressed the relationship between substance and ornamentation (质文 *zhi wen*). However, while Confucius placed equal emphasis on them, Dong stressed the ultimate importance of substance. Second, Dong analyzed and interpreted Confucius's use of hyperbole in the latter's comments on some historical events in the *Spring and Autumn*. Third, he noted that "cautious language" (慎辞 *shen ci*) was widely used in the *Spring and Autumn* to accurately signify hierarchical social relations, ultimately perpetuating Confucian morality (Yuan and Zong 33–35). Chen Guanglei and Wang Junheng note a few other perspectives by Dong, such as the rectification of names (文辞不隐情 *wen ci bu yin qing*), the use of concise language to capture the nature of and relations between matters (文约而法明 *wen yue er fa ming*), and the kairotic use of language (无通辞 *wu tong ci*) in the *Spring and Autumn* (203–213). While we agreed with these scholars about Dong's perspectives on language use, we consider their shared definition of rhetoric as the "methods and strategies of effective language use" (Yuan and Zong 1) too narrow for our present undertaking. We define rhetoric more broadly as the use of symbols in human communication. With a broader definition, we have identified a rhetorical theory that centers on the discourse of *dao* between Heaven and human subjects. Besides offering his perspectives on Confucius's use of language in the *Spring and Autumn*, Dong developed a rhetorical theory to facilitate humans in reading and responding to the evolving Heavenly mandate, or the inherent expression of *dao*.

HEAVEN AS THE MOST POWERFUL INTERLOCUTOR

In his interpretation of the *Spring and Autumn*, Dong reinforced history as an archetypical topos by including Heaven as the most powerful interlocutor of *dao*. He concurred with Confucius that historical knowledge possesses ritualizing power for cultivating a righteous leader. He claimed, for example, that as the *Book of History* recorded previous kings' achievements, it would familiarize the leader with government affairs; he also claimed that since the *Spring and Autumn* focused on telling apart righteous and wicked behaviors, it would teach a leader how to manage the masses morally and properly (*The Luxuriant Dew* 25–26). However, more emphatically than Confucius, Dong conceived the evolution of human history as directly correlating to the Heavenly mandate (天命 *tian ming*). He evoked Heaven as the mediator between the humans and *dao*, asserting that Heaven, earth, and humans share the same origin (元 *yuan*) (i.e., *dao*). In human society, the king is the son of Heaven, supposedly representing and operating in *dao*. Hence, the Chinese character for king (王 *wang*) consists of three horizontal stokes signifying Heaven, humans, and earth, with a vertical stroke signifying *dao* (295). On the one hand, the king needs to understand Heaven's will by studying history and the natural world, and then needs to enact the will in his human reign. On the other hand, if the king misunderstands Heaven's will and governs his people ruthlessly, Heaven will warn him with natural signs, punish him and his people with natural disasters, or even dethrone him. Thus, human society as led by the king was under the constant gaze of Heaven. The rise and fall of human history was framed as a result of following or disobeying the Heavenly mandate, rather than as following or not following the appropriate rituals, as Confucius so emphasized. By promoting Heaven as the mediator of *dao*, Dong seemed to have sidelined the mystic *dao*; in fact, he erected a powerful arbitrating divine to prevent the emperor from enacting any ruthless behaviors. In this neo-Confucian reformulation of human history, the emperor was legitimized as the leader of the Western Han Empire, but, dialectically, was held responsible to Heaven, the omnipotent mediator between humans and *dao*.

Dong evoked the new historical *topos* as consultant to Emperor Wu. For example, on one occasion, the emperor asked Dong to elucidate one of his concerns: "In terms of what the three great emperors have taught us about *dao,* they reigned in different times and they all made mistakes. Some say that *dao* does not change in time; but does *dao* mean different things for the emperors?" (Yao, Book 21, 9). Emperor Wu was most concerned about how to govern the empire in the true spirit of *dao.* Dong's response to the emperor's question not only reveals his thoughts on human history, but also his use of history as an archetypical *topos* in political discourse. Dong replied:

> When *dao* prevails, the world is devoid of corruption. Corruption rises when *dao* falls. The *dao* of previous emperors had its own deviations and inefficacy, thus their governance sometimes became stifled and they amended corruption with deviations. *Dao* of the three emperors occurred in different times. It is not that their *dao* was opposite but that they encountered different circumstances in salvaging the nation. Therefore, Confucius says, "Among those that 'ruled by inactivity' surely Shun may be counted."[6] Shun only changed the first month of the calendar and the color of court dress to comply with the Heavenly mandate. As he largely adopted the *dao* of Emperor Yao, why did he need to change anything else? Therefore, the emperors only changed some regulations, but not *dao.* However, the Xia Dynasty valued loyalty, the Yin Dynasty piety, and the Zhou Dynasty culture—such change of focus is the right way to amend the corruption left from the previous dynasty. Confucius says, "We know in what ways the Yin

modified ritual when they followed upon the Hsia (Xia). We know in what ways the Chou [Zhou] modified ritual when they follow upon the Yin. And hence we can foretell what the successors of Chou [Zhou] will be like, even supposing they do not appear till a hundred generations from now."[7] That means all emperors will emulate the three dynasties in their governance. The Xia followed the Yin without people speaking of any modification of ritual, because they share *dao* and value the same thing. The grandness of *dao* originates from Heaven. Heaven does not change, nor does *dao*. Therefore when Yu succeeded Shun, and Shun succeeded Yao, they passed the empire from one to the other, preserving the single *dao*. They did not have any major corruption to address; therefore we don't talk about how they modified *dao*. From this perspective, when inheriting a prosperous nation, the *dao* of governance stays the same. When inheriting a tumultuous nation, *dao* needs to be adjusted.[8] (11–12)

The heavy reliance on historical events and classical texts as the backing of Dong's exposition reveals a particular line of rhetorical reasoning, or enthymeme. In Dong's reasoning, history reflects the Heavenly mandate and *dao;* therefore what happened in the past can be a reference for the present and the future. This particular view of history constitutes the key premise of Dong's rhetorical syllogism. As Dong claims in the passage, "The grandness of *dao* originates from Heaven. Heaven does not change, nor does *dao*." In the same conversation with Emperor Wu, Dong also asked, "Heaven of the ancients is also the same Heaven of the present. Underneath the same Heaven, the country was ruled peacefully and harmoniously in the ancient times. . . . Gauging the present with the ancient standards, why is it that the present lags far behind ancient times?" (12). In other words, the *dao* of Heaven does not change; therefore the *dao* of the ancients can be studied and restored in the present. It is due to this view of history that Dong mobilizes historical events and sages' words as premises to back up his claim.

In Dong Zhongshu's rhetorical reformulation, Heaven was positioned as the most powerful interlocutor in the discourse of *dao*. When Confucius delineated his discursive system, he respected Heaven but virtually excluded Heaven as a discursive participant. Confucius's system chiefly involves three constitutive entities—the ritualized and learned gentleman, the ruler, and the masses. The gentleman counsels the ruler on how to govern the country by conforming to *dao,* and the ruler tries to convince the masses about his legitimate leadership position through wise and humane governance and proper ritual performance. In Dong's rhetorical reformulation, Heaven was ushered into the discursive system not only as an overseer and a protector of human beings, but also as an emotionally charged arbitrator of human affairs. It is in foregrounding a transcendent interlocutor with anthropomorphic quality, we argue, that Dong's discourse of *dao* departed from that of pre-imperial Confucians.

Understanding the Anthropomorphic Interlocutor

Once establishing Heaven as the fourth and the most powerful participant in the discourse of *dao,* Dong sought to identify the deity's "personality"—its values, intentions, and emotions. However, Dong's endeavor was not born out of pure scholarly interest, but from an interest in seeking state patronage for the Confucian school. Confucian scholars of the Western Han, including Dong, started to pay much more attention to the mystic power of Heaven than the pre-imperial Confucians. Sympathetic with the Confucian school, Emperor Wu trusted Heaven's tremendous power over his human reign. As the proclaimed son of Heaven, Emperor Wu was most concerned about how to read the mind of Heaven so that he could execute the Heavenly mandate without committing errors. In one of his inquiries of Confucian scholars, he expressed puzzlement as to how his reign was legitimated by Heaven. Dong capitalized on the occasion to expound the deity's anthropomorphic quality. The emperor's puzzle was given as follows:

> Over the last five hundred years, many kings, who upheld both culture and *dao,* endeavored to model previous emperors' regulations to bring peace to their people. However, none of them could reverse (their declining) course and finally faded away. Is it because what they clung to or performed was false that they lost their legitimation? Once Heaven issues a mandate, He will not withdraw but enact it to its fullest extent? Alas, even if I model ancient sages and attend to my duties from early in the morning to late at night, it still will not help? Three generations of my family have been conferred the Heavenly mandate, but where is the evi-

dence? Disasters and anomalies constantly occur, but where do they originate from? In terms of human lives and their propensities, some die young but some live long lives; some are benevolent while some are degraded. I often hear His name (being evoked to account for these phenomena), but I have not quite comprehended the way Heaven operates. (Yao, Book 21, 1–2)

The decline of previous kings constitutes a historical myth, which deeply perplexed the emperor. Over the prior five hundred years, many individuals were conferred the responsibility of the Heavenly mandate and rose to the throne, but none of them seemed to have successfully fulfilled the mandate. The emperor suspected that in spite of their earnest desire to bring peace to their people, the former kings must have misread the Heavenly mandate. He also hoped to rule the empire by complying with the mandate. However, he feared that he might fail to grasp the mandate and, thus, would follow the same path as the fallen kings.

In the emperor's inquiry, it is important to note several premises that Dong equally shared. First, the emperor acknowledged Heaven as the most powerful interlocutor in the discourse of *dao,* who would issue mandates and, with or without human agency, enact them to their fullest extent. The emperor's acknowledgment of Heaven's discursive role indicates that the Confucian and Daoist notion of Heaven being the ultimate arbitrator of human realm had been popularized in the Western Han. Second, when deliberating on the historical myth, the emperor saw the failings of previous kings, the disasters and anomalies, and the various kinds of human experiences being full of symbolic meanings. They were signs not only of an existent deity, but also of his anthropomorphic values and emotions. Third, by asking his consultants these questions, the emperor supposed that humans are not passive, obedient servants of Heaven, and that there exists a responsive, interactive relationship between humans and Heaven. By fully understanding Heaven's values, intents, and emotions and acting according to his mandate, the royal family would be legitimated by Heaven and avoid fates that previous kings experienced. But how could the son of Heaven discern the deity's values and emotions? The emperor was perplexed, and he awaited Confucian scholars' instruction, which Dong sought to offer in his answers.

In Dong's rhetorical construction of Heaven, he not only affirmed Heaven's anthropomorphic quality, but also infused Confucian morality into it. In his response to the emperor's inquiry, he agreed with the emperor that different phenomena are signs of Heaven's emotions and of His omnipotent power in both the natural and human realms. However, Heaven is not schizophrenic; His emotional expressions and ways of exercising power are both rational and ethical. As Dong explained, "When the state shows signs of losing *dao*, Heaven will admonish it by bringing some disasters. If the state does not self-reflect on its weaknesses, Heaven will alert it with anomalies. If the state continues to stay on the wrong course, harm and setbacks will ensue. Thus, Heaven expressly loves the human king with his benevolent heart (天心之仁 *tian xin zhi ren*), and He wants to stop human chaos" (Yao, Book 21, 2). While Dong confirmed these signs as being manifestations of Heaven's rationality, he also interpreted them by reading Confucian morality into Heaven's intents. Heaven's various intents originate from a benevolent heart, which the Confucian school had long held as being the origin and the center of humanity. Unlike some religions, such as Christianity, Confucianism holds that humans are born with a pure, benevolent heart. It is through the shared benevolent heart, which Dong assigned to Heaven, that humans can understand Heaven's values, emotions, and intents unmistakably.

To explicate the intents of Heaven, Dong mobilized the Daoist concept of yin-yang. He explained Heaven's moral values and His strategic uses of power as manifested in nature in the following terms:

> The grandness of Heaven's *dao* manifests in the forces of yin and yang. The vital force of yang is virtue (德 *de*) and that of yin is punishment (刑 *xing*). Punishment aims to destroy while virtue aims to generate. Therefore, yang often resides in summer, being charged with generating and nurturing. Yin often resides in winter, being stored somewhere not for use. Thus, we see that Heaven favors virtue over punishment. Heaven lets yang rise to the top to perform major tasks of the year, and he lets yin stay below to assist yang sometimes. Without yin's assistance, yang will not be able to complete its tasks alone. Yang is known for completing a year's cycle. That is Heaven's will. (Yao, Book 21, 4)

Through the dialectics of yin-yang, Dong unveiled Heaven's rationality, or the cosmic norms. The *Dao* of Heaven governs the change of seasons. By observing how summer and winter alternate, as Dong suggested, we could understand Heaven's moral propensity and His preferred way of governing the world (i.e., He places virtue/yang before punishment/yin in order to nourish life). Heaven's intentions account for the fact that He loves, nurtures, and benefits all living things. Thus, as Sarah Queen states, "Tung (Dong) read the location of yin and yang during a particular season, or the direction toward which they moved, as cosmological proof of Heaven's preference for virtue over punishment" (211). Through a Confucian reading of the natural signs, Dong ascribed Heaven a particular anthropomorphic quality, turning Heaven into a Confucian deity.

BETTERING COMMUNICATION WITH HEAVEN

Since Heaven shares a benevolent heart with humans, Dong believed that both parties were able to communicate with each other. First of all, as an erudite of the *Spring and Autumn Annals,* Dong had been initiated into such an ontological frame early in his intellectual life. Chronicles like the *Spring and Autumn* consist of notices that state ritual functionaries probably announced day by day, month by month, and year by year. As ancient Chinese historians carefully documented such state affairs as court divination, ceremony, and sacrifice, Queen posits that, "the religious dimension of the *Spring and Autumn* exemplifies the ancient Chinese belief that communication between the human realm and that of Heaven was not only possible but essential to Chinese civilization" (117). With a thorough training in the Gong-Yang lineage of the *Spring and Autumn,* Dong was extremely familiar with the ritualistic means that previous kings had employed to communicate with Heaven. When he expounded his view of history to the emperor, for example, he quoted an event recorded in the *Spring and Autumn* to show the human-Heaven communication— When Emperor Shun was conferred his reign, he only changed the first month of the calendar and the color of court dress to acknowledge the Heavenly mandate (Yao, Book 21, 11). Therefore, Dong was extremely concerned about the appropriate ways that state rituals are performed because, first, state rituals were institutionalized means of communication with Heaven, and second, appropriate performance of state rituals would indicate an accurate understanding of the Heavenly mandate and acknowledge hierarchical relations between Heaven and His human subjects.

According to *The Luxuriant Dew*, Dong sought to institute two state rites to reflect the relationship between Heaven and humans. First, he suggested that the king sacrifice to Heaven once a year at the suburban altar and sacrifice four times a year at the ancestral temple, and that the sacrifices at the ancestral temple follow the changes in the four seasons and the suburban sacrifice follow the beginning of the new year. Such a regimented schedule of ritual performance, according to Dong, is derived from the hierarchical relationship between Heaven and other minor deities. Heaven is the ruler of hundreds of Spirits, including the Spirit of deceased human ancestors. Heaven rules over human subjects, dead or alive. Second, Dong suggested that upon being conferred the Heavenly mandate, the emperor would need to change state regulations (改制 *gai zhi*), as Emperor Shun had done two thousand years before. He explained the change of state regulations as follows: "The founder of a new dynasty must shift his place of residence, assume a new title, change the beginning of the year, and alter the color of ceremonial dress—all for no other reason than that he dare not disobey the will of Heaven, and must clearly manifest [the Mandate conferred] on him."[9] The change of state regulations conveys to the supreme deity that His mandate has been received and will be enacted in the human realm. Thus, state rites served to honor the supreme leader of the universe, and to confirm human reception of His important messages.

When performing ritual acts, Dong emphasized the relationship between substance and form. Along with pre-imperial Confucians, Dong subscribed to the notion that ritual substance and ritual form ought to coexist in perfect harmony. As Confucius once admonished, only a well-balanced mixture of these two would result in a noble person (6.16). However, on occasions where such an ideal could not be realized, together with other exegetes of the Gong-Yang school, Dong expressed a preference for ritual substance. He said, "In setting out the proper sequence of the Way, the *Spring and Autumn* places substance first and form afterward; gives primary position to the mental attitude [of a person engaged in ritual] and secondary position to the external objects [of ritual]" (18).[10] That is, it is most important to have the right mental attitude or emotions when performing a ritual. The right mental attitude includes respect of both Heaven and hierarchical human relations.

To sustain such important communicative channels as the state rites, Dong argued that more exegetes of Confucian classics need to be trained. Dong made a suggestion to Emperor Wu that has shaped the Chinese educational system for more than two thousand years. He says,

> Nowadays people study different kinds of *dao* and hold different thoughts. Hundreds of schools teach different meanings about *dao*. As there is no unified thought in government and state regulations change constantly, the masses do not know which regulations to follow. I humbly think that those that fall out of the six arts and the Confucian school should be eradicated.[11] When heresies die off, thoughts in government will be unified, regulations will become clear, and the masses will know what to follow. (Yao, Book 21, 13)

Misled by other schools of thought, previous emperors changed state regulations constantly, which confused the masses and failed to serve Heaven properly. Therefore, Dong believed that only through subscribing to the Confucian exegesis of Heaven and human history would the Western Han avoid ritual transgressions. Thanks to Dong's eloquence, Emperor Wu took some of his suggestions and waged a series of reforms, one of which established the imperial academy to promote Confucian thought and to recruit Confucian scholars to study the *dao* of Heaven and earth.

CONVERGENCE OF RHETORIC AND POETICS

Dong formulated his rhetorical theory based on his interpretation of Confucius's use of language in the *Spring and Autumn*. When reading the chronicle, Dong identified some particular ways that Confucius, the alleged author, used language in his historiography. If we define rhetoric as the art of discursive production, as opposed to poetics broadly defined as the art of discursive interpretation, then rhetoric and poetics seamlessly converged in Dong's reading of the chronicle. Dong's Heaven-centered historical *topos* was derived from his weighing of Confucius's rhetorical practices manifest in the *Spring and Autumn*. His creative interpretation of Confucius's use of language rendered Dong not only a rhetorician but a literary critic. The *Spring and Autumn* was the surviving chronicle of the state of Lu, recording title accessions, marriages, deaths, diplomatic meetings, military campaigns, alliances, and other important events from 722 BCE to 481 BCE. To encapsulate a history of two and a half centuries with a little more than sixteen thousand Chinese characters, the entries are stylistically terse and laconic. The style offered Dong much interpretive space to expound on the text, discovering profound moral meanings in the terse language (微言大义 *wei yan da yi*).

In his interpretation of the chronicle, Dong was sensitive to Confucius's moralization of linguistic codes. As Xing Lu and George Xu have observed, the sage valorized language for its potentially moralizing and ritualizing powers. Writing a Chinese history from the vantage point of the Lu state, Confucius used different styles to encode his feelings towards various historical events. Dong interpreted Confucius's rhetorical strategies with an acute understanding of humaneness/humanity (*ren* 仁) that centered in the teachings of Confucius and Mencius:

> The *Spring and Autumn* groups the twelve kings of the Lu state into three historical periods: one that was witnessed, one that was heard of, and one that was learned as a legend by Confucius. . . . Regarding events that he witnessed, he recorded them in terse language. For events that he heard of, he lamented on the disasters that people had suffered. In terms of what was passed on as being legendary, his words were less emotionally charged. He used words in alignment with human feelings. . . . Variable human feelings correspond to elaborate or terse styles. As I have observed, Confucius used proper language to approach people close to him and to distance those far away from him in relationship. His language shows respect to the honorable but looks down upon the degraded. It treats the benign kindly and despises the frivolous. It praises the good but shows distaste for evil. It distinguishes between yin and yang (good and evil) but tells apart black and white (truth and falsity). Everything in the world has its proper nature. If two objects share the same nature, they should be joined. If not, they should be set apart.

> It is good that things are joined or set apart. (*The Lux-uriant Dew* 8)

This passage emphasized Confucius's careful use of language because, as Dong believed, different feelings towards historical events need to be expressed in corresponding styles. Further, Dong suggested that proper use of language not only reflects the author's variable feelings but also perpetuates an orderly human relationship. Through approaching those close to him and distancing those far away from him in his historiography, Confucius exemplified a morality—respecting hierarchical human relations—via language. Finally the last statement, "It is good that things are joined or set apart (偶之合之仇之匹之善矣 *ou zhi he zhi chou zhi pi zhi shan yi*)," rendered much interpretative power in Dong's use. On the surface, the statement emphasizes encoding objects according to their proper nature. Since the underlying tenet is that everything in the world is related in certain ways, Dong gained sanction to read his own meanings into events recorded in the Spring and Autumn.

However, Confucius did not employ different styles simply to denote his varying feelings towards historical events; instead, as Dong argued, the entire chronicle was meant to convey the profound meanings of righteousness (義 *yi*). Dong explained:

> Thus, the *Spring and Autumn* entertains profound meanings about righteousness. One may grasp part of them and study them in wider contexts. After examining their truthfulness, he will achieve just standards. After reading the terse language, he will understand the hidden meanings. Therefore, the chronicle recorded events that took place outside of the Lu state, but did not elaborate on them. When recording events inside Lu, the chronicle avoided kings' given names as a way of showing respect, but never omitted events simply because the involved persons were high-ranking or righteous. This is the way that the chronicle differentiated between inside and outside, the righteous and the wicked, and the high and the low. (8)

Thus, for Dong, historical events that happened inside or outside of the Lu state, the language styles employed, and the textual strategy of avoiding kings' given names ultimately embody profound meanings about righteousness. The *Spring and Autumn* is more than a book of history, but also a mystic book on the meanings of righteousness. For a reader intent on grasping the meaning of righteousness, he or she needs to, first of all, understand Confucius's rhetorical strategies used in the book. When developing his rhetorical theory on reading the Heavenly mandate, Dong first systematically studied the language strategies of Confucius, as modern Chinese rhetoricians have unfailingly noted, and then came to his own interpretation of the *Spring and Autumn*. Thus, we have argued that Dong was an excellent literary critic who harmonized rhetoric and poetics in his hermeneutic endeavor.

CONCLUSION

Since the Western Han rose as a united empire after the tumultuous Zhou and the short-lived Qin Dynasties, the emperors were eager to legitimate their reigns. Various schools of thought vied for state patronage as in previous dynasties. Dong's rhetorical theory, which appropriated rhetorical elements from various schools, was a response to the political and cultural demands of the time. When Emperor Wu summoned Confucian scholars to inquire about the Heavenly mandate, Dong found an opportunity to articulate his rhetorical theory systematically. In Dong's historical *topos,* Heaven was portrayed as the fourth, and also the most powerful, interlocutor in the discourse of *dao.* To comply with the mandate closely, an emperor must understand the anthropomorphic quality of Heaven—His values, intents, and emotions. An emperor must establish viable communication channels to discourse with Heaven—such as the performance of state rites and the interpretive work of Confucian erudites. Only erudites like Dong could assist the emperor in interpreting Confucian classics and reading Heaven's will properly; then they could suggest appropriate state rites and other proper actions. Dong's articulation of his rhetorical theory was grounded in his exegesis of the *Spring and Autumn.* In the interpretative process, he capitalized on Confucian rhetorical strategies in the chronicle to come up with a sensible discursive theory, which helped to legitimize and to strengthen Emperor Wu's administration. Ultimately, Dong's rhetorical theory is a discursive guide for the monarch.

Notes

1. Pre-imperial China, also called pre-Qin China, refers to China before the Qin Dynasty (221 BCE—206 BCE), after which China became a united feudal country. This statement describes chiefly the *status quo* of Confucian rhetoric studies in the United States. There are some important studies of Confucian intellectuals' thoughts on language and their political discourses in the imperial period, but these studies are conducted from the perspective of education (such as *Neo-Confucian Education: The Formative Stage*, edited by Wm. Theodore de Bary and John W. Chaffee); or philosophy/hermeneutics (such as Sarah Queen's study of Dong Zhongshu's interpretation of the *Spring and Autumn*). We are also aware that several Chinese rhetorical histories published in mainland China have offered quite an extensive treatment of Confucian figures in imperial China, such as *A Complete History of Chinese Rhetoric*, edited by Zheng Zhiyi and Zong Tinghu; and the *History of Chinese Rhetoric* by Yuan Hui and Zong Tinghu. Compared with our present study, we find that these rhetorical histories have adopted a relatively narrow sense of the term "rhetoric," focusing on the "methods and strategies of language use" (Yuan and Zong 1) rather than more broadly on the use of symbols for effective communication.

2. Since the text of the *Spring and Autumn* is terse and its contents limited, a number of exegetical schools emerged after Confucius's death to explain and expand on its meanings. The *Book of Han* lists commentaries by five schools, one being the Gong-Yang exegetical school. The Gong-Yang commentary was allegedly compiled during the second century BCE. It is phrased as questions and answers.

3. Confucius mentioned Heaven many times in the *Analects,* though usually fleetingly. On most occasions, his comments showed the power of Heaven and his respect for His mandate. For example, Confucius said, "He who has put himself in the wrong with Heaven has no means of expiation left" (3.13); "Whatsoever I have done amiss, may Heaven avert it, may Heaven avert it!" (6.26); "There is no greatness like the greatness of Heaven, yet Yao could copy it" (8.19).

4. See Arthur Waley's "additional notes" for divergent interpretations of Verse 14.16 (249–250).

5. The authorship of *The Luxuriant Dew of the Spring and Autumn* has been historically attributed to Dong Zhongshu. However, some scholars have questioned the authorship of the collection, and they suggest that only some chapters were penned by Dong (see both Arbuckle and Queen). In our rendering of Dong's rhetorical theory, we will mainly rely on his three renowned responses to Emperor Wu's inquiries, which were recorded in Ban Gu's *Han Shu (History of Han)*. We will draw on the early chapters of *The Luxuriant*

Dew, which are believed to be Dong's own writings, in our discussion of the exegetic strategies that he employed to read the *Spring and Autumn.*

6. The English translation of this verse is taken from Arthur Waley (Confucius 193).

7. The English translation of this verse is taken from Arthur Waley (Confucius 93).

8. All Chinese sources are translated by the two of us unless specified otherwise.

9. The English translation is adopted from Queen (203).

10. The English translation is adopted from Queen (190).

11 The six arts refer to six classics allegedly edited by Confucius, including the *Book of Songs,* the *Book of Change,* the *Book of History,* the *Book of Ritual,* the *Book of Music,* and the *Spring and Autumn.*

Acknowledgment

We would like to thank Carol Lipson, Roberta Binkley, and LuMing Mao for their constructive comments on an early draft. We also benefited from Kara Dean Zinger's copy-editing assistance.

Works Cited

Arbuckle, Gary. "A Note on the Authenticity of the *Chunqiu Fanlu.*" *T'oung Pao* 75 (1989): 226–34.

Chen, Guanglei, and Wang Junheng. *Zhongguo Xiucixue Tongshi: Xianqin Lianghan Weijin Nanbei Chao Juan [A Complete History of Chinese Rhetoric: Pre-Qin, Two Han, Wei, Jin, Southern, and Northern Dynasties].* Changchun: Jilin Jiaoyu Chubanshe [Jilin Educational Press], 1998.

Confucius. *The Analects of Confucius.* Trans. Arthur Waley. Vintage, 1989.

Dong, Zhongshu. *Chunqiu Fanlu Jin Zhu Jin Yi [A Modern Annotation and Translation of the Luxuriant Dew of the Spring and Autumn].* Commentary by Lai Yanyuan. Taipei: Taiwan Commercial Press, 1984.

Kennedy, George A. *Comparative Rhetoric: An Historical and Cross-Cultural Introduction.* New York: Oxford UP, 1998.

Lu, Xing. *Rhetoric in Ancient China, Fifth to Third Century, BCEE.: A Comparison with Classical Greek Rhetoric.* Columbia, SC: U of South Carolina P, 1998.

Mao, LuMing. "What's in a Name? That Which is Called 'Rhetoric' Would in the *Analects* Mean 'Participatory Discourse.'" *De Consolatione Philologiae: Studies in Honour of Evelyn S. Firchow.* Ed. Anna Grotans, Heinrich

Beck, and Anton Schwob. Goppingen, Netherlands: Kummerle Verlag, 2000. 507–22.

Oliver, Robert. *Communication and Culture in Ancient Indian and China.* Syracuse, NY: Syracuse UP, 1971.

Queen, Sarah A. *From Chronicle to Canon: The Hermeneutics of the Spring and Autumn, According to Tung Chung-Shu.* Cambridge, UK: Cambridge UP, 1996.

Theodore de Bary, Wm, and John W. Chaffee, ed. *Neo-Confucian Education: The Formative Stage.* Berkeley, CA: U of California P, 1989.

Xu, George. "The Use of Eloquence: The Confucian Perspective." *Rhetoric Before and Beyond the Greeks.* Ed. Carol S. Lipson and Roberta A. Binkley. Albany: SUNY P, 2004.

Yao, Nai, ed. *Gu Wen Ci Lei Zuan [A Sorted Collection of Classical Writings].* Taipei: Zhonghua Shuju [Zhonghua Press], 1965.

You, Xiaoye. "The *Way,* Multimodality of Ritual Symbols, and Social Change: Reading Confucius's *Analects* as a Rhetoric." *Rhetoric Society Quarterly* 36.4 (2006): 425–448.

Yuan, Hui, and Zong Tinghu, ed. *Hanyu Xiuci Xue Shi [History of Chinese Rhetoric].* Taiyuan: Shanxi Renmin Chubanshe [Shanxi People's Press], 1995.

Zheng, Ziyu, and Zong Tinghu, ed. *Zhongguo Xiucixue Tongshi [A Complete History of Chinese Rhetoric].* 5 Vol. Changchun: Jilin Jiaoyu Chubanshe [Jilin Educational Press], 1998.

7 "Why Do the Rulers Listen to the Wild Theories of Speech-Makers?"[1] Or *Wuwei, Shi,* and Methods of Comparative Rhetoric

Arabella Lyon

Men of the world who value the Way all turn to books. But books are nothing more than words. Words have value; what is of value in words is meaning. Meaning has something it is pursuing, but the thing that it is pursuing cannot be put into words and handed down.

Zhuangzi 1986, 152

In 1932, endeavoring to understand the Confucian scholar Mencius (372–289 B.C.) and his theory of mind, I. A. Richards asks,

> Can we in attempting to understand and translate a work which belongs to a very different tradition from our own do more than read our own conceptions into it? Can we make it more than a mirror of our minds, or are we inevitably in this undertaking trying to be on both sides of the looking-glass at once? . . . To put it more precisely, can we maintain two systems of thinking in our minds without reciprocal infection and yet in some way mediate between them? And does not such mediation require yet a third system of thought general enough and comprehensive enough to include them both? And how are we to prevent this third sys-

> tem from being only our own familiar, established,
> tradition of thinking rigged out in some fresh termi-
> nology or other disguise? (Richards 1932, 86–87)

These questions are at the core of translation and comparative work. To read, interpret, and analyze outside of one's home language and cultural traditions is a problem of ethics, cognition, and identity, more than simply one of method. Part of Richards' approach to the problem of translation is to provide multiple definitions of a word, attempting to ascertain its total meaning, a complex function of intention, feeling, tone, and sense. In sum, word-to-word correspondence is not adequate to understanding meaning from a different culture.

In the early efforts to recover the rhetorical theory of classical China, scholars struggled with translating "rhetoric." From a very early focus on *bian* (argue, debate) as the term that most closely approximated "rhetoric" between 500–200 BCE, through the acceptance of multiple terms—*shuo* (explain, speak), *shui* (speak effectively, convince), *quan* (urge), *jian* (remonstrate), *ming* (name, dialectics), *yue* (speak), *ci* (speech), and *yan* (say, language)—the field of comparative rhetorical studies has been concerned with identifying the Chinese words which approximate Western concerns and with developing "a language of ambiguous similarity" (Lu 1998, 91–3). A language of similarity, however, focuses on the cultural commonality and does not access what lies beyond similitude. That is, by using a method focused on similar linguistic terms, rhetoricians are limited in what they see and remain too mired in the presence and absence of Western concepts.[2] As Richards asks, are we seeing more than the mirror of our minds?

In this essay, I will give up the specificity of a disciplined and Western definition of rhetoric and develop two Chinese concepts relevant to thinking about political language. Certainly, there will be moments of similitude between Chinese communication theory and Western rhetoric, but my effort will be to develop an alternative vocabulary as a means of discussing the effects of language. In fact, to facilitate the goal of seeing more, I will be looking at "rhetorical" concepts that are not textual features, but rather wordless rhetoric. *Shi* (position or disposition) and *wuwei* (non-action) are not as concerned with text as tropes or enthymemes are, but are defining parts of a rhetorical situation, concepts along the lines of *ethos* or *kairos*. They are key concepts that cross the major schools of Chinese thought and are useful for analyzing political and strategic discourse. While both terms have been the subjects of books, at this point in the articulation of Chinese rhetorics, simply introducing the terms offers a new direction and methodology to the study of comparative rhetoric and issues of translation. I choose these two terms from other possibilities, for they are terms that Western readers might know. *Shi* could be familiar through *Sunzi* or *The Art of War,* and *wuwei* through popular Daoism, if not from the *Daodejing,* a classic of world literature.

A COMPARATIVE ORIENTATION

The centralized states of ancient China required different discursive practices than those of democratic Athens. Athenian rhetors, at least in the reigning imaginary, did things with words to change the world; through discourse's power to persuade others, the rhetor identified with the force of language. On the other hand, the Chinese speaker, most often speaking to a powerful ruler and his state institutions, tended to apply less forceful remonstration to affect the audience; rather than foregrounding his intentions, he identified with the process of decision-making, probably the audience's process of decision-making, but maybe, simply, all the forces engaged in decision-making. We can see how this power differential would affect the speaker's purpose and strategy in a comparison of Aristotelian persuasion and Confucian remonstration.

As I demonstrated in "Confucian Silence and Remonstration: A Basis for Deliberation," much of classical Chinese thinking eschews persuasion and argumentation. In Western notions of persuading, there is an audience to be moved, and the rhetor is working toward a better form of life as he imagines it. Many models of Western rhetoric value persuasion for the gain of the rhetor's (ethical) purpose and control of a political outcome. Rather than valuing persuasion, Confucius advocates remonstrating (*jian*) within a relationship of trust, and the Legalist Han Fei conceives persuasion as a cautious, narrow, middle path, edged with danger. While within authoritarian states and cultures that value stability, persuasion and political change may be an effect of remonstration or of walking the persuasive precipice, they well may not be seen as positive effects. The audience's power, as well as logical and interpretative skills, are more prominent because the speaker does not, in fact cannot, assume control. Rather than pursuing a truth at all costs, early Chinese speakers acknowledge the values of social stability and the authoritarian conditions under which the participants can manifest their particularities. The probable, though not necessary, effect of remonstration is engagement, very respectful engagement. In discussing China's potential for democracy, Virginia Suddath calls remonstration or *jian* "an indigenous means of protest" (Suddath 2006, 215). Remonstration, and even cautious persuasion, are not void of political effect, but the effect is not substantially driven by goals, conflict, and the power of rhetoric.

Each culture's assumptions can be revealed further with Gilbert Ryle's anatomy of verbs; he differentiates verbs of terminus and process. Process verbs, "seek" or "remonstrate," describe on-going action. Terminus verbs, "find" or "persuade," declare an end. If I claim, "I persuaded him that . . . ," there has been an end. The act of persuasion rarely occurs in the present tense, as an ongoing process. It is unusual to say "I am persuading him:" one can imagine this, but it is unusual. Almost always when one speaks of persuasion, someone already has swayed another's mind, and the act of persuading is finished. Since persuasion is concerned with dominance, goals, and outcomes, presenting persuasion as incomplete, as present tense, undermines its innate claim of achievement. Remonstration defines power and human relationship differently. Its criteria for success are in the act, not in the effect. If I say, "I remonstrate that . . . ," it is less clear that there has been an end or what would constitute an end. The ending of an act of remonstration is very different from the ending of an act of persuasion. In persuading, there is an end, a change in the audience. Remonstrating is a process without end: one can run out of time, energy, or materials, but otherwise one can continue the process. While an audience is implied in remonstration, the relationship is not innately hegemonic. Consequently, if we think of persuasion as a terminus verb and remonstration as a process verb, remonstration places the outcome of the situation in the considered actions of all the participants. Each decides how to proceed. One remonstrates to initiate a needed deliberative process, but the nature of that process is more responsive to the power of the audience. Remonstration in less engaged in forcing issues of betterment, change, and criteria of judgment. For these reasons, its contrast with persuasion can inform our understanding of *shi* and *wuwei*, rhetorical concepts which, despite their concern with strategy, indwell as *power potentials within a situation* rather than as cunning tools.

SHI (POWER/POSITION)

Shi has multiple definitions: position, power, potential, disposition, and strategic advantage, depending on whether its role is predominately in military strategy (*Sunzi*), political status (*Han Feizi*), or moral government (*Xunzi*). Its definitional ambiguity is not one of divided meanings, but one potentially synthesizing all connotations that might inhere in a particular case. In a book-length treatment of *shi,* Francois Jullien claims that, in translation, it falls between two poles—the static and the dynamic—and hence in its translations, creates paradoxes that are particularly productive for considering cultural differences. Haun Saussy criticizes Jullien's attention to difference as a Western tendency to transform "'the other' into 'our other,'" drawing attention to the difficulty of ever dealing adequately with another culture's vocabulary (Saussy 2001, 12). To minimize vocabulary abuse, I turn to Roger Ames who approaches *shi* in historical context. He argues that the accrued meanings of *shi* should not be read into the earliest military texts where *shi* is concerned initially with "advantageous terrain," nor should they be read into later military texts concerned with "conditions" or "circumstances" and "disposition" or "deployment," all connoting physical position, not simply location; rather *shi* should be read as "a fluid configuration ever responsive to its context"(Ames 1983, 66–67). Translators and interpreters should have historically, contextually appropriate meanings for the term. Following the need to understand terms within their specific historical locations, I discuss *shi* and *wuwei* in particular texts, in the case of *shi* in two texts: Sun's *Art of War* (*Sunzi bingfa*) to show its history and to place it within strategic discussions; and the *Han Feizi* to develop its political importance.

As opposed to the situation in the ritually, honor-bound, *tian*-ruled war of earlier times, strategy and tactics become important after the sixth century BCE in China. In the fourth century BCE text, *Art of War* or *Sunzi,* ascribed to the general Sun Wu, the art of war is seen as essential to the survival of the state. This survival depends on the intellectual work of analysis; hence, a good general's strategy is to calculate all factors in advance of the conflict so that the situation is controlled and victory is a predictable outcome. The kind of analysis needed to form a strategic advantage is based on broad questions such as "Which ruler has the way (*dao*)? Which commander has the greater ability? . . . Which side is more strict and impartial in meting out rewards and punishment?" (Chapter 1, 104). Since war is an intellectual and knowledge-based enterprise aided by a system of internal justice, not an enterprise of brute force, victory is determined before the battle or without the battle, not in the head-on clash. The text claims:

> It is best to preserve one's own state intact; to crush the enemy's state is only second best. It is best to keep one's own army, battalion, company, or five-man squad intact . . . the highest excellence is to subdue the enemy's army without fighting at all. Therefore, the best military policy is to attack strategies; the next to attack alliances; the next to attack soldiers; and the worst to assault walled cities. (Chapter 3, 111)

Even if the purpose of war is victory, unlike early Western generals, *Sunzi* integrates diplomacy with war, creating a comprehensive strategy of war, peace, and diplomacy. In broadening what constitutes military success to include relationships through peace and diplomacy, *Sunzi* conceives war not simply as victory, but as preservation and flourishing of the state (hence, its frequent embrace as a manual for business management). Its inclusive theory of strategy is why *Sunzi*'s concept of *shi* can be extended to speech situations and why it helps frame rhetoric more broadly concerned with position than with conquering.

In discussing *shi* or situational advantage, *Sunzi* states that "surprise" and "straightforward" operations present endless possibilities for strategy, but no fixed strategies, with each situation different. Still, like boulders rolling downhill (Chapter 5, 121), the force of strategic placement, not the demands on soldiers, wins battles. *Shi* has power beyond the human; "the expert at battle seeks his victory from strategic advantage (*shih*(sic)) and does not demand it from his men" and so strategic advantage defines cowardice and courage (Chapter 5, 120). That is, the soldiers' character is defined by the experts' ability to use strategic advantage. Neither courage nor war happen in the conflict, but rather in the good general's carefully planned strategic placement before the conflict. The military expert recognizes and creates *shi*. While military *shi* concerned with advantages of morale, justice, terrain, and opportunity may initially seem lacking in rhetorical implications, because of the expert's ability to recognize and create *shi*, the *Sunzi* has been picked up by any number of contemporary and Western authors and reinterpreted. Bookstore shelves are full of *Art of War* reinterpreted for business management, as military *shi* touches on the activities of skilled leaders who invent their speeches, assess their audiences, and develop the strategy, recognizing and creating *shi,* long before they stand and deliver.[3]

In early Chinese philosophy, the concept of *shi* also has more overtly political uses, and the work of the Chinese Legalists is one place to find it. Legalism, refined during the Warring States period (480–221 BCE), refers to a set of political theories which favor the objectivity and rigidity of the law over the instability of morality.[4] Han Fei (?289–233 BCE) is considered the greatest Legalist in his combination of law (*fa*), method (*shu*), and position/power (*shi*) as the approach to ruling a stable state. Suspicious of the ability of any individual, common or aristocratic, to manage the state, Han Fei places authority within the law, not in the rule of good men as Confucians would, not in nature as Daoists would.

While, at this time, *shi* still is used to reference military operations and prevailing conditions, Ames (1983) writes that it is most often used to indicate the advantages accrued to status. In the *Han Feizi,* Han Fei demonstrates how law (*fa*), method (*shu*), and position/power (*shi*) together provide a strategic approach to governing a stable state. In addition, using *shi* more than does any early text, the *Han Feizi* also is of particular interest to rhetoricians for an extended discussion of persuasion, a rarity in classical China.[5] Suspicious of human ability to administrate and worried about the dangers of persuasion, Han Fei places authority to rule within the law, method, and the ruler's *shi* and advocates for social stability through the power that the law and the ruler's position have to compel. While most authoritarian political models are concerned with "the right to rule" (God, lineage, or might), Han Fei theorizes that power and position (*shi*) are founded in the laws and that all matters should be decided on the law alone. The law founds the right to rule in the service of a safe, stable state. Hence, he writes "Were the ruler of men to discard law and follow his private whim, then all distinction between high and low would cease to exist" ("On Having Standards" 29). The whims of the ruler are dangerous to both his position and the power of the state.

Han Fei is sometimes seen as placing *shi* solely in the ruler's persona, but this reading minimizes how *shi* controls the ruler himself. More accurately *shi* accrues to the state through the laws. As he writes, ". . . for correcting the faults of superiors, chastising the misdeeds of subordinates, restoring order, exposing error, checking excess, remedy-

ing evil, and unifying the standards of the people, nothing can compare to law" ("On Having Standards" 28). The ruler functions as an
upholder of or place for the law who, through administrative method,
appoints other upholders of law so that together they effect a strong
and secure state. In critiquing *shi,* Han Fei repeatedly tells rulers not
to share their power with ministers, for it weakens their *shi.* Rather,
"the truly enlightened ruler uses the law to select men for him" ("On
Having Standards" 24). The law measures merit. Strategic political
position within the law makes the sovereign, not the individual acts
of the sovereign.

The Chinese concepts of *shi,* whether military or legalistic, offer
new means of analyzing both the rhetorical situation and the positions
of the rhetor or the audience. Certainly, Western rhetoric has related
concepts, but they are limited in their focus on the power of position-
ing. While *ethos* references the character of the speaker, it lacks focus
on the speaker's and the audience's relationship to power and sovereignty. One might imagine early, rough connections between *shi* and
either *kairos* or the rhetorical situation, but like *ethos, kairos* is inadequate in the senses of power differentials and strategy. In the twentieth
century, Michel Foucault (1977) argues that power is productive and
that the panopticon is a physical structure that disciplines through its
potential. Certainly, the importance of terrain and the productivity of
power are implied in both military and political *shi,* but the concept
of panopticon would only reveal one aspect of the terrain studied of
assessing *shi.*

More closely related is James L. Kastely's definition of rhetoric as
"the art of position"; he argues that this definition sees the world as
"necessarily a place of action, a place in which we need to figure out
who we are and how we have been positioned" (1997, 218). In discussing
the rhetorical play of two or more positions, he foregrounds rhetoric's
work of resisting ideologies, epistemological closures, and hierarchies
of persuasion and so, underscores the worldly action of rhetoric. He,
however, argues that one cannot understand rhetoric as "the repetition
of overturning positions, for since being positioned is unavoidable, one
must equally always be trying to do justice to new understandings of
past positions and to the consequences of newly assumed positions."
That is, positions must be justified and incorporated into histories.
When Kastely grounds rhetorical action in "the play of positions," he
offers a dynamic sense of position, not the position/power necessary

for a stable, safe state, but more like *Sunzi*'s military *shi*, which has endless possibilities and a concern with progress through refutation, not victory and closure. Since it emphasizes "newly assumed positions" and "understandings," Kastely's "play of positions" has only small similarity to the legalistic *shi*, which seeks to stabilize the state. Han Fei sees any individual's persuasion as potentially dangerous and disruptive to state stability, and Kastely describes persuasion as both the goal and the problem, asking what is one persuaded of and what are the difficulties of being too persuaded to continue playing positions. Both the ancient Chinese political theorist and the post-modern rhetorician share Kastely's concept that "we are inescapably positioned," but they perceive the power differentials within the positions differently. For Kastely, rhetoric's tension between praxis and irony creates the rolling-downhill potential power that can be generative. For Han Fei, persuasion's tension, seen through *shi,* is between the triad of ruler, the law, and state and the potential misperceptions and selfish desires of the minister; stability is preferable to the disruption of the power potential, the chaos of rolling downhill without control.

By foregrounding the material aspects and potential of place in strategic situations, *shi* focuses on political power differentials, questions of stability and inherent disruptions, definitions of authority for action, and factors outside of individual actors. Though similar to a variety of concepts in Western rhetorical traditions, concepts recent and traditional, *shi*'s differences—combined in rich knowledge of Chinese theories of communication, strategy, and power—help define what is uniquely Chinese in a cumulative theory of human communication.

WUWEI (NON-ACTION)

While some doctrine of *wuwei* or non-action predates Daoism, it is a principle of Daoist thought and permeates Chinese culture, since Daoism is, next to Confucianism, the most important Chinese classical philosophy. *Wuwei* or "non-action" is sometimes translated "effortless action," "doing nothing," "acting naturally," but more closely, if more problematically, translated "non-action." Following Anthony C. Yu's inclination to read *wu* as a nominal, not an adjective, it is translated as "that-which-is-not-action" (2003). This concept is important to understanding human communication for at least three reasons. One, *wuwei,* as read with regard to speaking effectively, embodies the idea that the process in a particular situation creates the change and not the powerful and skillful speech acts of a particular individual. Two, the political nature of *wuwei* makes it an interesting contrast to normative discourses of action, value, and judging. If human values, particularly political and legal values, are the criteria for judging acts, what does it mean to value not acting and not judging? Is *wuwei* simply a strange culturally specific concept, evasive of translation, or is it a paradoxical attempt to escape human criteria altogether? Ultimately, is it more than self-contradictory, rather an attempt to reference humanity beyond the motive and intent? Three, and perhaps the clearest reason for its significance, *wuwei* names the tensions between act and non-act. In English, it is all but impossible to find an antonym for act, deed, work, perform, do; there are representations only of the effort and effect, not their lack. So, too, in Chinese, it is difficult to deal with a negative compound word, lacking in denotation, but copious in connotation.[6] Humans have conceptual difficulty imagining human accomplishment through natural, not human-controlled patterns. *Wuwei* places before us the conceptual problem of what is an act or a non-act, what is an utterance or a non-utterance, what is human and what is non-human. What can we make of the problem?

Like *shi, wuwei* is a dynamic concept, changing from school to school and throughout history. To flesh out communicative representations of the concept, I will survey its appearance in three texts (*Analects, Daodejing, Han Feizi*) representing three schools (Confucian, Daoist, and Legalist) in the Warring States period. In both Daoist and Confucian traditions, there are associations between *wuwei* and virtue or moral potential (*de*)[7]; if *wuwei* is to work, the person must be virtuous in the sense of either attunement to nature's order (*Daodejing*) or cultivation of propriety and rites to create harmony between human achievement and the cosmos (*Analects*). Confucian virtue is dependent on situation; while there are not absolute reference points for morality, there is the consistent value of harmony and propriety. In the only specific use of *wuwei* in the *Analects*,[8] "The Master said, 'If anyone could be said to have effected proper order while remaining nonassertive (*wuwei*), surely it was Shun. What did he do? He simply assumed an air of deference and faced due south'" (15.5). Nonassertion or *wuwei* as "acting naturally" allows the ancient sage-king to lead without speech or act. He cultivates the proper relationship to the world and performs the relationship in the ritual stance of facing south as a ruler should. Through performing the relationship, making it into ritual, the Confucian ruler artlessly encourages his people's virtue.[9] His character (defined by stance), rather than his law, is the example that leads without compulsion or controls, and so creates a proper social world functioning effortlessly. Still, the lack of act is paradoxically achieved through personal cultivation. Hence, Confucius describes progress from being a teenager *set on learning* to being a seventy year old when "I could give my heart-and-mind free rein without overstepping the boundaries" (2.4). A seventy year old could act naturally without external rule or internal intention only after decades of virtuous education and the cultivation of propriety.

Daoism, an *alternative* to Confucianism, is a concept familiar to many perhaps because of the prominent texts associated with it (*Daodejing* (250–150 BCE), *Zhuangzi* (320 BCE?) and *Huainanzi* (140 BCE?)).[10] Conveniently, the *Dao* is often defined as "way" or "path," though it can more carefully be defined as a state of being, skillful or effective method, or a disposition. In discussing *Dao* in the *Daodejing,* Yu emphasizes that it is "referentially elusive" and points to four uses of *dao:* "path or road," "an ethico-political principle operative within a person, community, or an institution," "to guide or instruct," "to say or speak." (2003, 171, 177). Since my concern is not specifically with the concept of *Dao,* this essay will work with one broad definition: David L. Hall and Roger Ames's vision of *Dao* as "the incoherent sum of all names and forms" (1998, 245). In so doing, I also join Hall and Ames in seeing *Dao* not as an object, a what, or a noun (The Way), nor as an "effective" approach to life, but as a myriad of acts and processes which make the world. If Plato offers one best world or form, Daoism offers us a world that is boundless, giving no standpoint of critique, no place to imagine betterment. In Daoism, there is not cosmic unity, only process and becoming. When the *Zhuangzi* recommends we become "one with all things," David Hall and Roger Ames interpret this as not a call to dissolve into a united whole, but rather to recognize the *continuous* and *integrated* nature of phenomena within one's field of experience. No atoms and no boundaries, but no unified mush either. This particular translation helps us make further sense of the rhetorical aspects of remonstration (*jian*) and power/position (*shi*). While the earlier model of remonstration as a process verb contrasts it with persuasion and analyzes it within a Western frame of speech act, remonstration can be understood better within a Chinese worldview. The act of remonstration need not force a change, yet can still be understood as Suddath's "indigenous form of protest," because the experience of remonstration is received as a *continuous and integrated experience.* Despite being more a Confucian than Daoist concept, remonstration recognizes the interconnectedness of experience more than the fragmentation and diversity. In this frame s*hi,* military or political, also works in privileging the integrated nature of experience. Our positions are always potentials in continuous relationship with the positions of others.

While sometimes seen only as a religion by the West, it is unclear that Daoism even has transcendent aspects.[11] Aside from its well-recognized contemplative aspects, Daoism offers a robust political strategy in response to Confucianism; in "the incoherent sum of all names and forms," it is a political treatise aimed at showing that authoritarian methods will not attain political control, instead advocating natural order. In contrast to the training inherent in Confucian *wuwei,* Daoist *wuwei* is natural behavior, "the natural expression of interpersonal relationships" which precludes the need for prescribed norms of human behavior (Ames 1983, 38). If humans neglect *Dao* as "natural expression of interpersonal relationships" and instead focus on excellence, virtue, or rightness, then social norms and rituals arise, deforming organic order. In this vein, chapter 38 tells us

> Only when we have lost sight of the way-making (*dao*) is there excellence,
> Only when we have lost sight of excellence is there authoritative conduct,
> Only when we have lost sight of authoritative conduct is there appropriateness,
> Only when we have lost sight of appropriateness is there ritual propriety.
> As for ritual propriety, it is the thinnest veneer of doing one's best and making good on one's word,
> And it is the first sign of trouble.[12]
> Premeditation of what is virtue deforms *dao.* If naturalness and spontaneity is the primary characteristic of *dao,* then *wuwei* is its method. (Liu 1998)

Another way to think about the moral potential of *wuwei* as that-which-is-not-action is offered by Hans-Georg Moeller. Emotional separation and lack of action does not mean that the Daoist cannot discriminate between events, but rather that he cannot know what is the better event or what is the end-effect of an event. Moeller tells the *Huainanzi* tale of an old man, accepting of all events, whose life shows that the good can be bad and the bad can be good: finally his son is crippled, but spared being taken as a soldier for a devastating battle. Equanimity is born of not knowing, minimizing knowledge claims, and refusing one-sided attachments: this is what I would call epistemic skepticism. In not knowing, not privileging a side, and so not acting, the Daoist sage remains open to change and reversal, accepting of his position in the cosmos, and so he can lead the common people.[13] For if the *Daodejing* denies humanity as the center of the cosmos, it is concerned with very human politics and the relations of the ruler and the common people.[14] Discussing the method of a ruler, chapter 3 advises

> . . . in the proper governing by the sages;
> They empty the hearts-and-minds of the people and fill their stomachs.
> They weaken their aspirations and strengthen their bones,
> Ever teaching the common people to be unprincipled in their knowing (*wuzhi*)
> And objectless in their desires (*wuyu*),
> They keep the hawkers of knowledge at bay.
> It is simply in doing things noncoercively (*wuwei*)
> That everything is governed properly.

The sage ruler of the Daoist state places himself below the common people, so that they uphold him, yet do not find him burdensome. He puts his concern behind that of the people so that their way is not blocked and they regard him as harmless (chapter 66). Through his own refusal to contend, no one contends with him. This model of governing places authority in the ruler's openness, which allows space for the heart of the people, and so the sage ruler and the people are united. As Moeller writes, "the sage-ruler takes on the place of emptiness or non-presence while the people take on the place of fullness or presence" (2006, 58).

Concern with integrating experiences, not demarcating off individual subjects and privileging particular acts, makes *wuwei* a useful means of describing and affecting human experience. To this end, *wuwei* appeals to *Dao,* both in its contemplative and political or purposive aspects. In ignoring individualistic action and will-to-power, the Chinese communicator accepts *Dao* or the power of natural processes and integration (interdependence) of opposites. Rather than privileging his view, the Daoist sage accepts *the means and process as more significant than his desired end. Dao* as "the incoherent sum of all names and forms" authorizes, albeit strangely, the Daoist to speak, *to remonstrate,* to add to the names and forms, without privileging his actions and without determining goals, acts, and knowledge. Hence, there are Daoist texts advocating *wuwei.* Still, non-action, not-speaking, is difficult for rhetorical traditions of speech-as-action to accept or incorporate, but it is a problem for Daoist traditions too: "Rare are those in the world who reach an understanding of the benefits of teachings that go beyond what can be said and of doing things noncoercively (*wuwei*)" (Chapter 43).

In addition to its political and methodological importance in *Daodejing, wuwei* appears prominently in Legalist writing, especially in Han Fei's argument for ruling through *wuwei* or non-action. Han Fei, developing or rather deforming visions of Daoist sage-kings, writes, an "enlightened ruler reposes in non-action above and his ministers tremble with fear" ("The Way of the Ruler," 17). Rather than show ministers what the ruler values, which might lead to fawning, the ruler does not reveal himself, and hence the ministers will offer what they conceive to be the best advice and actions. The ruler's non-action is paradoxically a catalyst for action. However, we should not read this too simply as the idea that the lack of action in itself molds the actions of others. In *Effortless Action,* a book focusing on spiritual *wuwei,* not political, Edward Slingerland makes the important point that *wuwei* is a "set of dispositions," a cognitive and somatic training more akin to skill-knowledge than tranquility. That is, when Han Fei refers to the ruler's that-which-is-not-action, he isn't referencing a tranquil prince controlled and controlling through a panopticon. Rather, he is working in a tradition of describing an effective prince as perfectly tuned to his role. As early as *The Book of Odes* (tenth to seventh centuries BCE), rulers are described as reigning effortlessly (2003, 166, 214, 241). Slingerland suggests that Han Fei is imagining an institutional *wuwei* where the government works so smoothly that the ministers perform their jobs without any need for guidance (2003, 288). In effect, the ruler rules rather than becoming mired in the details of administration, and so he remains inconspicuous and safe (Creel, 1970, 67–8). I, however, think there is plenty of evidence that the ruler must guide ministers through what Han Fei describes as the "two handles" of reward and punishment and that Han Fei has a politico-legal, if not spiritual, ideal to offer the ruler. As I show below, Han Fei sees the ruler as developing "a set of dispositions" which allow him to rule efficiently and effortlessly.

Han Fei's non-acting emperor is not open and yielding to the natural way as one might imagine a contemplative Daoist sage as being, nor does he cultivate ritual propriety, as would Confucius, but rather he engages in a strategy of maintaining authority. Han Fei advises the ruler:

> Discard likes and dislikes and the ministers will show their true form; discard wisdom and wile and the ministers will watch their step. Hence, though the ruler is wise, he hatches no schemes from his wisdom, but causes all men to know their places. Though he has worth, he does not display it in his deeds, but observes the motives of his ministers. Though he is brave, he does not flaunt his bravery in shows of indignation, but allows his subordinates to display their valor to the full. Thus, though he discards wisdom, his rule is enlightened; though he discards worth, he achieves merit; and though he discards bravery, his state grows powerful. ("The Way of the Ruler" 16–17)

Han Fei is aware of the appeal of Confucian virtue and authority in a ruler conceived as a cultivated gentleman of moral worth. Against the rival philosophy, Han Fei argues for the development of "a set of dispositions" demonstrated through a refusal to act that, in turn, will make the state and the law strong. The act of non-action is not a contradiction, paradox, or following of the Way, nor is it the cultivation of proper social relationships, but rather a cognitive training to rule. The effect of *wuwei* is to force action—and the disadvantage—on ministers, a positive side effect. The laws and the cumulative actions of the ministers together enable the ruler's *wuwei* as a method protecting the stability of the state, but as well, the ruler can envision his *wuwei* as evidence of his wisdom, worth, and bravery. In summary, when Han Fei advocates *wuwei*, he conceives it as having the effects of an act

without the difficulty of the reality/word split, without the requirement of wisdom, without the prediction of consequence, and without
the dangers of persuasion.

Wuwei is a more difficult concept for Western rhetoric than *shi*.
Let me speculate, with the aid of another rhetorician on the complexity of *wuwei*. In an ongoing, e-mail exchange about the *wuwei*, John
Kirby asked me: Can one persuade without persuading? Can one teach
without teaching? Can one lead students to the *dao* without leading?
Inherent in these questions is a resistance to the idea that one cannot
act. If we define the human as action and accept a motion/action di-
chotomy, then a desire to be human pushes for a reading of *wuwei* as
effortless or natural action, not as non-action. Inherent is a belief, an
almost Confucian belief, that by one's existence and education, one's
proper life choices, one shows others the nature of good men (*junzi*).
Perhaps Kirby's questions are aimed at revealing that humans read
the world and that each human act has symbolic impact. This is in
keeping with the rhetorical tradition of persuasion which privileges intended act and minimizes unexpected possibility and openness. Given
its vision of a conscious cultivation of character, Kirby's questions connect with Confucian *wuwei*. However, *wuwei* itself plays a tiny part
of the *Analects* and is a major concept, and a different concept, in the
political theory of both *Daodejing* and *Han Feizi*. We cannot take the
easy answer here.

In fairness, I think his questions are not just sophistry or resistance,
but more questions of grammar, perhaps a bit the type of grammar
that reveals a form of life, but as well the type of sophistic, philosophical, muddling grammars that Ludwig Wittgenstein abhorred (though
a type the writer(s) of the *Daodejing* adored). Kirby's questions perhaps
can help reveal forms of life, but first let me muck with the muddle. In
response to the difficulties philosophers had in attaching language to
a material world, Wittgenstein wrote that his aim was showing "the fly
the way out of the fly-bottle" (remark 309). To this end, let us think
with him a moment to see if we can find a way out. If the grammar of
our language allows us to say "non-existence is existence" or "one can
act without acting," what is the nature of these propositions? (1) Are
they simply play, as when "language *goes on holiday*" (remark 38) and
theorists need the friction of real language situations (remark 107), or
(2) have we entered the labyrinth of language "from another side and

so are lost" (remark 203), or (3) do they exist in a different language game, an ancient form of life that we cannot speak well (remark 23)?

Now one might agree with all three possibilities. Without a doubt, there is a sense of playfulness and holiday within the *Daodejing*, but forms of language are deep (remark 111), surviving millennia, far too long to be an ordinary "holiday." I suggest that "act without acting" is more significant than the poetic play of *I Know Who Killed Me* (a variation on "I heard a fly buzz—when I died"). The ineffable is very different than sophistic puzzles. The limits of language are not the limits of my world, simply the limits of my spoken world. If there are many ways of and consequences to not acting, but no accepted (possible) way to describe the negative of acting, then access to that side of the human is unavailable to critique. One might walk better with the friction of language, but there is no friction for what language doesn't say. Perhaps *wuwei* can't be spoken, but then in some way, it has been. Then is one lost and wandering in the *Daodejing*'s labyrinth of language and Kirby's questions? I think we are lost only if we want the pleasure of seeing how poorly language attaches to human experience. Entering from the other side of the labyrinth has confused us, but it also has revealed experience anew, the new direction showing the backside of old patterns and acceptances. If we seek to find the other side and understand the labyrinth from a different perspective (hear echoes of the *Dao*), then being lost is only an intermediate stage. The wandering provides a chance to think again about what was once accepted. Having been lost, we can now approach *wuwei* and the paradox of its effectiveness, seeing it as "an ancient form of life" that we cannot speak well and maybe never did.

If I live my life and you see it as exemplary and you follow it, have I led you? If I live my life and you fear it, have I led you? Have I persuaded you? Certainly not in any way that is facile. Rather, though I may have done something resembling action in the world, I have not directed my path toward you or the world. You have followed the path as it has opened, and maybe it has been opened by one of three conceptions of *wuwei*, by my "effortless action," a set of dispositions, or all that-is-not-action, but that opening does not represent strategy, intention, control, persuasion, or power. The opening refuses both rhetoric and reference. If there is a rhetorical theory in *wuwei*, it is not of trope, identity, position, or persuasion, but of openings, perhaps openings of intuition, but also openings of happenstance, ambiguity, and unconsciousness. By playing with the contradictory potentials of grammar, *wuwei* suggests the possibility of a rhetorical theory or a discourse theory that anticipates the undecidable and uncontrolled nature of the future. The three senses of *wuwei,* each with a different implication for communication and for the weak link between speech and experience, together offer moments of radical potential for re-imagining political discourse and community.

CONCLUSION

When Richards ponders translation, asking "Can we make it more than a mirror of our minds, or are we inevitably in this undertaking trying to be on both sides of the looking-glass at once?," he, in effect, wonders if the looking glass can tell us that we are not the fairest in the land, that there are texts, ideas, and beauties beyond our own (1932, 87). In an effort to escape the binary of the West and the Other and to understand the theories of political discourse in other cultures, rhetorical theory—a Western concept replete with other Western concepts—has to give up persuasion, deliberation, identification, and the whole truckload of words that made rhetorical study possible in the first place. New words and concepts that note communicative processes invisible to the traditions of the West have to be understood within their traditions.

Shi and *wuwei* are concepts that contribute to understanding Chinese communication theory as not just textual signs and symptoms, not persuasion and sophistry, but as far more than similitude. Grasping the political implications of s*hi* and *wuwei* requires a third system that repudiates the assumptions of "our own familiar, established, tradition of thinking" so that it doesn't come back to us "rigged out in some fresh terminology or other disguise" (Richards 1932, 87). The third system can never be the world of classical Chinese philosophy. Indeed, we are unlikely to be addressing emperors. That world is gone. Still, a rational reconstruction of the rhetorics of ancient empires tells us things relevant to current worries about empire. The analytical movement beyond a New Critical translation of terms into a historical placement of ideas breaks the looking-glass into smaller pieces and forces the Western spectator to study harder in attempting to see a whole.

Notes

1. Han Fei, *Basic Writing,* 113. "Why do the rulers listen to the wild theories of the speech-makers, and bring destruction to the state and ruin to themselves? Because they do not distinguish clearly between public and private interests, do not examine the aptness of the words they hear, and do not make certain that punishments are meted out when they are deserved." Han Fei's skepticism about the value of rhetoricians and speech is in keeping with much of early Chinese thinking about communication. In the context of this paper, it draws attention to the divide between spoken words and the more subtle implications of *shi* (power/position) and *wuwei* (nonaction).

2. For a longer discussion of comparative method, see Sue Hum and Arabella Lyon.

3. Blaine McCormick criticizes *The Art of War* as a model for business because of the implications of the war metaphor and the promotion of deception, but for the most part, it is widely accepted.

4. The dominant image of China presents China without the rule of law, but in fact, there is a long history of Chinese literature showing it does have Chinese rule of law. The rule of clans and guilds were somewhat more arbitrary and breakable than Western law, but as well, China had governmental systems of rites and justice that provided a basis for law (Des Forges and Qiang 2006). While the "rule of law" question is beyond the scope of this paper, it is a key area for understanding the place of public discourse in China (Liu 1998; MacCormack 1996).

5. For an extended discussion of "The Difficulties of Persuasion," see Arabella Lyon's "Imagining Rhetorical Authority."

6. In some length, Liu Xiaogan (1998, 217–21) discusses this problem as does Anthony C. Yu (2003, 172–6).

7. Others define *de* as potential or power potential. This is important, as virtue is not transparently a goal of the *Daodejing.*

8. Both Roger Ames (1983) and Slingerland (2003) have lengthy discussions of *wuwei* historical evolution and permutations. Both of them interpret *wuwei* within the *Analects* and the broader Confucian tradition despite its relative absence. I follow them in part to set up Daoist *wuwei* as a response to Confucianism.

9. See also *Analects* chapters 2.1, 2.2, 2.3, 15.5, 12.7, 12.17.

10. See Robert Oliver (1971), Lu Xing (1998), and Steven C. Combs (2005) for broader discussions of the relationship between Daoism and rhetoric.

11. David L. Hall and Roger T. Ames (1998) provide a survey of the controversy and a cogent argument against transcendence. Rather than thinking about the intersection between immanence and transcendence, *Daodejing* is concerned more with the relationship between what can be said or known and the ineffable, defined in the context of nature (*tian*), deeply skeptical of culture. It is surprising that an argument for nature offers a political theory, but it does.

12. According to Michael LaFargue and Julian Pas (1998), as of 1993, there were about 250 translations of *Daodejing* in Western language. Many more have appeared since then. Having seriously considered half a dozen, I have chosen Roger Ames' translation. While it is not the closest to my understanding of *wuwei*, it is philosophically focused and informed by recent Chinese research.

13. See also *Daodejing* chapters 30 and 40 for examples of reversal.

14. See also *Daodejing* chapters 2, 7, 20, 22, 34, 37, 48, 49, 57, 58, 66, and 72.

Works Cited

Ames, Roger T. *The Art of Rulership*. Honolulu: U of Hawaii P, 1983.

—. "Introduction." *Sun-Tzu: The Art of Warfare*. Ed. and trans. Roger Ames. NY: Ballantine Books, 1993.

Confucius. *The Analects of Confucius: A Philosophical Translation*. Trans. Roger T. Ames and Henry Rosemont, Jr. New York: Ballantine, 1998.

Coombs, Steven C. *The Dao of Rhetoric*. New York: SUNY P, 2005.

Creel, Herrlee G. *What is Taoism? And Other Studies in Chinese Cultural History*. Chicago: U of Chicago P, 1970.

Dao De Jing "Making This Life Significant": A Philosophical Translation. Ed. and Trans. Roger T. Ames and David L. Hall. New York: Ballantine Books, 2003.

des Forges, Roger V., and Fang, Qiang. "Were Chinese Rulers above the Law? Toward a Theory of the Rule of Law in China from Early Times to 1949 CE." Buffalo Legal Studies Research Paper No. 2006–006. Available: http://ssrn.com/abstract=896910.

Foucault, Michel. *Discipline and Punish: The Birth of the Prison*. Translated by Alan Sheridan. New York: Pantheon Books, 1977.

Hall, David L. and Roger T. Ames. *Thinking from the Han: Self Truth, and Transcendence in Chinese and Western Culture*. Albany: SUNY P, 1998.

Han Fei. *Basic Writing of Han Fei Tzu*. Translated by Burton Watson. NY: Columbia UP, 1963.

Hum, Sue and Arabella Lyon. "Recent Advances in Comparative Rhetoric." *The Handbook of Rhetoric*. Ed. Jim Aune and Andrea Lunsford. Thousand Oaks, CA: Sage, Forthcoming.

Jullien, Francois. *The Propensity of Things: Toward a History of Efficacy in China.* New York: Zone Books, 1995.

Kastely, James L. Rethinking the Rhetorical Tradition: From Plato to Postmodernism. New Haven: Yale UP, 1997.

Kirby, John. Emails to author, 2007.

LaFargue, Michael, and Julian Pas. "On Translating the *Tao-Te-ching.*" *Lao-tzu and the Tao-te-ching.* Ed. Livia Kohn and Michael Lafargue. Albany: SUNY P, 1998. 277–301.

Liu, Xiaogan. "Naturalness (Tzu-jan), the Core Value in Taoism: Its Ancient Meaning and Its Significance Today." *Lao-tzu and the Tao-te-ching.* Ed. Livia Kohn and Michael Lafargue. Albany: SUNY P, 1998. 211–228.

Lu, Xing. *Rhetoric in Ancient China, Fifth to Third Century BCE: A comparison with Classical Greek Rhetoric.* Columbia: U of South Carolina P, 1998.

Lyon, Arabella. "Confucian Silence and Remonstration: A Basis for Deliberation." *Rhetoric Before and Beyond the Greeks.* Ed. Carol Lipson and Roberta A. Binkley. Albany: SUNY P, 2004, 131–45.

—. "Rhetorical Authority in Athenian Democracy and the Chinese Legalism of Han Fei." *Philosophy and Rhetoric.* 41 (2008): 51–70.

McCormick, Blaine. "Make Money, Not War: A Brief Critique of Sun Tzu's The Art of War. *Journal of Business Ethics* 29 (2001): 285–86.

Moeller, Hans-Georg. *The Philosophy of the Daodejing.* New York: Columbia UP, 2006.

Oliver, Robert. *Communication and Culture in Ancient India and China.* Syracuse, NY: Syracuse UP, 1971.

Richards, I. A. *Mencius on the Mind: Experiments in Multiple Definition.* London: Kegan Paul, Trench, Trubner, 1932.

Ryle, Gilbert. *Dilemmas.* New York: Cambridge UP, 1954.

Saussay, Haun. *Great Walls of Discourse and Other Adventures in Cultural China.* Cambridge, MA: Harvard UP, 2001.

Singerland, Edward. *Effortless Action: Wu-wei as Conceptual Metaphor and Spiritual Ideal in Early China.* New York: Oxford UP, 2003.

Suddath, Virginia. "Ought We Throw the Confucian Baby Out with the Authoritarian Bathwater?: A Critical Inquiry into Lu Xun's Anti-Confucian Identity." *Confucian Cultures of Authority.* Eds.i Peter D. Hershock and Roger T. Ames. Albany: SUNY P, 2006.

Sunzi. *Sun-Tzu: The Art of Warfare.* Trans. Roger Ames. NY: Ballantine Books, 1993.

Wittgenstein, Ludwig. *Philosophical Investigations.* Trans. G. E. M. Anscombe. New York, NY: MacMillan Press, 1953.

Yu, Anthony C. "Reading *The Daodejing:* Ethics and Politics of the Rhetoric." *Chinese Literature: Essays, Articles, Reviews* 25 (2003): 165–87.

Zhuangzi. *The Complete Works of Zhuangzi.* Translated by Burton Watson. New York: Columbia UP, 1986.

8 The Right Use of True Words: Shinto and Shingon Buddhist Rhetoric in Ancient Japan

Kathy Wolfe

INTRODUCTION

I have been involved for some time in the study of pre-modern Japanese rhetoric, employing a broad understanding of "rhetoric" that encompasses the study and use of persuasive strategies (language-based and not) as well as theories regarding the relationship between language and meaning, or knowledge (Bizzell and Herzberg 1). In this essay, I will share and illustrate some principles of language use, and more general linguistic philosophies, that developed in ancient Japan as integral parts of the Shinto and Shingon Buddhist traditions, focusing on the span of time between 500—1000 CE.[1] Other perspectives on language and persuasion certainly existed at this time, in various other Buddhist and also Confucian schools of thought; I link Shinto and Shingon Buddhism in this limited exploration in part because of their mutual dependence during this period, and in part because several of the ideas within them regarding rhetoric appear to linger in Japanese culture today.

Joseph Kitagawa asks whether "Japanese tradition, before it came under the powerful influence of the West, possessed a worthwhile system of meaning that was an alternative to that of the Europocentric [sic] modern world" (xviii). Much scholarship on Japanese rhetoric and communication, while acknowledging and delineating the rhetorical strategies characteristic of modern Japanese discourse, answers him by presuming that there was no rhetorical tradition in Japan prior to the opening of the country with the Meiji Restoration of 1868 (after which

Western-style rhetoric was aggressively imported (Okabe, "Japan's" 281)). For example, John L. Morrison argues that "some 1,350 years of recorded history . . . evidence no [Japanese] rhetorical tradition" (89); Roichi Okabe agrees, saying, "Japan has been rhetorically barren, with no development of an indigenous rhetorical theory" ("Impact" 1). Two of the several assumptions built into these claims are first, that "rhetoric" means only the canons and practices that developed in ancient Greece and Rome, and second, that anything resembling rhetoric in premodern Japan was derived from other cultures.

Both of these assumptions have some merit. Addressing the first, Carol Lipson and Roberta Binkley ask, "If we use the term rhetoric and its associated analytical system to examine a set of texts from a culture whose approaches and values differ markedly from those of Aristotle, are we in fact violating the term, as Arabella Lyon suggests" (10)? Kitagawa seems to answer in the affirmative: ". . . useful though Western-inspired methodology may be, it is based on a particular, provincial taxonomy and cannot be employed indiscriminately in what amounts to a cookie-cutter approach to analyzing non-Western traditions" (xiii). However, I agree with Lipson and Binkley in feeling that *rhetoric* has developed into a sufficiently broad term to be appropriately used in cross-cultural analyses, if it is usefully contextualized and one is careful to acknowledge the "prejudgment and historical distance" obscuring one's full comprehension of any "alien or ancient text" (Kitagawa xxix). Lipson and Binkley argue that "We can never entirely leave our own cultural system and its analytical categories, and we can never fully experience the ancient cultures we study and their systems of thinking" (11). Accordingly, in my examination of ancient Japanese rhetorical principles, I will be moving between Xing Lu's "hermeneutic" method (using native Japanese terms for rhetorical principles), and George Kennedy's method of applying classical rhetorical vocabulary to describe non-Western examples of rhetoric (Lipson and Binkley 11).[2, 3]

As to the second assumption behind the notion that Japan had no indigenous rhetoric (that its communicative norms came from elsewhere), the difficulty of discerning what is native in ancient Japanese traditions must be acknowledged. Prior to the introduction of Chinese writing in the fifth century (and along with it, aspects of Chinese philosophy and government), Japanese culture was transmitted orally. All written texts from Japan's ancient period will have been penned by authors influenced to varying degrees by the Chinese language and culture of the time. However, the importations were most often carefully chosen, and inevitably shaped by indigenous Japanese cultural norms and expectations which had developed in a relatively isolated geographic area, so that local and foreign assumptions about language and persuasion merged to form new and unique philosophies (Meyer 2). Therefore, though the earliest history is muddy, I believe it is possible to speak at least tentatively of something called *Japanese* rhetoric that existed before the country's exposure to and study of the discourse principles of other cultures, and which evolved with the inclusion of new ideas, yet retained a measure of its original identity, however difficult that may be to tease out of the existing evidence.

Often, a Western understanding of rhetoric is "based on the peculiar Western convention of dividing human experience into semi-autonomous pigeonholes, such as religion, philosophy, ethics, aesthetics, culture and society" (Kitagawa xiii). Kennedy tells us, however, that historically, rhetoric has not always been thoroughly abstracted from its many contexts (3), and that was also the case in pre-modern Japan, where rhetoric was intertwined with other areas of thought. But when we examine the terminology and theories concerning persuasion and language within the Shinto and Shingon Buddhist traditions (and their related aesthetics), we quickly find in Japan a long tradition of theorizing the relationship between language and reality and weighing the most proper or effective uses of communication. This tradition is first illustrated in the ancient period through the importance of language that inheres in the philosophy of Shinto.

Shinto Rhetoric

Early Development of Shinto and its Use as Political Rhetoric

Shinto, or *kami no michi* ("way of the gods"),[4] was the religion of the earliest Japanese, and persists in the culture today.[5] In prehistoric times, it was comprised of a diverse set of practices, including animism, nature and ancestor worship, and fertility rites. It shared elements with religious practices found in Northeast Asia and the South Seas, which may give some indication of where the first inhabitants of Japan came from (Tsunoda 24, Saunders 262). The ancient Japanese "affirmed that the natural world was the sacred, original world, and that there was no order of meaning behind the world experienced by them" (Kitagawa xxi). The basic belief in Shinto is of the kinship of human beings with all of creation, including the anthropomorphic gods (*kami*)[6] affiliated with natural objects and forces.

Shinto evolved with the culture of the early Japanese, growing to include agragrian *kami* and *kami* that became associated with specific clans (*uji*) and were venerated within specific sacred spaces (Matsumae 335). Gradually, as the Yamato clan became more powerful, its members adopted the sun goddess, Amaterasu, as their *kami,* and "promoted [her] to the highest seat in the . . . pantheon" (342), commissioning histories (the early eighth-century *Kojiki* and *Nihon Shoki*) that repeatedly described them as the goddess' descendants. Thus, they historically legitimized their rule: "The court realized that recording the divine lineage of the royal family was indispensable and thus obligated the compilers to meld history with myth" ("Kojiki"). Here are just a few examples of this manipulation, from the *Nihon Shoki* (also known as *Nihongi*):

> The Emperor Kami Yamato Ihare-Biko's . . . mother's name was Tama-yori-hime, daughter of the Sea-god. From his birth, the Emperor was of clear intelligence and resolute will. [. . .]

> [T]he Heavenly deity had simply generously bestowed the Empire on the Heavenly Grandchild. [. . .]

> The God Incarnate, the Emperor Yamato-neko, who rules the world, gives Command to the Ministers assembled in his presence. [. . .]

> The Empire was entrusted by the Sun-goddess to her descendants, with the words: 'My children, in the capacity of deities, shall rule it.' For this reason, this country, since Heaven and Earth began, has been a monarchy. (Ashton)

The weaker clans in service of the Yamato ruler were assigned rituals that institutionalized their subservient roles (Matsumae 350). For example, because the mythical histories described their founding deities as taking on particular responsibilities, the Inbe clan prepared and administered offerings, while the Nakatomi were the authorities regarding recitations ("Norito"). *Shoshu* (recitation) of folklore and mythology was performed for the monarch "by the *kataribe,* families of reciters" (Meyer 33, Konishi 254). The *Nihongi* relates the origin of these families:

> On the day on which he first began the Heavenly In-
> stitution, Michi no Omi no Mikoto . . . was enabled,
> by means of a secret device received from the Emperor,
> to use incantations and magic formulas so as to dissi-
> pate evil influences. The use of magic formulas had its
> origin from this. (Ashton 24)

Shortly after the publication of the *Nihon Shoki,* or *Nihongi,* scholars were summoned to give public lectures on the chronicles to affirm
their ideology (Hall 352).[7] Local nature worship was to some degree
subsumed under a centralized, state-sponsored religion, with a specific
office and set of laws (the *Jingikan* and *Jingiryo*) governing *kami* worship procedures ("Ritsuryo Jingikan").

The Power of Words and Intuition in Shinto: *Kotodama* and *Aware*

Shinto can be called a "religion" only in a loose sense, for it has no
founder or official text. Like most faiths, however, it does acknowledge
the power of words. In his examination of speech in oral cultures,
Kennedy notes a common reliance on ritual magic—attempts to control nature through chants and recitations (74). This is a key characteristic of Shinto practice, exemplified by the concept of *kotodama,* "the
spiritual power residing in words" or "the right use of words" (Herbert
39, 71) that was released by the reciting of a spell, or *kotoage* ("lift-
ing up words") (Konishi 101).[8] Jin'ichi Konishi notes that the term
kotodama was not found in writing until its use in some of the poems
of the *Man'yoshu,* compiled in the eighth century, but argues that the
concept had to have existed in archaic times (103). *Kotodama* could
not be elicited through writing, but only through a human voice, using only the Japanese language, spoken with a solemn tone and style
(101). However, "Whether invoked for good fortune or calamity, . . .
the *kotodama* was not to be unleashed frivolously" (104).

The *kami* were thought to reside in nature and to be somewhat
akin to humans, which meant that they could both speak and react
to human language that addressed them correctly (Konishi 107); but
if a *kotoage* was directed toward an inappropriate audience, the spell
would not work, and might cause harm to the speaker (105). In addition, if *kotoage* were used too often, the strength of the *kotodama* might

Still very western focus of "effective speech" to an audience

decline (109). "One of the attributes commonly acknowledged as belonging to the *Kami* is *koto agesenu,* the 'non-raising of words,'" which
would avoid the weakening of the *kotodama* and is connected to the
Shinto virtue of *makoto,* sincerity or conscientiousness, in which "true
words become true deeds" (Herbert 33, 71). It is less difficult to live
according to one's words if one doesn't talk excessively.

Koto agesenu may be linked, as well, to a Shinto aesthetic norm,
aware, originally an expression of pleased surprise which later came to
be "tinged with sadness," meaning a sensitivity to beauty and change,
and to the deep emotions that can be stirred by simple, transient things
(Tsunoda 176–77).[9] Such sensitivity is a well-known expectation for
readers of imagistic Japanese verse. *Aware* is, I think, an unsurprising
aesthetic for a culture in many ways homogenous, in which strong
group orientations create common contexts and speech codes, leading
to the feeling that excessive detail or explanation is a stylistic defect
(Konishi 15):

> If too much normal language intervenes in an expres-
> sion of animistic beauty, its spirituality will risk debili-
> tation. Over the centuries, Japanese verse has moved
> toward ever shorter forms, from the choka to the thir-
> ty-one-syllable tanka, and from there to the seventeen-
> syllable haiku. . . . [T]he attitude that *kotoage* were
> best left unspoken . . . figured in the process of ab-
> breviating the Japanese lyric. To those brought up in
> the tradition of rendering description as minutely as
> possible—a Western tradition . . .–-the drive to reduce
> a poem to a mere seventeen syllables may be impos-
> sible to understand. (Konishi 109)

Kotodama in Action in the Shinto *Norito*

In the Japanese poetic tradition, the *norito* are brief ritual prayers in
which designated orators—Shinto priests, members of appropriate
clans, imperial messengers, and on occasion the Emperor himself—
addressed the *kami* on behalf of the people, or personified the *kami*
and transmitted their messages to the people. (When the *kami* were
the audience, the reciter took care to say, "I humbly [or fearfully, or
reverently] speak"; however, if the orator was addressing the people on

behalf of the *kami,* he commanded, "Hear me" and declared straight-forwardly, "Thus I speak" (Philippi).)

The *norito* were recited at regular festivals, held at court or at shrines around the country, at which court nobles, clergy, and some common people were gathered. The liturgies themselves were usually preceded by an explanation of the origin of the festival, praise for the virtues of the deity being honored, offerings of food or other gifts, and an announce-ment of the *norito's* purpose ("Norito"). The rituals were performed to celebrate planting and harvest of the rice crop, to congratulate new rul-ers, to consecrate new priests, palaces, or shrines, to pacify the deities in times of trouble, and to purify the people (especially those serving the imperial family). Each *norito* also included elements that justified impe-rial rule by reiterating the Emperor's divine lineage—he is usually called "the Sovereign Grandchild," for example, who was commanded to rule as "an incarnate deity" (Philippi):

> The eight myriad deities . . . caused him to descend from the heavens,
> Leaving the heavenly rock-seat,
> And pushing with an awesome pushing
> Through the myriad layers of heavenly clouds—
> Thus they entrusted [the land to him].
> The lands of the four quarters thus entrusted,
> Great Yamato, the Land of the Sun—Seen-on-High,
> Was pacified and made a peaceful land;
> The palace posts were firmly planted in the bed-rock below,
> The cross-beams soaring high towards the High Heavenly Plain,
> And the noble palace of the Sovereign Grandchild constructed,
> Where, as a heavenly shelter, as a sun-shelter,/he dwells hidden,
> And rules [the kingdom] tranquilly as a peaceful land.
>
> (Philippi 45–46)

The main corpus of 27 *norito* was not compiled in written form until 927 CE (in the *Engi-Shiki,* a book of laws), but at least some of them are assumed to predate the seventh century (Bock 57–58). They were recorded in a phonetic script called *senmyo,* which consisted of Chi-nese characters chosen for their phonetic value, and arranged in Japa-nese word order with a gloss of Japanese particles and inflections. This script was considered the most precise for recitation of these important prayers; an effort was made to bring the language as close as possible to that assumed to have been spoken in the past, so that a person performing the rituals would still be attuned to the *kotodama* (Konishi 64, 207).

In Shinto, the power of language had to be applied in an orderly way, to ensure the tranquility of the nation. It was believed that in ancient times, the *kami* had to silence the land in order to control it, before entrusting it to the emperor:

> The very rocks, the stumps of trees,
> The bubbles of water all speak,
> And it is truly an unruly land.
> But I shall pacify and subjugate it,
> And shall have it ruled
> tranquilly. . . . They silenced to the last leaf
> The rocks and the stumps of the trees,
> Which had been able to speak. (Philippi 73, 45)

Belief in *kotodama* "is borne out in the language of the *norito*" (Bock 59),[10] some of which were speech acts of a sort, in which what was said would come to pass; this characteristic is reflected in titles such as "Words for the Great Purification" and "Ritual to Dispel a Malevolent *Kami*" (Bock 62, 99). In the first, the prayer is invoked to exorcise "the various sins perpetrated and committed/By those who serve in the Emperor's court":

> Let him [the great Nakatomi] pronounce the heavenly ritual, the solemn ritual words.
> When he thus pronounces them,
> the heavenly deities will push open the heavenly rock door
> [. . . and] will hear and receive [these words].
> . . . When they thus hear and receive,
> Then, beginning with the court of the Sovereign Grandchild,
> In the lands of the four quarters under the heavens,
> Each and every sin shall be gone. (Philippi 47)

The sins were transported into strips of sedge reeds attached to pieces of wood, and then appointed diviners were to "Carry them out to the great river/And cast them away" (Philippi 49).

In the second *norito* mentioned above, offerings of garments, a mirror, a jewel, a bow and arrow, a sword, a horse, wine, rice, herbs, game, and fish are prepared in an effort to placate a vengeful deity:

I place these noble offerings in abundance upon tables
Like a long mountain range and present them
Praying that the Sovereign Deities
Will with a pure heart receive them tranquilly
As offerings of ease,
As offerings of abundance,
And will not seek vengeance and not ravage,
But will move to a place of wide and lovely mountains and rivers,
And will as deities dwell there pacified.
With this prayer, I fulfill your praises. Thus I humbly speak.

(Philippi 70)

The style of the prayers, perhaps even more than their content, was thought to account for their efficacy: "[T]he archaic and majestic-sounding verbiage was to be intoned with solemn and sonorous syllables designed to please the *kami* and also to be awe-inspiring and magic-provoking within the minds of the celebrants and audience" (Bock 59). Unfortunately, the sonority of the language is lost in translation (as well as by being put on a page), though scholars generally praise Donald Philippi's version of the *norito* for its retention of the poetry (Havens 2). As Philippi writes, "It is clear from the title of a Kamakura period work called *Senmyoru* (Rhythm Chart of Senmyo) [. . .] that the reading of these edicts required a standard meter"; however, the documents containing the musical notation did not survive ("Senmyo," Philippi 2).

Philippi notes that two of the most common stylistic techniques found in the *norito* are repetition and metaphor, which emphasize unity of purpose and lend beauty to the recitation. Throughout the collection are found stock phrases such as "By the command of the Sovereign Ancestral Gods and Goddesses/Who divinely remain in the High Heavenly Plain," "as the morning sun rises in effulgent glory," and "as far as the toad can crawl/And as far as the briny bubbles can reach" (Philippi 17, 38. Naumann writes that ". . . fixed figurative passages are handled like set pieces, inserted and grouped as required in order to produce new rituals" (62).

The predominant metaphors and similes in the *norito* make use of nature imagery, apropos of the centrality in Shinto of the kinship between humans and the natural world. We find guardian deities and the emperor's reign compared to "sacred massed rocks"; the ruler likened to the radiant sun and moon, and to a young pond; collections of nobles serving the sovereign described as "luxuriant, flourishing trees"; offerings piled up "like a long mountain range"; a priest or other supplicant humbly looking "like a cormorant bending [his] neck"; and sins or pollutions made to disappear like mist blown away by the wind, or as a stand of trees cut away with a sharp sickle (Philippi 19–48).

Other comparisons found in the prayers include the ruler being likened to jewels of red, blue, and white (representing health, divinity, and long life), as well as to a strong sword, firm cloth, and a smooth, clear mirror (divine symbols in the Shinto faith which represent the ruler's skill, strength, and authority to oversee the land) (Philippi 66–78). Finally, in an ancient blessing formula (*yogoto*) recorded in the *Nihongi,* the parts of a house symbolize the heart, life, and wealth of the ruler:

> The pillars built up/Are the mainstay of the heart of the lord of this house.
> The beams laid in place/Are the flourishing of the heart of the lord of this house.
> The rafters laid in place
> Are the setting in order of the heart of the lord of this house.
> The crosspieces laid in place
> Are the levelness of the heart of the lord of this house.
> The ropes tied in place
> Are the firm securing of the life of the lord of this house.
> The grass thatched on the roof
> Is the abundance of the wealth of the lord of this house. (80)

These prayers were invoked for the benefit of the nation as a whole, which was to be achieved through the longevity of the emperor's reign, prosperous harvests, and the people's purification. The function of speech (or *kotomuke,* the directed word) was to create and maintain peace and harmony (*wa*), furthered by each person devoting him- or herself to the common interest *(kenshin)* (Herbert 72, 74).

The *norito* may compare, somewhat, to classical Western epideictic discourse, as one of their purposes was to praise and honor the gods and rulers; however, they could also be considered deliberative (in the sense of exhorting others to perform a future action), as their other goals were to petition the *kami* for prosperity and protection for the people in the immediate future, and to encourage the loyalty of the people themselves. Though Shinto rituals contain clearly rhetorical elements, Shinto did not rely on spoken or written persuasion to propagate itself among the people; if one had to be persuaded to follow one's *kami*-nature, this ceased to be natural and therefore was not Shinto. However, though "Shinto influence cannot be found through any search for formal propaganda" (Mason 178), its central concept of *kotodama*, exemplified in the simple yet moving *norito*, offers evidence of an understanding among the ancient Japanese people of the crucial importance of words, addressed properly to the *kami*, to bring good results.[11] Kigawa explains that ". . . *norito* was not a book of doctrines or dogmas from which people learned the meaning of life and the world; its aim was to provide people with proper orientations for the practical performance of rituals, prayers, and charms" (Kitagawa xxvii). This focus on the spiritual power of language would help an imported faith, esoteric Buddhism, to gain a following in the nation.

SHINGON BUDDHIST RHETORIC

Rhetorical Considerations in the Early Development of Buddhism in Japan

Buddhism was introduced to Japan not directly through China, but by a Korean regional ruler likely seeking Japanese friendship and military assistance, in the sixth century CE (a commonly accepted "official" date of transmission is 552, though some Japanese may have been exposed to Buddhism earlier through envoys to both Korea and China) (Saunders 91–92). Over the objections of the Nakatomi and Mononobe Shinto adherents, the powerful Soga clan accepted the Buddha figure and the scriptures that had been sent, and undertook a "test conversion" to ensure that their audience of native Shinto gods would not be angered by the worship of Buddhist deities. An epidemic occurred and Buddhism was temporarily abandoned; however, subsequent misfortunes came to be seen as being caused by the rejection of the Buddha (itself a powerful audience), and so Buddhism was once more allowed (Eliot 199–200). Along with precepts of Confucianism, Taoism, and other schools of Chinese thought, Buddhism represented a culture that the Japanese imperial court sought to emulate in part because its civilized respectability would be helpful in further consolidating the hegemony of the ruling family over the collection of clans in the country.

Many parts of the Chinese culture being introduced reinforced what the Japanese already felt and did; for example, both societies were hierarchical and valued social harmony over individual gain. Esoteric Buddhism's many deities and rituals, reliance on intuitive insight, and "doctrine of the harmonious whole" (Meyer 46) would likely have seemed familiar to Shinto devotees, and in any case, Shinto espoused a belief in *musubi*, a dynamic synthesis of tradition and progress that resulted in an openness to new ideas (Herbert 68). Early on, Buddhism in Japan "was largely concerned with exterior, magical powers and material advantage—in other words, a viewpoint much like that of the native religion" (Saunders 100). However, during the life of Prince Shotoku (regent from 593–622), the Shinto practice of "affirming the present life" may not have rung as true (at least among the political elite), as he lived "amongst corrupt relatives in a new nation filled with dissent, intrigue, and political rivalry" which may have led him to "seek something beyond the sphere in which he lived to fulfill his ideal of peace and harmony" (Matsunaga 146–47). Buddhism's negation of earthly life in favor of nirvana would have represented a new idea to most Japanese, and indeed, the Shinto belief in death as a kind of pollution would have an impact on the degree to which Buddhist negation of life could become part of the Japanese philosophical outlook.

Prince Shotoku was a devout Buddhist scholar, and "As a Buddhist holding a position of power . . . it might well have been possible for [him] to crush the indigenous faith. . . . He also had ample excuse, considering that major proponents of the native faith were the enemies his clan had to defeat prior to their rise to power" (Matsunaga 147). But he continued to support the worship of native gods, almost surely in part because his family's claim to authority (their ruling ethos, so to speak) derived from the people's belief in the rulers' descent from Amaterasu (148). As mentioned above, the two faiths had not been difficult to combine, since Shinto was so flexible in its acceptance of "deities of practically every variety and nature"; a tangible manifestation of this mixture were the *jinguji* (combinations of Shinto shrines and Buddhist temples), whose building had already been sponsored by previous rulers to signify their official support of both sets of gods (Matsunaga 151).[12]

True to the "principle of the unity of religion and state" (Kitaga-wa xxiii), during the Nara period (710–794), the imperial court tried hard to control the various Buddhist sects' access to land and other resources. "Under Emperor Shomu, Buddhism was used as symbolic support for political centralization," and the imperial court controlled the ordination of clergy while supporting its official temples through taxes and land donations; this meant great agricultural wealth for Buddhist leaders, some of whom were even able to maintain private armies ("Japanese Buddhism"). The "superior type of magic" in the learned Buddhism of the court was to be practiced to benefit the ruling class (and by extension, the state) (Matsunaga 168).

But commoners discovered Buddhism through the preaching of priests—an activity recorded in the histories that obviously contra-dicts the notion that there was no public speaking in ancient Japan. These "people's priests" were neither trained, nor ordained, and often mixed elements of Shinto and Taoism with their Buddhism, but they were popular and often criticized the "academic" Buddhism of the capital (Harderwijk). This more democratic and individualistic Bud-dhism made people, potentially, somewhat independent of the gov-ernment—which therefore prohibited priests from "propagating their magical rites among the common people, since it was a cause of dissen-sion and unrest" (Matsunaga 170–71).

In the early Heian period (794–967) the rulers' hold on Buddhism was weakened somewhat, in part because the leaders of the two new-est Buddhist sects (Tendai and Shingon) located their monasteries in the mountains, away from the urban influence of the new capital. However, in order to have sufficient support, the new sects needed to maintain the simultaneous approval of the nobility and the common people, whose lives were still mostly governed by Shinto practice.

The Role of Ethos in Kukai's Successful Establishment of Shingon Buddhism

Matsunaga argues that "syncretism" was the defining feature of the Heian Buddhist sects, which incorporated aspects of Confucianism and Taoism in their frameworks. This tendency to assimilate many philosophies under one umbrella was also applied to the indigenous faith. The *shinbutsu-shugo* and *honji-suijaku* concepts (essentially, two levels of unification in which Buddhist deities are ultimately seen as absolute, true nature and the Shinto gods as trace manifestations of

them) began to develop at this time (Matsunaga 2).[13] This merging of
Shinto and Buddhist deities (later to be termed *Ryobu Shinto,* or Dual
Shinto) made it easier, obviously, for more Japanese people to accept
Buddhism without fearing retribution from their native Shinto gods.
However, at the same time that the common people were being led to
Buddhism, the disseminator of any new philosophy still had to secure
the approval of the government to have access to sufficient resources
for monasteries and temples.

The Heian Buddhist priest who was arguably most successful at
appealing to both imperial and common audiences was the propa-
gator of Japanese Shingon Buddhism, Kukai (774–835, later known
as Kobo Daishi, "Great Teacher Who Spread Widely the Buddhist
Teachings"). Kukai was one of the most prominent intellectuals in the
history of Japan; being involved in philosophy, art, linguistics, engi-
neering, poetry, and other disciplines, he possessed an exalted reputation at court, where his aesthetic refinement was admired (Saunders
157). He was renowned for his skill with spoken and written language;
he is recorded as having publicly disputed doctrinal questions with
Nara priests (a rhetorical activity that evolved with the integration of
a wide variety of philosophical traditions), and was often called to the
imperial palace so that Emperor Saga "might hear his beautiful language" and have Kukai write his imperial messages (Reischauer 94,
Matsunaga 186).

Kukai was also popular with the common people, for whom he
founded a general-education school and implemented other beneficial
social programs (Matsunaga 186), thereby bolstering his ethos with a
different constituency. But what made Shingon itself (and its contemporary school, Tendai) so attractive was its radical egalitarian notion
that any person could achieve enlightenment in his or her lifetime
("Shingon"). For Kukai, language was the most important key to this
process.

Philosophy of Language in Shingon Buddhism

At his monastery on Mount Koya, Kukai taught his disciples the doctrine of Shingon, or "True Word," which seems uniquely suited to
synthesis with Shinto for a variety of reasons. Shingon is a form of
Vajrayana Right-Handed Tantric Buddhism, the chief deity of which is
Mahavairocana (in Japanese, Dainichi), the "Great Illuminating Sun"
of whom all things are a manifestation, surely a useful link to Shinto's

sun goddess, Amaterasu, along with the great profusion of other *kami* (Saunders 161). (Interestingly, in the *Nihon Shoki,* Kukai's Otomo clan was depicted as having been the guards of the sun deity (Green)). This sect argues that truth, or reality, possesses both exoteric and esoteric forms; the apparent doctrine, or *Ken-gyo,* is likened to "formal conversation with a guest," while the hidden doctrine, or *Mikkyo,* is compared to "intimate family talk between relatives" (Nanjio 82). The words denoting the exoteric truth are "open and brief, and adapted to those taught" (i.e., the common people) (qtd. in Tsunoda 148), but the esoteric truth is only accessible through the ritual of the Three Mysteries (*sanmitsu*) of body, speech, and mind, taught orally by a master to his disciple(s). In this sense, esotericism was elitist; but its elements of magic and mystery apparently appealed to many people ("Japanese Buddhism").

Speech was not considered as solely inherent in humans: "Since all beings and all things are of the same essence, and since logical reasonings, discussions, and dialectics only scratch the bark of things, one should, by thought and other means . . . strive to feel and to understand the cosmic life and become conscious of our intimate and universal communion" (Shinzai Harashi, qtd. in Steinilber-Oberlin 104). This perception of the "speech" of the world, the ability to hear, intuitively, what the universe is saying, is accomplished in three ways. The first way is through mudras (symbolic gestures and postures that represent teaching, protection, and other movements of the cosmos); the second, through mandalas (Japanese *mandaras,* diagrams which evoke the structure of the universe) (Steinilber-Oberlin 109, 113). Finally, a disciple should utilize mantras—syllables such as "aum" or "hum" consisting of a vowel and nasal consonant, which "tend to produce through continuous pronunciation a resonance in the head [recall the sonority of the *norito* releasing *kotodama*], a kind of profound inner echo, leading to a mystical rapture wherein the practitioner is aware of the vast overtones of the universe and the laws inherent in the nature of things" (Saunders 77).

Kukai believed that reality could only be comprehended through art and voice: he said, "The law [dharma] has no speech, but without speech it cannot be expressed. Eternal truth [tathata] transcends color, but only by means of color can it be understood. . . . In truth, the esoteric doctrines are so profound as to defy their enunciation in writing" (qtd. in Tsunoda 141–42). Shingon Buddhist monk (bonze) Shinzai Harashi explains:

> Speech is omnipresent. . . . Each body lives by a thought of which it is but the material expression, or which seems so to us, and each thought expresses itself in words, in sounds, in gestures. Silence does not exist, but the 'mental murmur' subsists, which explains why beings can sometimes understand each other by silence itself. (qtd. in Steinilber-Oberlin 107)

In the sense that all beings could make themselves understood if the listener utilized the proper modes of perception, everything was thought to possess a mode of communication; this understanding Shingon had in common with Shinto. The difference was that in Shingon, one did not direct the communication toward a *kami,* but went further and attempted to reproduce the communication of the universe, to experience absolute reality by becoming one with it and comprehending both emptiness (all things exist only in reference to other things) and oneness (all things are part of the cosmic order, as in Shinto animism) (Abe 280, 284).

Kukai presumed, in his insistence on the importance of spoken sound, an integral relation between language and reality; in this way, he can be considered an early structuralist. In his essay, *The Meanings of Sound, Word, and Reality (Shoji jisso gi),* he explains that

> No sooner does the inner breath of living beings vibrate the air of the external world than there arises voice (*sho*) . . . when voice . . . expresses the name of a thing, it is called letter (*ji*). The names thus revealed unfailingly evoke objects, which are so-called reality. That each voice, letter, and reality divides itself into myriad parts is called meaning (*gi*). (qtd. in Abe 282)

Not only does Kukai assert a fundamental connection between language and reality or truth, but he also attempts an exhaustive illustration of the many layers of truth that can be expressed in words—indeed, in each individual sound, and letter, that helps to constitute a word.[14] This knowledge of, and concern for, phonology is one reason Kukai is traditionally believed to have invented, or at least standardized, the Japanese kana system, which made use of abbreviated Chinese characters to represent Japanese sounds.

Japanese Shingon rhetoric shared and reinforced the native Shinto understanding of the power of language (which, along with the links between the two faiths' deities, made the new philosophy more palatable to its potential audiences), and also took that understanding to a new level by asking adherents to use *mantra* to become one with the universe. The life of Kukai serves as a clear illustration of the importance of ethos in the establishment and maintenance of any religion and philosophy in ancient Japan, as does the concern for ethos in Shingon Buddhism generally (exemplified by an expression of good will for and acceptance of Shinto, as well as by the mysterious and exclusive nature of its esoteric teachings). Esoteric Buddhism echoes Shinto in finding the style of communication to be of utmost importance in the pronunciation of mantras and extends that concern to distinguishing the formal and intimate natures of Buddhist teachings. Though both faiths were manipulated by the imperial court to some degree to help justify the political status quo, both were also concerned with the well-being and salvation of individual adherents.

LINGERING TRACES

Several of the characteristics of ancient Shinto and Shingon Buddhist rhetoric appear to have persisted in more modern Japanese communicative concepts and techniques, though a direct line of causation may be difficult to discern. For example, the ideas of benevolence and unity—and the relation of language use to these principles—which permeate each philosophy are manifested today in the concept of *amae,* which can be loosely translated as "dependence on (or presumption of) another's love." Stella Ting-Toomey tells us that Japanese speakers are generally "expected to be verbally indirect and non-verbally circumspect because their every word and utterance have large group implications" (33). Thus, *amae* can account for some of the hesitancy and ambiguity characteristic of much Japanese discourse; being indirect will allow one to avoid stepping on another's feelings, or violating his or her *amae.*

The taciturnity and indirectness of many Japanese may also be due in part, according to Akira Tsujimura, to the relatively high level of ethnic and linguistic homogeneity in the country. This kind of social context can mean that excessive verbal elaboration is often unnecessary, as the people are often able to understand each other with fewer words of explanation (120) (recall here Konishi's discussion of brevity as an aesthetic ideal in Japanese poetry).

> According to Satoshi Ishii (1992), Japanese discourse, due to the influence it received from Buddhist teachings, follows discourse patterns different from English. Ishii points out that an American usually organizes his or her ideas explicitly and directly in a linear order as if building a bridge from points A to B. On the other hand, a Japanese often organizes his or her ideas implicitly and indirectly, as if arranging stepping stones from points A to B [. . . .] interpretation depends heavily on contextual information. (Maynard 115)

In fact, many Japanese place high value on being able to understand each other with no speech. This communication occurs at the level of mood instead of words, when the people involved in a given rhetorical situation are so well-attuned to one another's feelings, and to the attendant context, that verbalization is not necessary. This phenomenon is known as *ishin-denshin,* "heart-to-heart" communication (Tsujimura 17).

A similar phenomenon is that of *kuuki.* The word refers to the aura responsible for the mental concurrence that emerges when the members of a group, without discussion, simply come to a decision together. Tsujimura attempts to explain *kuuki* as "the prevailing atmosphere in both a physical and a social sense" (126). Perhaps it could be understood as corresponding somewhat to the "mental murmur" associated earlier with Shingon Buddhism. The great value placed by the Japanese on such a subjective form of communication can be puzzling to many Westerners, who are often more accustomed to making all of the components of a decision-making process verbally explicit. To many Japanese, such explicitness, or obviousness, is harsh and unnecessary, and actually insulting to an audience because it does not allow them active participation in the making of meaning.

Indirectness in Japanese discourse is also evident in the fact that many Japanese, in order to preserve a sense of group harmony, will often maintain that they agree with one another when in actuality they do not. This duality is comprised of *tatemae,* or "principle" (the surface attitude), and *honne,* or "true mind" (the internal attitude).

The duality is somewhat reminiscent of the apparent and hidden doctrines espoused in Shingon, as well as the "true nature" part of the *honji-suijaku* theory. John Condon explains it this way:

> *Tatemae* is literally the outward structure of a building; the term refers to what is outwardly expressed . . .
> *honne* is literally one's 'true voice,' and it refers to what one really thinks or feels. The Japanese assume that there may be a difference between what one says and what one thinks. How else could it be in a society that values harmony . . . that discourages individualistic outspokenness, and that restrains the bold expression of personal feelings? (25–26)

Seiichi Makino notes that among younger Japanese speakers, *tatemae* now seems to be losing ground to the expression of *honne,* though "the distinction between the two concepts still remains potent in the Japanese mentality" (32–33).

While some Westerners may view this duality as "two-faced," in Japan it is considered a sign of maturity to adjust to this discrepancy (Doi 183). It must be remembered, too, that even when a Japanese individual keeps her true feelings to herself, others often recognize when this is taking place (consider *ishin-denshin*), so the practice is not really dishonest. A Japanese audience, accustomed to taking a large measure of responsibility for the success of any communication, is expected to know a speaker's real meaning from nonverbal or contextual clues. According to Makino, "Japanese culture has often been said to be a *sasshi no bunka* (a guessing culture). . . . meaning that a Japanese must either anticipate or conjure the intentions of another. . . . requir[ing] social sensitivity [. . . . which] underlies *amae*" (37).

Conclusion

It should be clear from even this very limited exploration that ancient Japan was anything but a "rhetorical vacuum" (Morrison 89). A broad conception of what constitutes "rhetoric," and an examination of one context where rhetoric is acknowledged to function in all cultures (religion) quickly reveals a wealth of early Japanese ideas regarding language, persuasive techniques, and their relation to knowledge and reality. The way in which the Yamato clan manipulated Shinto histories to bolster its authority, the reverence with which Shinto priests released the *kotodama* to benefit the people, the care that Shingon Buddhist adherents took with the mystery of speech in order to better commune with and understand the universe, the understanding that Kukai had of the need to appeal to aristocratic and common audiences—all of these are just a few examples of the understanding and practice of rhetoric in ancient Japan, pieces of which have seemingly evolved to influence modern Japanese language norms and expectations. (It will be interesting to see whether ongoing changes in Japanese culture—for example, increasing Westernization—might weaken these links.) In this ancient hierarchical society, Japanese monarchs and priests skillfully developed their ethos in order to advance their respective causes, and were awed by, and respectful of, the immense power of language.

NOTES

1. There is a wealth of historical and political context that I do not have space to include here; I encourage readers to consult any reputable history of Japan (such as *The Cambridge History*) to gain a fuller understanding of the conditions under which Shinto and Buddhism developed in that nation.

2. I will maintain my sources' methods of romanizing Japanese words throughout, minus the macrons illustrating long vowels.

3. Although I have managed a low-intermediate use of modern spoken Japanese, I am not a specialist in the earlier form of the language; therefore, I am working with what are considered authoritative English translations of primary texts and English-language critical commentaries. I am hopeful that future work in ancient Japanese rhetoric will involve collaboration with scholars of classical Japanese.

4. The term "Shinto" is of Chinese origin (*shen-tao*).

5. Kuroda Toshio has claimed that what is now termed "Shinto" was not an original religion at all, but rather a form of Taoism imported from China that obliterated the indigenous faith (Breen and Teuwen 5). However, John Breen and Mark Teuwen (and others) argue that native "habits of faith" were not wiped out, but were grafted onto the forms of worship imported from elsewhere and altered them in ways that make it possible to discern what is likely indigenous (7).

6. *"Kami"* is a term whose meaning has been long debated. A famous 18th-century Shinto scholar, Motoori Norinaga, wrote:

> I do not yet understand the meaning of the term *kami*. Speaking in general, however, it may be said that *kami* signifies, in the first place, the deities of heaven and earth that appear in the ancient records and also the spirits of the shrines where they are worshipped. It is hardly necessary to say that it includes human beings. It also includes such objects as birds, beasts, trees, plants, seas, mountains, and so forth. In ancient usage, anything whatsoever which was outside the ordinary, which possessed superior power, or which was awe-inspiring was called *kami*. (qtd. in Tsunoda 23)

7. Documentation of these lectures is found mostly in unpublished manuscripts kept in libraries in Japan (Cambridge History 352).

8. Other examples of ancient Japanese language-magic terminology are *kotowaza* (word charms, proverbs) and *wazauta* (spell song) (Konishi 107).

9 Now, *aware* means "wretched" (Tsunoda 177).

10. Cognates of *noru* [to tell, recite, command, reveal, decree] are: *inoru*, to pray; *nori*, law, rule; *norou*, to curse, to imprecate; *noroi*, a curse, malediction; *noberu* or *noburu*, to tell, express, relate, narrate, state; *notama(f)u*, to speak, to tell (superior to inferior) and so forth. Cognates of the archaic word *to*, a spell, are: *tona(f)u*, to make sounds, and the verb *tonaeru*, to name or call" (Bock 62, note 291).

11. This faith in the *kotodama* persists today, for example, in the avoidance of "bad-luck words" at weddings held at Shinto shrines (Konishi 107 note 24). However, since the *kotodama* specifically manifests the "spirituality inherent in nature" and "Nature has almost completely disappeared from the cities," Konishi fears that "The *kotodama* therefore faces imminent extinction" (108, note 25).

12. In addition, priests had requested (and allegedly received) the sun goddess' approval of a Buddhist image in the temple at Todaiji. According to some accounts, she not only approved, but also linked herself, as the Sun, to the "illuminating" nature of the Buddha. The Shinto war-god Hachiman is then said to have worshipped the Buddha image (in the person of a Shinto priestess), thereupon becoming the Todaiji temple's guardian deity (Matsunaga 164–65).

13. The first stage was the indication that native gods accepted and would protect Buddhist ones (see note 9 above); in stage two, Shinto gods allegedly requested Buddhist instruction so as to overcome their existence in godly form; stage three saw some native deities recognized as having reached Buddhist Enlightenment (for example, Hachiman's history was revised so that he was seen as always having been a bodhisattva); and in stage four, all

Shinto gods were viewed as manifestations of Buddhas and bodhisattvas, so
that "if we view the Japanese gods, we are in effect visualizing the Buddha
from our position in the relative world" (Matsunaga 218–227).

14. The rich depth conveyed in Sanskrit sounds and characters is enu-
merated in Kukai's essay "The Meanings of the Word H[A]UM." The surface meaning of each character is given as follows: "H" (standing for the
word hetva), means "cause;" "A" (the original sound, without which no other
sound could exist) stands for emptiness; "U" (una, "wanting"), evokes im-
permanence; and "M" (atman, "entity") stands for the self (Hakeda 247–48).
The hidden meanings of each character contain even more depth:

> The letter H connotes that the first cause of all things is
> unobtainable. . . . As the sound A is inherent in all other
> sounds, the mother of all as it were, so what is truly meant
> by the letter A pervades all things. . . . The letter A signi-
> fies 'the enlightened mind,' 'the gateway to all teachings,'
> 'nonduality,' 'the goal of all existences,' 'the nature of all
> existences'. . . . the letter U . . . stands for that which is free
> from any alteration. . . . interpenetration of many in one
> and one in many is the ultimate meaning of the letter M.
> (qtd. In Hakeda 248–58)

Taken together, the surface and hidden meanings of each character connote
the summary and unity of all religious teachings, practices, and attainments.
For Kukai, "The world is made of texts and only of texts—not of their representational function but of their materiality" (Abe 276).

Works Cited

Abe, Ryuichi. *The Weaving of Mantra: Kukai and the Construction of Esoteric
    Buddhist Discourse.* New York: Columbia UP, 1999.
Aizu History Project. "Japanese Buddhism: A Historical Overview." James
    M. Goodwin. n.d. 22 Aug. 2007 <http://www.cs.ucla.edu/~jmg/ah/
    budd.over1.html>.
Ashton, W. G., trans. *Holy Nihongi.* Internet Sacred Text Archive. 1896. 1
    July 2005 <http://www.sacred-texts.com/shi/>.
Bizzell, Patricia, and Bruce Herzberg. *The Rhetorical Tradition: Readings from
    Classical Times to the Present.* 2nd ed. Boston: Bedford, 2001.
Bock, Felicia Gressitt. *Engi-Shiki: Procedures of the Engi Era, Books VI-X.*
    Tokyo: Sophia UP (Monumenta Nipponica), 1972.
Breen, John, and Mark Teeuwen, eds. *Shinto in History: Ways of the Kami.*
    Honolulu: U of Hawaii P, 2000.

Condon, John C. *With Respect to the Japanese*. Yarmouth, ME: Intercultural, 1984.

Doi, L. Takeo. "The Japanese Patterns of Communication and the Concept of AMAE." *Quarterly Journal of Speech* 59 (April 1973): 180–85.

Donahue, Ray T., ed. *Exploring Japaneseness: On Japanese Enactments of Culture and Consciousness*. Westport, CT: Ablex, 2002.

Eliot, Sir Charles. *Japanese Buddhism*. London: Broadway House, 1935.

Green, Ron. "Kukai, Founder of Japanese Shingon Buddhism." 7 Aug. 2007. 22 Aug. 2007 <http://www.ronnygreen.us/kukai.htm>.

Hakeda, Yoshito S. *Kukai: Major Works, Translated, With an Account of His Life and a Study of His Thought*. New York: Columbia UP, 1972.

Hall, John Whitney, et al., eds. *The Cambridge History of Japan*. 6 vols. Cambridge: Cambridge UP, 1999.

Harderwijk, Rudy. "History of Japansese Buddhism." A View on Buddhism. 23 Nov. 2006. 22 Aug. 2007 <http://buddhism.kalachakranet.org/history_japanese_buddhism.html>.

Havens, Norman. "Review of Donald Philippi's *Norito*." *Japanese Journal of Religious Studies* 19.4 (Dec 1992): 398–402. <http://www.ic.nanzanu.ac.jp/SHUBUNKEN/publications/jjrs/pdf/384.pdf>.

Herbert, Jean. *Shinto: At the Fountainhead of Japan*. London: Allen, 1967.

Kennedy, George. *Comparative Rhetoric: An Historical and Cross-Cultural Introduction*. New York: Oxford UP, 1998.

Kitagawa, Joseph M. "Preface." Ed. Donald C. Philippi. *Norito: A Translation of the Ancient Japanese Ritual Prayers*. Princeton, NJ: Princeton UP, 1990. Orig. pub. Institute for Japanese Culture and Classics, 1959, vii-xxxviii.

"Kojiki and Nihon Shoki." *Encyclopedia of Shinto*. Kokugakuin University. 2006. 22 Aug. 2007 <http://eos.kokugakuin.ac.jp>.

Konishi, Jin'ichi. *A History of Japanese Literature, Volume One: The Archaic and Ancient Ages*. Trans. Aileen Gatten and Nicholas Teele. Ed. Earl Miner. Princeton, NJ: Princeton UP, 1984.

Lipson, Carol S., and Roberta A. Binkley, eds. *Rhetoric Before and Beyond the Greeks*. Albany: SUNY P, 2004.

Makino, Seiichi. "*Uchi* and *Soto* as Cultural and Linguistic Metaphors." *Exploring Japaneseness: On Japanese Enactments of Culture and Consciousness*. Ed. Ray T. Donahue. Westport, CT: Ablex, 2002. 29–64.

Mason, Joseph Warren Teets. *The Meaning of Shinto: The Primeval Foundation of Creative Spirit in Modern Japan*. New York: Dutton, 1935.

Matsumae, Takeshi. "Early Kami Worship." Trans. Janet Goodwin. *The Cambridge History of Japan, Volume One: Ancient Japan*. Ed. Delmer M. Brown. Cambridge: Cambridge UP, 1993. 317–358.

Matsunaga, Alicia. *The Buddhist Philosophy of Assimilation: The Historical Development of the Honji-Suijaku Theory*. Tokyo: Sophia UP, 1969.

Maynard, Senko K. *Principles of Japanese Discourse: A Handbook.* Cambridge: Cambridge UP, 1998.

Meyer, Milton W. *Japan: A Concise History.* 3rd ed. Lanham, MD: Rowman and Littlefield, 1993.

Morrison, John L. "The Absence of a Rhetorical Tradition in Japanese Culture." *Western Speech* 36 (Spring 1972): 89–102.

Nanjio, Bunyiu. *A Short History of the Twelve Japanese Buddhist Sects.* Trans. from the original Japanese. Tokyo: Bukkyo-Sho-Ei-Yaku-Shuppan-Sha, Meiji, 19th Year [1886].

Naumann, Nelly. "The State Cult of the Nara and Early Heian Periods." *Shinto in History: Ways of the Kami.* Ed. John Breen and Mark Teeuwen. Honolulu: U of Hawaii P, 2000. 47–67.

"Norito." *Encyclopedia of Shinto.* Kokugakuin University. 2006. 22 August 2007. <http://eos.kokugakun.ac.jp>.

Okabe, Roichi. "Japan's Attempted Enactments of Western Debate Practice in the 16th and the 19th Centuries." *Exploring Japaneseness: On Japanes Enactments of Culture and Consciousness.* Ed. Ray T. Donahue. Westport, CT: Ablex, 2002, 277–291.

—. "The Impact of Western Rhetoric in the East: The Case of Japan." Paper presented at the Seventh International Conference of the International Society for the History of Rhetoric. Gottingen, Netherlands, July 1989.

Philippi, Donald C. *Norito: A Translation of the Ancient Japanese Ritual Prayers.* Princeton, NJ: Princeton UP, 1990. Orig. pub. Institute for Japanese Culture and Classics, 1959.

"Ritsuryo Jingikan." *Encyclopedia of Shinto.* Kokugakuin University. 2006. 22 Aug. 2007. <http://eos.kokugakun.ac.jp>.

Saunders, E. Dale. *Buddhism in Japan, With an Outline of its Origins in India.* Philadelphia: U of Pennsylvania P, 1964.

"Shingon Sect." Japan Reference. 2007. 22 Aug. 2007 <http://www.jref.com/culture/shingon_sect_buddhism.shtml>.

Steinilber-Oberlin, A. *The Buddhist Sects of Japan.* Trans. Marc Loge. London: Allen, 1938.

Ting-Toomey, Stella. "Rhetorical Sensitivity Style in Three Cultures: France, Japan and the United States." *Central States Speech Journal* 39 (Spring 1988): 28–36.

Tsujimura, Akira. "Some Characteristics of the Japanese Way of Communication." *Communication Theory: Eastern and Western Perspectives.* Ed. Lawrenc D. Kincaid. San Diego: Academic, 1987. 115–26.

Tsunoda, Ryusaku, Wm. Theodore de Bary, and Donald Keene. *Sources of Japanese Tradition.* New York: Columbia UP, 1958.

Rhetoric from Ancient India

9 Storytelling as Soul-Tuning: The Ancient Rhetoric of Valmiki's *Ramayana*

Mari Lee Mifsud

In an ancient Hindu world, circa 500 BCE, the poet Valmiki composed an epic of the travels (*ayana*) of Rama. Rama was born the son of King Dasaratha, young prince of idyllic Ayodha, as an avatar of the god Vishnu. As an avatar, Rama is human, but filled with the strength of the gods. With this strength, he is to kill the demon (*rakshasa*) Ravana, and to save the universe from evil.[1]

Audiences of this epic, entitled *Ramayana,* experience the ways that norms of culture are created, communicated, reinforced, and obeyed; the ways that personal and public relations are constituted and negotiated; the ways decisions are made in the face of dilemmas; and the ways that meaning-making is orchestrated. Moreover, because the *Ramayana* proceeds through the guiding context of the universal divine, masters and gurus from antiquity to contemporary times state that experiencing the *Ramayana,* whether as audience or reader, tunes one's soul, bringing it into harmony with the divine. Translator Ramesh Menon writes that listening to or reading the *Ramayana* "serves to exorcise one's sins, from this life and others, and to purify one's soul." (2001, xi).

In this essay, I illuminate rhetorical dimensions of storytelling as soul-tuning in Valmiki's *Ramayana*.[2] I explore how the story's historical, reflexive, and paratactic rhetoric invites experiencing it not just as Rama's story, but as the *telling* of Rama's story. The *telling* is the tuner of the soul, as it creates an indelible impression on human memory of divine revelation.

Through this illumination emerge additional questions related to the history and theory of rhetoric. How is it that Valmiki's *Ramayana* can be considered rhetoric? How can the history and theory of rhetoric be guided by cultural pluralism, rather than by continued dominance of Greek models? What particular textual considerations should be given to reading the rhetoric of the *Ramayana?* These questions ought to be addressed first for the sake of orientation.

ORIENTATIONS TO THE *RAMAYANA* AS AN ANCIENT RHETORIC

This is an inquiry into rhetorical dimensions of storytelling as soul-tuning in Valmiki's *Rayamana*. By "rhetorical dimensions," I mean those practices of symbolic exchange and influence that constitute and orchestrate individual and cultural meanings, understandings, actions, identities, and relations. For the purpose of focus in this study, I narrow my definition of these practices to storytelling.

Storytelling is a (if not *the*) primary means by which ancient Hindu culture initiates exchange, whether of goods, ideas, actions, or relations. By "exchange," I do not mean to call forth notions of speech being a transfer of ideas as goods in the most mechanistic, abstract, dyadic kinds of ways.3 Rather, by "exchange" I call forth notions of the gift. Gift exchange is what Marcel Mauss identifies as a total cultural phenomenon. From Mauss's classic anthropological study of archaic gift cultures, a total cultural phenomenon is defined as one that constitutes and orchestrates legal, economic, moral, religious, spiritual, political, interpersonal, epistemological, ontological, and aesthetic dimensions of culture.4 In ancient Hindu culture, speech, in particular storytelling, is such a gift. The god Brahma, the creator himself, gives Valmiki both the story of Rama, as well as the sacred *sloka* verse in which to tell the story (Menon 2001, 6). In exchange for these gifts of story and style, Brahma requests Valmiki to compose the epic of Rama through the sloka meter into the first story of the earth (*Adi Kavya*) (6–7). This story is given (revealed) as a means of bringing ancient Hindu culture into harmony with *dharma,* a notion as old as the Indian tradition, with meanings ranging from divine "duty, work, righteousness, morality, justice, cosmic law and harmony, and eternal truth" (x). This symbolic exchange of speech for divine harmony is a rhetorical phenomenon shaping ancient Hindu culture.

Dharmic speech, though, should not be so quickly rendered "rhetoric." Inquiry into the *Ramayana* as rhetoric requires a disruption of an assimilative orientation comparing and judging what is other to what has been the norm, namely ancient Greek rhetoric. In place of an assimilative orientation must be an aggregate one, so that ancient Hindu rhetoric can be recognized as distinct from yet equal to ancient Greek rhetoric. Such an experience requires a certain figuration of thought and speech, what the classical Greeks called but did not embrace as a rhetorical norm—*parataxis*.[5] An awareness of parataxis emerges from reading ancient epic poetry like the *Ramayana*.[6] Audiences can experience the rhythm of the paratactic speech: the way this speech weaves together ideas without the aid of logical connectors beyond *and,* mixing big stories with small, equalizing the importance of side stories and the central story. Because the rhetoric of the *Ramayana* is itself paratactic, something I will illuminate more fully in the next section of this essay, a paratactic approach to inquiry into this text seems appropriate and fitting. To start, a paratactic approach would inquire into this text as a distinct rhetoric, adjacent to ancient Greek rhetoric, the latter neither assimilating nor subjugating the former, the two being a part of the multiplicity of the unity of what rhetoric can be.

Of course, such an inquiry is a challenge considering the dominance of ancient Greek norms in the study of rhetoric at large. The ancient Greeks offer the language of rhetoric, not only the term *rhetorike* but the philosophical vocabulary for the idea and practice of rhetoric, including the aforementioned *parataxis*. To recognize the Greek norm of rhetoric, though, does not necessitate that all rhetorics be judged through these norms. We can recognize the distinctions and similarities between rhetorics without having to judge one in terms of the other.

Let's consider a prominent dimension of ancient Hindu rhetoric, as distinct from ancient Greek. The ancient Greeks favored argumentation and persuasion about probabilities; the ancient Hindus favored exhortation and didacticism about dharma. Sanctioned speakers in Hindu culture speak the dharma as a way of instructing and teaching others the way of and to the divine. There is no room for probability in dharma. Dharma is dharma, unquestionable and absolute. Yet, the human experience of probability persists. The rhetoric of dharma is designed to halt the weighing of probabilities and to guide experience to the dharmic way. Dharma is spoken, primarily, in deliberative passages, where characters facing a dilemma speak to themselves and others about the dilemma and work to achieve a dharmic resolution.

A dharmic resolution is a decision in the face of a dilemma that recognizes the way of and to the divine. An example from the *Ramayana* will help to illuminate this point.

When Rama is sixteen, the great brahmarishi Viswamitra visits Rama's father, King Dasaratha. Dasaratha, in quintessential gift culture practice, initiates the ritual of guest/host relating by speaking as host, showering Viswamitra with praise, and offering to grant the brahmarishi whatever he wishes. But when Dasaratha hears Viswamitra's request for the young Rama to go kill two rakshasas, Dasaratha regrets having given his word. Dasaratha recognizes his dharma to honor his word, yet, not knowing his son is an avatar, he cannot resolve himself to sending Rama on such a dangerous journey. He is wrought with conflict over his dilemma: either break his word to Viswamitra, or risk his beloved son's life. In his turmoil, he decides to get more information. He goes through a period of questioning Viswamitra about the rakshasas and their reign of terror, searching for a way out of the dilemma. He opts to break his word, with a slight adjustment: he will not send Rama, but he will go in Rama's place.

In response to this negotiation, Viswamitra speaks in a voice like doom announcing Dasaratha's vice: his broken word and his speech filled with empty flattery. To bring Dasaratha into a dharmic resolution, Viswamitra amplifies the poles of Dasaratha's dilemma: "I will return from where I came, and you can live in your fool's paradise, until Ravana arrives at your gates one day. But I say to you, Dasaratha, if you want to tread the path of destiny written in the stars, send Rama with me!" (17).

Dasaratha is driven back into confusion by Viswamitra's speech. Blind with a father's love, he hardly knows what he has done or what he needs to do. He is enveloped with fear of both poles of his dilemma. So his guru Vasishta gives him counsel: Dasaratha should fear only one of the poles of his dilemma, namely breaking his word. He should not fear the other because Rama is not a normal human boy, and clearly Viswamitra makes his request with a wisdom and divine plan beyond what Dasaratha knows. With this culminating counsel, finally "the light of reason dawn[s] on Dasaratha" (17). He announces his resolve to send Rama and asks Viswamitra for forgiveness.

Dasaratha's dharmic resolution is based on a rhetorical feat, namely of exhortative and didactic speech. Three speeches, each with their own way of leading Dasaratha to dharma must be given before he can see and accept the way: 1) Dasaratha's speech to himself on the sacred-ness of having given his word; 2) Viswamitra's speech amplifying the poles of Dasaratha's dilemma, in particular the dharmic pole; and 3) Vashishta's counsel. Dasaratha cannot resist his desire to protect his son when he has only his own recognition of his dharmic obligation to honor his word. Viswamitra must offer an exhortation to ampli-fy the poles of Dasaratha's dilemma and to advise that the dharmic pole is the only choice. Because Viswamitra's exhortation has univer-sal power, the urgency of selecting the dharmic pole has the rhetori-cal tone of necessity. But still, Dasaratha is incapable of accepting his dharma. Visishta must speak, as Dasaratha's guru, to show Dasaratha the way. This speech is didactic, teaching Dasaratha how breaking his word would corrupt destiny, not only the destiny of the Ikshvaku line to remain noble, but of Rama to serve as he is meant to serve in ac-cordance with dharma.

Dasaratha's resolve is brought about by both exhortative and di-dactic rhetoric to urge, advise, teach, and guide him to dharma. Even Dasaratha's own reflections on the sacred gift of his word to Viswami-tra take on an exhortative rhetorical quality, as these reflections urge him to act in accordance with what he knows to be the truth. Where-as Dasaratha attempts to discern probabilities in the face of dharma, dharma refuses such attempts. Rhetoric, then, is employed as a means not to judge and persuade among probabilities, but to advise, teach, and guide one to accept dharma.

This rhetoric is not a lesser rhetoric, or a proto-rhetoric, simply because it operates outside of the Greek norm of probabilistic argu-ment and persuasion. It is, however, a different rhetoric, and difference matters. Inquiry into rhetoric as a human and cultural phenomenon requires a multiple and diverse understanding of its various perfor-mances, the many ways it constitutes and orchestrates meanings, un-derstandings, identities and relations, whether on an individual, inter-personal, or cultural level. Those of us fascinated with rhetoric as a way of studying, better yet imagining, what it can mean to be human must do more than just study the Greeks and their rhetorical theory and practice.[7] And when we study rhetorics beyond the Greeks, we must recognize that while the legacy of the Greeks cannot and should not be abandoned—for their language and theories are not only unavoidable but useful—we must engage this legacy in paratactic style.

The final orienting issue is that of the text. Valmiki's *Ramayana* is an oral, Sanskrit, epic poem that I am reading as a literary, prosaic, English translation. So many differences separate these respective "texts." One is oral, the other written; one is performed, the other read; one is ancient, the other contemporary; one is Sanskrit, the other English; one is verse, the other prose, etc. We do not have a stable text in Valmiki's *Ramayana*. What we have is a tradition. This tradition consists of multiple layers of textualization, from layers upon layers of ancient Sanskrit oral storytelling sung in meter for live audiences, to the multiple translations of these stories into the written word as literature for an audience of readers both within and beyond Hindu culture, to the many diverse performances of the *Ramayana* that range from plays, to dances, temple carvings, comic strips, television shows, and syndicated newspaper columns.

The multiple textualities of the *Ramayana* are elaborated further when we recognize that Valmiki's is just one among many tellings of Rama's story. There exist, in addition to Valmiki's, tellings throughout Southeast Asia, to Sri Lanka, Nepal, Bangladesh, Malaysia, Laos, Vietnam, Thailand, Cambodia, and Indonesia (Menon xiii). Besides Valmiki's, four tellings of the *Ramayana* into other Indian vernacular languages are classics: Kampan's *Iramavatara,* the Tamil Ramayana (twelfth century); the Bengali *Ramayana* of Krittibas Ojha (late fourteenth century); Tulsidas's *Ramacharitmanas* in Hindi (sixteenth century); and Exhutthachan's *Aadhyatman Ramayanam* in Malayalam (sixteenth century) (Menon 2001, xiii).[8] As translator Ramesh Menon comments,

> The epic has come to us through countless generations of gurus and sishyas, masters and disciples, transmitted through the ages in the ancient oral tradition. Since its original composition there have been many interpolations and embellishments by numerous, now nameless, raconteurs—from saints and bards to grandmothers passing the story on to their grandchildren during long summer nights—in many languages and traditions. (xii)

Moreover, each telling of the Rama story relates to particular theological, social, political, regional, performative, and/or gender contexts (Richman 1991, xi). Each telling is ideological, so, for example, in Valmiki's *Ramayana* we encounter the ideology of Brahmin Hindu culture, not all Hindu culture.

The challenges of textuality are many, but embracing paratactically the resources of multiple notions of textuality, we can see that these challenges are not so much problems to overcome, as possibilities. Paula Richman describes the approach used in *Many Ramayanas,* her collaborative project with leading *Ramayana* scholars:

> We accept the idea of many *Ramayanas* and place Valmiki's text within that framework. Some scholars assume, either implicitly or explicitly, that Valmiki has written *the* definitive *Ramayana*. Hence, the diverse non-Valmiki *Ramayanas*—the "other *Ramayanas*"—have often been assessed against that standard, according to their angle of divergence from Valmiki's version. While Valmiki's importance is undeniable, we learn more about the diversity of the *Ramayana* tradition when we abandon the notion of Valmiki as the *Ur*-text from which all the other *Ramayanas* descended. We need instead to consider the "many *Ramayanas*," of which Valmiki's telling is one, Tulsi's another, Kampan's another, the Buddhist *jataka* yet another, and so forth. Like other authors, Valmiki is rooted in a particular social and ideological context. His text represents an intriguing telling, but it is one among many. (1991, 9)

The singular privilege of Valmiki's version is being questioned in indology, as is the privilege of studying the epic from the Sanskrit critical editions. Drawing from the work of noted scholar A. K. Ramanujan, contemporary indology questions the appropriateness of a singular privilege of Sanskrit texts for scholarly work on the ancient Hindu epics (Kaskikallio 1996, 146). Ramanujan writes of the *Mahabharata,* companion epic to the *Ramayana,* "No Hindu ever reads the *Mahabharata* for the first time. And when he does get to read it, he doesn't usually read it in Sanskrit (A. K. Ramanujan, as quoted in Kaskikallio 1996, 146)."

The diversification of *Ramayana* texts points to the resourcefulness of "going local" rather than "universal" when encountering the *Ramayana.* Indian epics as a source of tales or teachings have been

experienced primarily through local language for a long time (146). As
a result, a Sanskrit scholar and a folklorist or anthropologist or rhetorician or average audience might have very different ideas about the
world of Indian epic, and each of these ideas needs to be paratactically
ordered to show the aggregation of ways to experience the epic. The
privilege of scholarly methods defining as the norm, or the original,
the Sanskrit texts of Valmiki's *Ramayana* comes undone in paratactic
style. The *Ramayana* is not so much a "text" as a "tradition," one that
should be entered locally, but recognized as bigger than the local, so
big as to constitute a magnificent array of diverse cultures and ideologies. To experience the *Ramayana* paratactically would be to recognize
the locality of one's entrance, along with the proliferation of possible
entries into the tradition. This proliferation of possibilities creates the
grand paratactic multiplicity in the unity of the *Ramayana* tradition.

So I, too, experience the *Ramayana* tradition locally. This means
using the version of the *Ramayana* most prevalent in my local culture
of western scholarship on the *Ramayana,* namely an English translation of Valmiki's version of Rama's story. The English translation I
use, too, comes from my local culture. The translation I use is the
translation selected by a group of my faculty colleagues for inclusion
in our university's year-long humanities seminar for first-year students: Ramesh Menon (2001), *The Ramayana: A Modern Retelling of
the Great Indian Epic.* I recognize that this translation does not represent the whole of the *Ramayana* tradition, but rather Menon's telling of
various tellings of Valmiki's telling. Menon admits that, though he has
taken few liberties with the story or its sequence as it has come down
in India, his *Ramayana* is not a scholar's translation, but a novelist's recreation of the legend according to Valmiki. His telling does not work
from a Sanskrit text, nor a critical edition, but rather from other English versions (xiv). In using Menon's telling of Valmiki's *Ramayana,* I
do not mean to continue the privilege of Valmiki's version, but only to
enter the *Ramayana* tradition locally, in a paratactic style. In eliminat-
ing hierarchy, parataxis does not eliminate those norms ruling at the
top of the hierarchy, but rather situates these norms alongside other
norms, in an equal, horizontal style. Valmiki's version and Menon's
telling are, for me, not *the Ramayana* but my local entrance into the
tradition.

With these orientations, let's begin our inquiry into the rhetoric
of storytelling and its soul-tuning qualities, including its historical,

reflexive, and paratactic style. Because this inquiry is suggestive rather than exhaustive, I will focus, primarily, on the first book of the *Ramayana*, the *Bala Kanda*. This book will give us insight into the whole of Valmiki's *Ramayana,* as well as offer the most striking example of reflexivity in the poem, namely Valimiki's story of his coming to tell the *Ramayana.*

STORYTELLING AS SOUL-TUNING

Valmiki's *Ramayana* is a repository and memory bank of Hindu culture. It is a history and is categorized as such within the canon of Hindu scripture. Its scriptural category is called *Itihasa,* which literally translates, "so indeed it was," and has meaning ranging from talk, to legend, tradition, history, traditional accounts of former events, and heroic history. *Itihasa* is a sub-category of the *Smriti* scriptures.[10] *Smriti* scriptures are one of two categories of Hindu scripture; the other category is called *Sruti. Sruti* scripture is that which is heard, akin to revelation. *Smriti* is that which is remembered, akin to tradition, not revelation. *Sruti* scripture is constituted by the Vedas. *Smriti* scripture is Post-Vedic. In other words, in Hindu scripture, first the truth is revealed, then the story of the revelation is told. This historical storytelling serves to tune the soul to divine revelation.

The telling, then, is a defining characteristic of Valmiki's *Ramayana.* Indeed, we know this not only from the poem's categorization as *Smriti* scripture, that which is told, but also from its elaborate reflexive stories about storytelling. These stories offer details about the rhetorical situation of storytelling: how the tellers speak, how audiences listen, how hospitality figures the occasion, how content is shaped, and how effects are, in short, soul-tuning.

We know from these reflexive passages, that storytellers are sanctioned speakers for a culture—primarily kings and rishis, as well as messengers. The audiences consist of everyone and everything, from royalty, to commoners, to devas, gods, and rishis, to the stars in the sky, and the jungle, always in the background. The occasions for storytelling arise as part of an elaborate ritual of hospitality, a primary feature of archaic gift cultures. To be a guest was as much of an honor as to be a host, and the occasion of being either set forth an elaborate ritual of gift-exchange, largely orchestrated through speech performances, primarily storytelling. We are told as well that these stories are compositions of the past, designed to make present that which has fallen into oblivion. The effect is a soul-tuning memory of posterity, of all prior descendants and all future generations, that creates an indelible impression on the memory of the human race.

In a string of reflexive passages in the *Bala Kanda,* we are told as much. When Rama arrives at the Kamasrama he is "regaled with stories" by his host (20). In other scenes of host practice, both King Janaka, Sita's father, and Sadananda offer stories to guests as a form of proper hosting. Stories are told to guests by hosts not for entertainment only (but certainly for entertainment), but as a ritual way of creating general relations. These stories are intimate gifts given by the host that will allow guests to know the divine past, and to carry this past, along with the host as storyteller and his people, into future generations. As Sadandanda announces, he will tell the story of Viswamitra's life to his guests "for the sake of posterity" (46).

We are told that stories speak of a long-ago, near forgotten, past. The stories at the Kamasrama, for example, were of times out of mind, of the bygone millennia. Viswamitra's story of the Ganga bore his audience "back to primeval times, dim and magnificent, when sovereigns of unearthly lineage ruled the kingdoms of the earth" (38). By these stories, we are told, audiences are captivated, amazed, and impacted in the most meaningful and awesome ways. During the storytelling at the Kamasrama, "the Stars traversed the sky ever so slowly, for their keenness to eavesdrop on the shining tales" (20). Viswamitra's story of the Ganga, "held princes and rishis in thrall (38)" ; in addition, "Whenever he paused, the others sat with bated breath, lest they disturb his flow of inspiration beside the holy river" (38). We are told, as well, that Viswamitra's audience of kshatriyas and munis sat in silence long after Viswamitra had finished speaking, for they were "claimed by the past," and "they sat unmoving by the mystic river that once fell from their sky, and the whispering of her currents bore them far from themselves" (41–42). And we are told of how the audience listened to Sadanandas's story of Viswamitra: "Twilight fell and the audience didn't stir from their listening to Sadananda. Encouraged by their eager silence, he continued until darkness fell, and lamps were brought out, and it was late when the Brahmana finished his extraordinary tale" (46). The impact of these stories on audiences might be most powerfully expressed in the description of Dasaratha listening to the stories of Rama and Lakshmana upon the return of the boys to Ayodha. Dasaratha is described in terms of a guest at the feast of storytelling. We are told he made the boys tell their stories over and over again, and each time he listened as if the stories were food, drink and air to him (53).

Perhaps the most striking reflexive story on storytelling in the epic is the elaborately detailed story of how the *Ramayana* comes to be told. This story merits a closer look for the meta-rhetoric of its offerings—its illumination of the speaker, audience, occasion, composition, and effects of the telling of Rama's story.

Narada, the God Brahma's son, is sent by his father to visit Valmiki. Upon his arrival, Narada initiates the guest/host ritual of exchange by granting his host, Valmiki, a blessing for his thoughts. Valmiki responds by asking if any man born into the world was blessed with all the virtues. After naming the virtues for Narada—integrity, bravery, righteousness, gratitude, dedication, flawlessness of character, compassion for all the living, learning, skill, beauty, courage, radiance, control over anger and desires, serenity, and lack of envy (4)–Valmiki is granted a blessing from Narada. This blessing, this gift, is the story of Rama, the man who is blessed with all the virtues.

Narada's storytelling begins with a beckoning to Valmiki and his disciples to come close for the story. The audience sits entranced, as heedless of the time that passed as they were of the flowing river. Valmiki sits in the lotus posture with his eyes shut to listen to the tale. Darkness comes, then twilight turns to night, then moonlight to darkness, then darkness to scarlet dawn, all the while he and his disciples sit entranced. Narada tells not of the Ramarajya, when Rama ruled Ayodhya as the world's very heart, but of a time before, during the exile of Rama. Of those years he speaks for their "indelible impression upon the memory of the race of men" (5). When Narada finishes, not a dry eye could be found among his listeners.

Valmiki is so affected by the story that even months after hearing it he continues seeing images of Rama. We come to learn that Brahma is preparing Valmiki to be the first poet of Rama's story. As mentioned earlier, Brahma visits Valmiki and reveals that he blesses his tongue with the sloka verse, and his eyes with the vision to tell the tale: "You will see clearly not only into the prince's life, but into his heart; and Lakshmana's, Sita's, and Ravana's. No secret will be kept from you and not a false word will enter your epic" (6–7). Brahma's gift of speech to Valmiki is so significant that it will carry with it immortality, something Brahma pronounced he was unable to grant to mortals when Ravana asked him for that boon. But, to Valmiki, unlike Ravana, Brahma grants immortality: "As long as Rama is remembered in the world of men, so shall you be. The epic you are going to compose will make you immortal" (7). By creating such memory, storytelling creates Valmiki's immortality. Immortality, like the achievement of nirvana, means that his soul lives on in perfect and everlasting divine harmony.

Valmiki accepts Brahma's gifts (blessings), and sets out to compose the tale of Rama. Elaborate details of his epic composition continue the introduction of the *Bala Kanda*. First, the setting for Valmiki's creativity is described. He sits on the banks of the Tamasa, facing east on a seat of darbha grass, his "mind still as the Manasa lake upon the northern mountain, so the images of Narada's inspiration played on it like sunbeams" (7). The noble words spring in a crystal stream from his heart, as his disciples sit around him, listening breathlessly (7).

We are told his composition takes one week, and eventuates in 24,000 verses. This great composition, which is sometimes what the *Ramayana* is called, comes to him as if he were just an instrument, and the real poet were another, far greater than himself (7). He divides the poem into six books, and five cantos, and names it the *Ramayana* upon completion of "his work of genius" (7). Valmiki's genius is his telling. The revelation is the genius of the gods.

Upon finishing, two handsome young men appear to Valmiki, as twins of heaven, with voices like gandharva minstrels. He teaches them the poem, and they learn it, immediately and perfectly, just as they hear it from the Valmiki's lips. They sing it as Valmiki himself could not, for Brahma had chosen them to tell the story throughout the sacred land. The twins go from asrama to asrama, clad in tree bark and deerskin, their voices matching as one, speaking the *Ramayana* in a stream that flows like another Ganga. Rishis who hear them are enchanted and bless the beautiful boys. The twins eventually sing the poem to a king, who turns out to be Rama, who turns out to be their father.

This elaborately detailed, extensive story about how Rama's story comes to be composed and told helps us to experience the *Ramayana*, not just as a story of Rama, but as a story of storytelling. We are audience to a story about the sanctioned speakers of stories, the enthralled audiences, the guest/host occasion for stories, the content and form of composition, and the overall effects. And of the composition we are given the most elaborate details of what would be known in classical western canons of rhetorical creation and performance: invention, disposition, style, memory, and delivery. Valmiki tells us that storytelling is not so much invented by the speaker as inspired by the divine, that the speaker's agency lies more in shaping the formal rhetorical dimensions than in inventing the story, that the story's composition consists of 24,000 verses organized into six books and five cantos, that its style is a sacred verse and metre placed on Valmiki's tongue by Brahma, and that it is delivered by Rama's twins in perfectly voiced song, from memory created instantly upon the boys' hearing the poem.

The story of the telling of Rama's story offers a meta-rhetoric of storytelling as soul-tuning. Story and style are divine gifts that must be repaid with a great composition, an *Adi Kavya,* and told throughout the lands and generations of people. We know this telling is of the highest importance to the gods, for Brahma repays the telling with immortality, the greatest of all gifts. This telling allows audiences to know and remember the divine past, and to know and remember the model of the man with perfect virtue. The effects of the story make an indelible impression on human memory of divine harmony.

To illuminate further how this memory is rhetorically created, let's consider again the paratactic style of the story. Alongside the telling of Rama's story are told dozens upon dozens of other ancient Hindu stories. These stories are placed at the side of the Rama story, yet no overt logical connections are given. The general introduction of a story other than Rama's begins with a question, such as when Rama asks Viswamitra upon approaching the Kamasrama, "Whose asrama is this?" (20). Rama's question leads Viswamitra to tell the story of the Kamasrama, the sacred land of the rishis made from the ashes of the love Deva Kama when Siva glared open his third eye on her for piercing him with shafts of lust. When Viswamitra finishes the story, no commentary is given, and Rama and Viswamitra enter the asram. Rama's story continues from there. No overt connection between the story of the Kamasrama and Rama's story is articulated. The logic of their relations, or the lesson of the Kamasrama beyond its being an answer to Rama's question, is left unspoken.

In addition to the story of the Kamasrama, the *Bala Kanda* tells the tale of the Rakshasa Tataka, a woman once beautiful cursed for shamelessness by rishi Agastya and turned into a flesh-feasting monster, hated by all the creatures of the earth, void of speech, capable only of making vile noises.[11] The legend of Vamana, too, is told, namely

how his evil rule is ended by a trick played upon him by the dwarf boy
Mahabali, an avatar of Vishnu. The magnificent story of the Ganga,
and how she was brought down to flow upon the earth is told, as well
as the story of the great Viswamitra's kingdom, the myth of Siva's bow,
the story of Sita being discovered as a baby, and the legend of Indra's
thousand phalluses as his punishment for being an adulterer.

The interplay of Rama's story with other stories creates a paratactic
style of storytelling. This style holds multiple related and divergent
things in mind simultaneously, not as one unified entity, but as an aggregate. A paratactic style allows for aggregation, and in turn creates a
cultural memory of general relations.[12] Multiple and divergent things
can be seen as touching. The possibilities of connection proliferate. An
intimacy emerges in the process, a feeling of connection and connect-
edness, a feeling of closeness, and both particular and general awareness of one's situation. This intimacy is a creation of gift exchange and
forges a memory of general relations. Exchange cannot be studied in
isolation as an independent act, and we could learn from the practices
of ancient gift cultures the way in which a general economy of relations
is always at work in exchange. Gifts always bear the traces of others,
hence of the past. When exchange is wrought through the gift, memory proliferates. To consider the general economy of relations at work in
exchange is to consider not just the particular operations of an action,
but the more general economy in which the action is situated (Bataille
19). Cultural memory presupposes a cultural intimacy where elements
on which action is brought to bear are not isolated from the whole of
the world, but are brought into contact with the whole, brought into
presence from oblivion—and a memory is forged of general relations,
not merely of operations, at play in action.

Rama's entering the Kamasrama with Viswamitra is not merely
about Rama's next action that he will take on his dharmic path of
duty. It is about the whole of that space in which the action will take
place, the whole which is brought out from oblivion by the story of
the Deva Kama. We are not told the lesson Rama is to learn from this
story, nor are we told in any overt and stable way how the action Rama
is about to take upon entering the Kamasrama is related to the story,
or how it will—if it will—be shaped by the story. The two stories are
just placed, side by side, equally, in an aggregative, not assimilative,
way. Their touching creates cultural intimacy and memory, and leaves
to the audience the logic(s) and lesson(s) to be learned. In a paratactic

style, Valmiki's tale of Rama is of his actions in their general economy of relations, rather than in their isolation as virtuous acts. The memory forged through such telling is of general relations, not merely operations. Such a memory in an audience comes with great responsibility, to see fully these general relations, to carry them forward, and to allow them to guide one to dharma.

The historical, reflexive, paratactic rhetoric of Valmiki's *Ramayana* offers to audiences the virtues of storytelling, along with the virtues of Rama. This storytelling tunes the soul by creating a cultural memory of general relations, and an indelible impression of revelation on this memory. Yet, storytelling does not eclipse human agency in finding the way to this revelation. The audience must discern the logic(s) and lesson(s) of these general relations and acquire the vision requisite for achieving dharma. Moreover, storytelling is the principal means of symbolic exchange of speech for divine harmony. This exchange is part of the general economy of the gift, and gives rise to the tradition of storytelling as soul-tuning in ancient Hindu culture.

NOTES

1. See Goldman (1984, 1, 23); Parpola (2002, 361); Brockington (1998, 379). The dating of the *Ramayana* is a debatable issue. Goldman makes the case that the old core is dated c. 750–500 BCE, and Brockington makes the case that the old core is dated c. 500–300 BCE.

2. Thus far scholars of rhetoric have done little with ancient Hindu texts including the *Ramayana*. Only Oliver (1971) and Kennedy (1998) make mention of the *Ramayana* in their studies, and both do only that, namely make brief mention of the epic as a significant rhetorical text. Oliver and Kennedy attend more to the *Mahbharata*, just as most Western scholars of rhetoric attend more to the *Iliad* than the *Odyssey*. The *Mahbharata* and the *Iliad* are both epics of war, with ample speeches orchestrating the public and personal spheres in a time of war. The *Mahbharata* speeches offer the protocol of negotiations and diplomacy, and instructions for call to arms, conciliation, subversion of allies, bribery, and punishment. In the *Mahbharata* we also find speeches of lamentation and debate among nobles on political issues.

3. See Peters (1999) for a history of theories problematizing the notion of speech as exchange.

4. For a linguistic study of gift exchange in ancient Hindu culture, see Benveniste (1997).

5. It is worth noting that while the classical Greeks identified this rhetorical style, they did not sanction it for civic speech. Instead, they sanctioned hypotaxis, or vertical thought/speech that structures meaning through overt logical connectors. In sanctioning hypotaxis as the proper style of civic speech (speech that constitutes and orchestrates culture), the classical Greeks were rejecting their archaic epic past, which was styled paratactically.

6. See Lord (1960) for the foundational study of parataxis in oral epic poetry.

7. For critical essays addressing and responding to the need for rhetorical scholarship beyond the Greeks, see Lipson and Binkley (2004).

8. For critical essays on the many *Ramayanas,* see Paula Richman (1991), (1995), (2001).

9 In addition to Richman see also Kaskikallio (1996, 145); Sullivan (1990, 13–21); Doniger (1992, 28).

10. The other text in the category of Smriti scriptures is the *Mahbharata.*

11. Perhaps most striking for rhetorical interests is the punishment of Tataka in the form of removing her speech and replacing it with the vile noises of a monster. Speech is told through this story to be a virtue of beauty, and its absence a condition of the monstrous.

12. I have addressed this issue in other writings: Mifsud (2006), and Mifsud, Sutton, Fox (2005).

Works Cited

Bataille, Georges. *The Accursed Share.* Vol. 1. Trans. Robert Hurley. New York: Zone Books, 1991.

Beneveniste, Emile. "Gift and Exchange in the Indo-European Vocabulary." *The Logic of the Gift.* Ed. Alan Schrift. New York: Routledge, 1997, 33–42.

Brockington, John. *The Sanskrit Epics.* Vol. 12. Handbuch der Orientalistik. Leiden, Netherlands: Brill, 1988.

—."The Textualization of the Sanskrit Epics." *Textualization of Oral Epics.* Ed. Lauri Hanko. Berlin: Mouton de Bruyter, 2000, 193–215.

Doniger, Wendy. "Deconstruction of the Vedic Horselore." *Ritual, State, and History in South Asia: Essays in Honour of J. C. Heesterman.* Ed. A. W. van den Hoek, D. H. A. Kolff, and M. S. Oort. Leiden, Nettherlands: E. J. Brill, 1992. 275–308.

Feyerabend, Paul. *Against Method.* Atlantic Highlands, NJ: Humanities Press, 1975.

Kennedy, George. *Comparative Rhetoric: An Historical and Cross-Cultural Introduction.* New York: Oxford UP, 1998.

Koskikallio, Petteri. "From Classical to Postclassical: Changing Ideologies and Changing Epics in India." *Oral Tradition* 11.1 (1996): 144–53.

Lipson, Carol and Roberta Binkley. *Rhetoric Before and Beyond the Greeks.* Albany: SUNY P, 2004.

Lord, Albert Bates. *Singer of Tales.* Cambridge: Harvard UP, 1960.

Mauss, Marcel. *The Gift: The Form and Reason for Exchange in Archaic Societies.* New York: W. W. Norton, 1990.

Menon, Ramesh. *The Ramayana.* New York: North Point Press, 2001.

Mifsud, Mari Lee. "On Rhetoric as Gift/Giving." *Philosophy and Rhetoric* 39.4 (2006): 89–107.

Mifsud, Mari Lee, Jane S. Sutton, and Lindsey Fox. "Configurations: Encountering Ancient Athenian Spaces of Rhetoric, Democracy, and Woman." *Journal for International Women's Studies.* 7.2 (2005): 36–52.

Oliver, Robert. *Communication and Culture in Ancient India and China.* Syracuse, NY: Syracuse UP, 1971.

Parpola, Asko. "Pandaíe and Sita: On the Historical Background of the Sanskrit Epics." *Journal of the American Oriental Society* 122.2 (2002): 361–73.

Peters, John Durham. *Speaking Into the Air: A History of the Idea of Communication.* Chicago: U of Chicago P, 1999.

Ramanujan, A. K. "Repetition in the *Mahâbhârata.*" *Essays on the Mahâbhârata.* Ed. Arvind Sharma. Leiden, Netherlands: E. J. Brill, 1991. 429–43.

Richman, Paula and Thapar, Romila, eds. *Questioning Ramayanas: A South Asian Tradition.* Berkeley: U of California P, 2001.

Richman, Paula. "Epic and State: Contesting Interpretations of the Ramayana." *Public Culture* 7.3 (1995): 631–54.

—, ed. *Many Ramayanas: The Diversity of a Narrative Tradition in South Asia.* Berkeley: U of California P, 1991.

Sullivan, B. M. *Krsna Dvaipâyana Vyâsa and the Mahâbhârata. A New Interpretation.* Leiden, Netherlands: E. J. Brill, 1990.

10 Argument in Classical Indian Philosophy: The Case of Śankara's Advaita Vedānta

Scott R. Stroud

Ancient and classical India was a vigorous meeting-place of rival philo-sophical/religious systems, including those stemming from the Vedic tradition (varieties of classical Hinduism), those rebelling against this tradition (the varieties of Buddhism and Jainism), and those arriving from the Islamic west. Rival thinkers had to argue for their cases in public forums, as well as in texts that would be read by a relatively wide audience. This intense atmosphere fostered a variety of inter-esting rhetorical tactics for spreading one's *darśana,* or philosophical worldview. Of particular interest to this study is the case of Advaita Vedānta, a classical school of Indian philosophy that reaches its argu-able high-point in the thought of Śankara (b. 788 CE). Śankara trav-eled widely through ancient India, founding centers of learning along the way and debating opponents from many different traditions. What is remarkable is the success that he had in spreading a philosophy that George Thibaut would later describe as "the most important and in-teresting one which has arisen on Indian soil"—one that argued that the world and all the objects that seem to comprise it are ultimately illusory (Thibaut, 1992, xiv).

What is of rhetorical interest is the way that Śankara pushes this rather counter-intuitive doctrine. Unlike common "mystical" stereo-types of eastern thought, Śankara was quite devoted to the methods of making rational arguments and countering objections. There is a point, though, at which Śankara employs a powerful strategy—that of using rhetorical tropes to complete these "rational" arguments that are said to be about knowledge of what is ultimately real. In other words,

240

the challenge centers on how one can argue a point that is beyond language by using linguistic means.[1] Śankara, like other thinkers in the ancient and classical Indian philosophical tradition, answers this challenge by incorporating what can be called *experiential argument*—arguments that evoke and depend on the experience of an auditor in the determination of the argument's truth or reasonableness. Such an approach can be contrasted to abstractly valid and schematized forms of argument that can be said to have a truth value, regardless of a specific audience's attending to them. This study will examine some of the trends of experiential argument in Indian philosophical texts and how they are used to make points that "transcend" language. Elsewhere, I have analyzed two general types of narrative that can be found in Indian philosophical traditions that necessitate audience involvement in their reconstruction, and therefore in confirming their "truth" value (Stroud, 2002a; 2002b; 2004). Here, I am interested in a putatively "philosophical" and argument-based approach that still makes an important use of audience experience in the pushing of a certain point. Thus, I will examine the interesting case of Śankara, who makes much use of reasoned argument to explicate and defend scriptural sources and claims in the Indian tradition. What is interesting, though, is how amidst his use of argument, one finds recurring analogies and examples. Why does he continually appeal to such sources of proof? How do they function in a rhetorical context? What will be argued is that his employment of examples and analogies are used not because they accurately represent the world or *Brahman,* but because they involve the reader or listener in an experience that elucidates the claim that is being made about the nature of a subject's taking an illusion to be real (viz., taking the world of objects to be *Brahman*). Thus, these examples and analogies, as well as a type of first-person address that I will discuss, are vital parts to his message in both form *and* content, since they provide rhetorical means of evoking and instantiating the sort of mindset he wishes to impart upon his hearers.

The Milieu of Indian Philosophical Discourse

A vitally important fact about the Indian philosophical tradition is that virtually all of its major schools base their thought on what has already been given—the scriptures called *śruti* ("what is heard") and the collection of texts called *smrti* ("what is recalled"). The former include the ancient chants and hymns in the four *Vedas,* along with expository texts and the *Upaniṣads*, whereas the latter include texts such as the *Bhagavad Gita*. The unorthodox (*nastika*) schools that did not accept these texts (especially *śruti*) included major traditions in Indian thought such as Buddhism and Jainism. Part of the interesting dynamic that developed in later Indian thought (particularly around Śankara's time) is the debate between *astika* (orthodox) and *nastika* philosophical views. Such a diverse and pluralistic culture is bound to foster tolerance, but it also encourages a discussion among these factions, especially when it comes to garnering support among pupils, followers, or local officials.

While the ancient *Rig Veda* was largely focused on ritualistic practices and their hymns, it began the focusing of the Indian tradition on interactive communication that would reach a crescendo in Śankara's time of classical Indian philosophy. The *Rig Veda*, as Robert Oliver points out, contains "question-and-answer dialogues or discussions" that provide the predecessor for the extended dialogues between individuals in the later *Upaniṣads* (Oliver, 1971, 53). The *Upaniṣads* featured a shift in Indian thinking away from the emphasis of the *Vedas* on ritual action to secure boons in the afterlife, to a more ascetic, monistic view of the self and the world. The Buddhists and Jains complicate this picture later by their own rejection of Vedic methods of pursuing worldly goods for the individual self. Much of this disagreement occurred in the composing of texts focusing on maintaining, educating, and/or gaining adherents, as well as in debates between such expounders of philosophical systems.

By the time of Śankara (b. 788 CE), major patterns of thought in Hinduism proper and contrary traditions such as Buddhism had gathered some inertia. As with many things in Indian intellectual history, however, the prevalence of a wide variety of subjects and stands complicated matters for those who wanted to harmonize and solidify the strands of Indian philosophy stemming from Vedic thought. Śankara was one such thinker, and he fully carried the burden of the term "Vedānta"—literally, the "end of the *Veda*." As Govind Pande puts it, "He reflects that peculiar combination of orthodoxy and radicalism which is characteristic of the truly great reformer," which resulted in his nuanced position interpreting the ritualistic portions of the *Veda* and the nondualistic claims of the *Upaniṣads* (1994, 171). Contra the Buddhists, Śankara tries to maintain that the *Upaniṣads* are correct in their revelation that the self of a person (*Atman*) is the same as the underlying foundation of reality (*Brahman*). Contra Indian philosophers that argued for a separate theistic god, Śankara maintained that, at base, *Brahman* was without division—even from the individual creature. Against schools such as *Mīmāmsa*, Śankara argued that rituals and their performance were not the important aspect to reaching *moksha* (enlightenment or release), but instead that mere knowledge that *Atman* is *Brahman* was sufficient enough to remove the "illusion" of individuation in this world (the ignorance causing such an illusion is called *avidya*). As one commentator puts it,

> Śankara's main aim, which he wishes to fulfill through his critique of rival theories, is neither dialectical nor cosmological; rather, it is, in our opinion, metaphysical in nature. By refuting antagonistic metaphysical systems, Śankara intends to establish such a metaphysical doctrine as can give human beings perfect knowledge and can thereby make them realize the *summum bonum* of their life (i.e., liberation or *Moksha*). (Verma, 1992, 162)

While these other schools employed strategies based in fairly rational argument and methodological textual exegesis, Śankara's texts emphasize a further point while making his case about the metaphysical nature of the world—the importance of the individual being addressed. This will be shown to be directly related to the position he is arguing, namely that the self of the individual *is* the ultimately real self. While I will explore this point in more detail in the remainder of this study, it is important to see how the rhetorical features of his argumentative strategies are related to his conception of the rhetorical situation he was in—that of teacher or guru.

Teaching has a long and interesting history in India, and many of the texts mentioned above (especially the *Upaniśads*) center on the interaction between a guru and student. Even in situations such as public debate, a common spectacle in the time of Śankara, the endgame was still educative—the "loser" of the debate on philosophical matters was often required "to adopt the very doctrines against which he had unsuccessfully argued" (Bader, 2000, 183). This was not the case in every debate, but the stakes were always high, since a guru's reputation and disciples were closely connected to that guru's ability to display in action the fruits of that wisdom. The audience in most cases was composed of royalty, monks, and laypersons, all potential or actual students of patrons of the debating gurus (Solomon, 1978, 833). It is well-known that public debates were widely held and attended as spectacles in ancient and classical India, but specifics about their execution are little known. In some cases, the adjudication of winners seemed to lie with the audience as a whole, whereas in other cases (such as Śankara's supposed debate with Mandana) they were depicted as being adjudicated by one selected judge (Oliver, 1973, 53; Solomon, 1978, 834). Either way, a detailed literature evolved in India concerning the types of arguments one should use in such debates, and such argumentative strategies and formats became evident in written texts (Solomon, 1976, 15). In Śankara's case, it is evident that he engaged in four types of rhetorical activities—teaching, preaching, debating, and writing. The first was addressed to his known disciples who often followed him in his wanderings, whereas the second involved potential disciples—other mendicants or, in some cases, a more common audience. Debating took him into the company of rival gurus, as well as lay audiences of people and royalty. The last sort of activity, writing the various texts attributed to him, often met the requirement that a teacher pass down his teachings to his pupils now and in the near future. These texts often mirrored the dialectical form of a vigorous debate.[2] In all of these cases, one sees Śankara's dedication to pushing one point—that a certain knowledge he had could enlighten the audience, if they could but see it and realize its truth.

Whatever Śankara wrote or discussed was knowingly placed in a context of education of pupils and conversion of disciples, thus adding an important rhetorical dimension to his teachings. The burdens of this situation, of course, are not one-sided. While teachers, such as Śankara, pushed hard for their points, students were expected to be trusting and to stay with their guru until they reach the point of liberation (*moksha*)—the point at which they realize the truth of the guru's teaching and are able to extend that tradition in their own teaching. The teacher was to encourage this by revealing the meaning of scripture, to eliminate ignorance (*avidya*), and to transmit knowledge that was liberating for the pupil. By "liberating," the soteriological goal of Śankara's teaching is implied—the dissipating of the illusion of individuation (viz., the separateness of one's self from other selves), and the pain and suffering it causes. This is what makes teachers like Śankara more than merely philosophers in the Indian tradition; they are spiritual masters, as they articulate positions on issues that directly relate to the achievement of the sort of experience that one ought to desire (viz., liberation) (Cenker, 1983, 45).

Thus, the rhetoric of this period of India, which Śankara exemplifies, can be labeled as not merely oriented toward persuasive ends, but can be seen as an *educative rhetoric*. His point was to educate and enlighten individuals such that they could then educate others in a continuation of the Indian guru-tradition. While Śankara continues the use of reasoned argument in his writings and commentaries on the vital texts of the Hindu tradition, he also employs appeals to experience in ways that other traditions do not. The argument I will make in the following section is that his use of certain rhetorical devices in his argumentative texts is not merely a superfluous "rhetorical" means; instead, the position he is arguing for (viz., nondualism) necessitates such strategies, since these methods provide experiences to his auditors, who are then involved in the confirmation of that position.

CHALLENGES POSED BY SANKARA'S RHETORICAL SITUATION

Śankara faced an interesting challenge during his lifetime in India. The Buddhists were still attacking the reading of Self (*Atman*) that Śankara wished to defend and emphasize from the Upaniṣadic heritage, and other schools loyal to the ancient *śruti* texts still insisted on emphasizing "worldly action." On the one side were the Buddhists with their doctrine of *anatman,* or no-self; on the other side were those that emphasized the fulfillment of ritual obligations by individual selves. The major opponent in this latter category was the *darśana* (school) of *Purvamīmāṃsa*, a tradition of exegesis that emphasized the role of ritual and *dharma* (duty) in proper human action. Śankara, having become a wandering ascetic early in his life, was diametrically opposed to such an emphasis and its presupposition of individuated selves who were the bearers of such duties. Of course, his reading faced not only the challenge of such opponents, but the plain fact that much in the *Vedas* was dedicated to ritual action; even the *smrti* texts such as the *Bhagavad Gita* seemed to favor the path of action over his path of knowledge of *Brahman*. Thus, Śankara was faced with the challenge of how to enunciate his point and defend it in such a way as to distinguish it from the Buddhists, who denied the reality of the self (or soul), and those that over-emphasized the individual ritual and action-based tendencies in the primary texts of the tradition.

Add to this issue the difficulty of the position that Śankara was committed to, and one sees how these various challenges could become increasingly difficult. Śankara was, to a large degree, responsible for breaking the hold on popular thought that Buddhism held in ancient India, as well as in establishing a refined tradition of Vedānta that mirrored the monastic training of the Buddhist community (*sangha*) (Isayeva, 1993, 87–88). In order to do this, though, he had to persuade religious leaders and teachers, as well as the parts of the public and leadership that he preached to. What position was he striving to convey to his audience? The very difficult one that is committed to the following basic points: (1) what is ultimately real is *Brahman,* (2) one's self (*Atman*) is the Self of all (viz., *Brahman*), (3) the world of individuation and change was illusory (viz., not truly real), and (4) knowing the truth about *Brahman* is efficacious in destroying the illusions created by ignorance (*avidya,* also translated as "nescience") of the unitary nature of the real. For Śankara, all the suffering and transmigration associated with life (a common target of effectively all Indian philosophical systems) was caused by a failure to see that all is *Brahman,* including one's self (*Atman*). In Śankara's *Upadeśāhasrī,* he quickly makes this point in the first few verses:

> *Karmans* [as the results of actions, good or bad, in the past existence] produce association with a body. When there is association with a body, pleasant and unpleasant things are inevitable. From these result passion and aversion [and] from them actions . . . [From actions] merit and demerit result [and] from merit and demerit there results an ignorant man's association with a body in the same manner again. Thus this transmigratory existence rolls onward powerfully forever like a wheel. (*Upad* I.1.3–4)[3]

Śankara is not just referring to reincarnation here; his point is the larger one that our continuing identification of the self with the empirical body is the source of all our struggles (and eventual suffering), in this life or the next.

This is a difficult point to argue, of course, primarily due to the fact that most people readily adhere to the belief that they are individuated from other "selves" and that their actions matter. Śankara pushes the path of knowledge (or more precisely, the way of removing

ignorance about the nature of the self) as it does not presuppose action and its individuated constituents—"Only knowledge [of *Brahman*] can destroy ignorance; action cannot [destroy it] since [action]
is not incompatible [with ignorance]. Unless ignorance is destroyed,
passion and aversion will not be destroyed" (*Upad,* I.1.6). Śankara is
clear that action is a vicious circle insofar as it presupposes commitments to doership (viz., that this *individual* self is acting, and that this
action will have a real impact on the nature of that self). Trying to
become enlightened merely gets one deeper into the pool of illusion.
Śankara's self-imposed rhetorical challenge concerns how to argue the
point that all individuation is illusory and that one's *Atman* is the Self
of all (*Brahman*), a point that even impugns the ability of language to
communicate it:

> Nor again is [*Atman*] expressed by words denoting an
> object, by saying [of It] "it is known." *Atman* is never
> taken to be expressible by words or cognizable, accord-
> ing to those who [realize that] *Atman* is only one, free
> from pain and changeless. (*Upad,* I.18.56–57)

How can Śankara argue such a point? He definitely uses what can
be called reason-based argument for much of his work, such as in his
elaborate commentary on the cryptic text, the *Vedānta Sūtras* (also
referred to as the *Brahmasūtra*). What I will examine in the following
section are some ways that he appeals to the experiences of his audience to convey these challenging and counterintuitive claims, thereby
rendering the extreme more palatable.

EXPERIENTIAL ARGUMENT IN SANKARA

While I do not want to make the mistake of claiming that Śankara's
argumentation strategies do not involve the giving and challenging of
reason-based claims, I do want to highlight alternative strategies in
his texts that assume a particular importance in light of the rhetorical
challenges he faces to accepting the above claims. In particular, I will
explore Śankara's use of two rhetorical tactics to convey his claims
about *Atman* and the individual—the use of first-person address and
his appeal to specific analogies and examples. These strategies do not
exhaust all of his rhetorical resources, but they are crucial insofar as
they address something that his other arguments cannot—the evoking
of an experience of a sort of nonduality in the audience.

Before I explore these devices, I want to detail the problem that underlies ignorance or nescience, and which poses the challenge to individuating (or dualistic) uses of language to discuss *Brahman*. The core problem is what Śankara calls "superimposition" (*adhyāsa*). In his *Brahmasūtra Bhāsya*, or commentary on the *Brahmasūtra*, Śankara defines "superimposition" as "an awareness, similar in nature to memory, that arises on a different (foreign) basis as a result of some past experience . . . [it] regards the appearance of one thing as something else."[4] What Śankara is elaborating here is the basis of ignorance—the seeing of the unified, nondivided world (viz., *Brahman*) as individuated into ever-changing parts. The individuation or duality is superimposed on the unity of *Brahman*. Of course, Śankara and later *advaitins* had to deal with the problem of how we superimpose qualities on something (viz., *Atman-Brahman*) that we don't have direct experience of (in the way that we seem to have experience of ordinary objects). What is important here, however, is the fact that this doctrine explains why arguing about *Brahman* is so difficult—language seems to presuppose subject/object dualities, as well as individuation among constituent parts of the world. Thus, saying *"Brahman* is x" is just as bad (unenlightening) as blindly going through life and acting as if one's self is separate from the self of all. Superimposition as a concept diagnoses the problem behind "ignorance" (*avidya*); beyond this, J. G. Suthren Hirst rightly indicates that it shapes Śankara's educational attempts in both content and method. Hirst largely means that Śankara qua guru aims to prevent the superimposition of individuating qualities on *Atman,* and thus designs his pedagogy to eliminate such superimpositions of qualities on the self (Hirst, 2005, 86–87). I would extend this sort of analysis to his rhetorical tactics—how can Śankara talk about the nondual nature of *Atman/Brahman* without thereby individuating it? This will prove to be a key point not only to his educational method, but to his rhetorical practice, since it too was aimed at the enlightenment of pupils.

Nondualistic First-Person Address

Śankara uses a tactic I call *nondualistic first-person address* to a stunning effect in some of his works, particularly the prose portions of the *Upadeśāhasrī.* A vital and recurring sentence in the *Upaniṣads* is *"Tat tvam asi,"* or "Thou art that."[5] This is a "great sentence" (*mahavakya*) that Śankara makes much of in his commentary, since it effects the vedāntic truth that "you" (the one being addressed, the *Atman*) are "that" (*Brahman*, the ultimate reality of the world). This second-person address is still dualistic insofar as it presupposes and furthers an individuation between subject qua speaker and subject qua object of communication (the addressee). Indeed, the endpoint of Śankara's pedagogy even seems to include the nondualistic union of the teacher and pupil (Cenker, 1983, 58), so it is not difficult to imagine that Śankara would wish to move beyond such means of communicating his nondualistic point. He even goes so far as to indicate that all such conceptions of self as used in thought and speech stand as a superimposition on the *Atman*—"Everything seated in the intellect, as well as the bearer of the 'I'-notion, is [a qualifying attribute] of the Witness" (*Upad*, I.18.94). The "Witness consciousness" referred to here is one's actual self—*Atman*—which is always a subject and never an object of knowledge (thereby individuated). The way Śankara transcends this sort of dualism is by adapting a technique implied by another great sentence from the *Upaniṣads*—"*Aham Brahman Asmi*" or "I am Brahman."[6] What will be seen to be unique is how he employs such a first-person claim in a rhetorical fashion, effectively combining the force and meaning of both "I am Brahman" and "Thou are that."

In such texts as the *Upadeśāhasrī*, one sees Śankara's way of arguing the point that the self of the individual (the *Atman*) is the self of all (*Brahman*)—the speaker uses a first-person mode of address, but with a double reference. Simply put, if the speaker's self is the self of the hearer, she only needs to refer to the "I" to cover all involved. For instance, Śankara starts *Upad* I.13 with the following fascinating verses:

> As I am eyeless, I do not see. Likewise, as I am earless, how shall I hear? As I have no organ of speech, I do not speak. As I am mindless, how shall I think? As I am devoid of the life principle, I do not act. Being without intellect, I am not a knower. Therefore I have neither knowledge nor nescience, having the light of Pure Consciousness only. (*Upad*, I.13.1–2)

Obviously, there is some sort of reality to the claim that the human individual "Śankara" has eyes, speaks (or writes), thinks, knows things (as a guru, say), and so forth. This "truth," however, is only a "conventional" sort of truth; like the realities of a dream, it disappears on waking to a higher level of "knowing." The point Śankara is trying to make vis-à-vis the superimposition of qualities on the *Atman* is crucial. *He* does not act, as Śankara's true self is not individuated or on the same level as the world of individuated actors, acts, and projects. From this perspective, it would be a mistake to say "he is ignorant" or "he is knowledgeable," as both of these judgments presuppose (and reify) the superimpositions of individuated qualities on the undivided *Atman/ Brahman*. Indeed, those individuals who take seriously claims about *their* enlightenment or illusion are instantiating the sort of *avidya* Śankara wants to erase—"Through deluded [seeing] all people think, '[I am] deluded,' and again through a pure [seeing] they think, '[I am] pure'; for this reason they continue in transmigratory existence" (*Upad*, I.13.10).

When Śankara uses such tactics as first-person address, there are two sorts of reference being invoked. First, there is the obvious reference to the "person" of Śankara—viz., he is making claims about his own self, psychical state, and so on. Beyond this, however, the reader adds Śankara's statements that one's self is beyond all individuation to this sort of address and can thereby *experience* the other sort of reference—the self of Śankara *is* the self of the hearer. When he indicates that "I am x," he is indicating both (1) that the hearer is also x, and (2) that the hearer is Śankara (qua "I" that is not individuated from other subjects). This is a crucial accomplishment in Śankara's educative rhetoric, as grasping this maneuver means that one *sees* what a nondual sense of self is like; the meanings of "Śankara," "myself," predicates such as "ignorant," and so forth all collapse in the unity of *Atman/Brahman*. This coheres with the importance he puts on hearing in teaching, and takes seriously the claim that "teaching is useful [only] when it is directed to a hearer. If the Overseer is not taken as the hearer, who would be the hearer" (*Upad*, I.18.111)? What is meant by "Overseer" is the *Atman,* or the witnessing consciousness that is always subject and never an object (say, of judgment or perception). By using *nondualistic first-person address,* Śankara can maintain his point of nonduality between the self of one and the selves of others, as well as retain the assertoric force that is essential for his teaching. Only under such a radical system of monism could a claim about "I" be a claim about "you." It is the experience of such a double-reference by the auditor that makes this tactic different from many other ways of arguing assertoric claims, in the Indian tradition or elsewhere.

Experiential Analogies: The Rope-Snake Analogy

A second tactic Śankara employs in his commentaries on the *Upaniṣads* and other texts is the use of analogies. His use of these varies from a mere mention (viz., "like mistaking a rope for a snake . . .") to a more sustained explanatory usage. Either way, I would argue that these are functioning as *experiential analogies,* since they call upon the hearer's experience to foster her own reflective and imaginative engagement with the ideas Śankara is presenting. I will explain this point, but first I will provide an example of one of the two common analogies I will detail—the rope-snake analogy.[7] Quite often, Śankara uses this example of perceptual illusion to make a point about *avidya*—the superimposition of qualities and distinctions upon the unified *Brahman*. One sees a rope on a dimly-lit path and mistakes it for a snake. One *really* reacts to it as if it were a dangerous snake, but these reactions and the perceptions that lead one to the judgment, "this is a snake," disappear once one *knows* it is really a rope. Śankara's explanation is that the qualities relevant to a snake have been superimposed on the object of the rope. Knowledge dissolves this superimposition, however. Thus, Śankara invokes this analogy when talking about the efficacy of knowledge of *Brahman*:

> From this [self-]established [*Atman* which is indicated
> by the word] "I" the attribute "you" is excluded—just
> as the notion of a serpent [is excluded] in application
> to a rope—by means of reasoning and such teachings
> as "Thou art That" and so forth. (*Upad,* I.18.4)

The serpent qualities should not be superimposed on the rope, nor should one react to it as if such were the case; likewise, one should not superimpose individuation on the self (the *Atman*) by cutting it up into objects (the empirical self and the selves of others).

The rope-snake analogy was common among a variety of schools of thought in India, even Śankara's Buddhist opponents (Hirst, 2005, 107–108). This may explain why he often defaults to it—it would have common currency in terms of being understood by audiences and opponents alike. The key part to Śankara's use is his commitment to a pre-existing reality as revealed by the analogy; this is a point to which the Buddhists do not push the same analogy. One may reasonably wonder if either the analogy's meaning is underdetermined, or if one of the parties (say, Advaita Vedānta or their Buddhist opponents) are misusing the analogy. Such a dilemma is only forced, though, if one takes the analogy to be (1) self-standing and (2) a model of the theoretical point being made. If one believes that the analogy has a simple core and can be supplemented in terms of meaning, there is less of a need to adjudicate who is using the perceptual-error analogy "correctly." Additionally, if one takes it in a *rhetorical* sense as opposed to a *theoretical-descriptive* sense, such problems can be avoided. This latter point is crucial and must be explained.

One common criticism among contemporary commentators of Śankara is that the analogies he employs (such as the rope-snake analogy) fail to model the reality he is arguing for. For instance, Karl Potter criticizes the analogy on such terms in a straightforward fashion:

> What becomes free, Brahman or the self? I.e., is the rope in the model analogous to Brahman or to the individual self? We need an analogy which explains a three-way relation—among Brahman, self, and world. How can we use an epistemological model of illusion, which presupposes the existence of a knower and a known, to throw light on the relation among Brahman, a knower, and the known? A more sophisticated analogy seems to be called for. (Potter, 1999, 163)

Potter brings up a valid structural critique of the analogy, if it is to be taken as a representation or model of reality and the *Atman/Brahman* relation. Stephen Kaplan takes Potter's comments quite seriously, noting that "The artifacts employed in these analogies do not provide insight into the nature of Brahman," and thereby pursues the modern analogy of the hologram as a more sophisticated advaitin trope (Kaplan, 2007, 180).

What these critiques miss, however, is the *rhetorical* purpose of such analogies—as devices that evoke a certain experience in the auditors for a specific argumentative purpose. I classify the rope-snake analogy as an *experiential analogy* because it not only elucidates one thing in relation to some relevant structural or content-based similarity in another thing, it does so by evoking a certain experience that has persuasive value. This claim needs justification, but such an account should not be too far removed from Śankara's general approach to philosophical argument. Even Potter notes that "Śamkara, like the Buddha, apparently was more interested in teaching his pupils to overcome ignorance than in discovering the proper account of the relation between Brahman, the self or selves, and the world" (Potter, 1999, 165). If such analogies could be used not to model the world, but instead in a melioristic employment—namely, evoking an experience in order to affect an educative change in the auditor—then rhetorical sense can be made of Śankara's continual reference to analogies such as the rope-snake.

This seems to be an unhelpful way to take such analogies, a path toward which western commentators often incline. In such a reading, these analogies are taken as a way of illustrating a modeling relationship. This is the way that Potter and Kaplan approach Śankara's analogies—as supposedly *describing* the nature of the world, the self, and so forth. These commentators seem to assume an intellectual or conceptual purpose behind the analogies that use everyday situations (viz., mistaking a rope for a snake), and they then proceed to criticize the specific analogy in question on the grounds that it does not hold much epistemic value in elucidating the nature of *Brahman* and *Atman*. Instead of beginning with an assumption that such analogies are used in a *descriptive* fashion, I would submit that they are better seen as employed in a *reconstructive* or *melioristic* fashion. The latter type of employment is what is captured in Śankara's *rhetorical employment* of the rope-snake analogy. I would argue for the following points in his use of such *experiential analogies:* (1) they play a vital role in Śankara's overall argument, (2) the experience of thinking through the analogized matter in relation to the argumentative claim expands knowledge, (3) the reason they expand knowledge of some subject matter is that they evoke auditor activity, and (4) this activity is an instantiation of the key thrust of Śankara's argument against superimposition.

The clue to the value of Śankara's use of analogies is to consider what his pedagogical goal is, and how the experience of "thinking through" these analogies connects to that. If their goal is not to accurately *model* the world, what do they do? Eliot Deutsch argues that "Advaitic literature is replete with analogies and with elaborate analyses of them. They function not so much as a means of *convincing* one in any shallow rationalistic sense but as a means of *awakening* one to new possibilities of experience" (Deutsch, 1973, 94). I would extend this sort of analysis by arguing that they awaken through evoking a familiar experience in imagination that is then linked to a novel point. Śankara acknowledges at one point that illustrations and analogies are not identical in all details to the phenomena described, but they are similar in *some* aspects.[8] The key point, in Śankara's case, is the act of superimposition of qualities on something and their subsequent elimination. In the case of the rope-snake analogy, the auditor imaginatively sees what it would be like to remove the superimposed qualities of snakes from the harmless rope, and then see it and act toward it accordingly. The snake that one reacted to, in a very real sense, has *disappeared*. In the case of *Atman/Brahman,* one starts in the midst of illusion—"Even before knowing Brahman, everybody, being Brahman, is really always identical with all, but ignorance superimposes on him the idea that he is not Brahman and not all."[9] The way around this is not by positing something specific about *Brahman* that is the case; instead, it lies in the method of "superimposition and its refutation,"[10] or the removal of qualities that one has overlaid on the truly real. The analogy of the rope-snake is so powerful precisely because it highlights what it is like to remove superimpositions, not because it actually tells us something positive or concrete about *Brahman.* Instead, it *shows* us something about the experience of superimposition and its removal.

Śankara discusses the efficacy of knowledge of *Brahman* and its lack of connection to *producing* anything; in his commentary to the *Bṛhadāraṇyaka Upaniṣad* (I.iv.10), he notes that "This knowledge has never been observed either directly to remove some characteristic of a thing or to create one. But everywhere it is seen to remove ignorance" (Madhavananda, 2004, 102). What is this ignorance? The mistaken belief that these individuated objects (including one's postulated ego or self) are truly *real.* The use of perceptual illusion analogies (viz., the rope-snake analogy) is integrally linked in Śankara's argument with the metaphysical notion of *Brahman.* One can see this linkage, as well as the point of the *experience of removing ignorant beliefs about what is real* in the following passage from Śankara's commentary on the *Brahmasūtra* (III.ii.21):

> Both of these objects [viz., the "act of knowing Brahman" and "the act of sublating the universe"] will be fulfilled from the very instruction that Brahman that is free from the universe of manifestations is one's Self. For from the very revelation of the nature of the rope, mistaken as a snake, follows the knowledge of its real nature, as also the removal of the manifestation

of snake etc. on it brought about by superimposition through ignorance. (Gambhirananda, 1965, 621)

Notice that Śankara wants to claim little about Brahman besides its *not* being individuated and divided as is the world of ordinary sense. The act of negating these superimpositions is explicitly like the realization of the rope instead of the snake, not in content, but in experiential quality—both involve the individual removing what was formerly taken to be real. This is the path of negation, and it is one that Śankara is keen to push; in his commentary on the *Brhadāranyaka Upanisad* (IV.iv.20), he notes this tendency of scripture to negate qualities supposedly of *Brahman,* and asks:

> When everything is the Self, what should one see, . . . know, and through what?—and not by resorting to the usual function of a sentence in which something is described by means of names. Therefore even in the scriptures the Self is not presented like heaven or Mount Meru, for instance, for it is the very Self of those that present it. A presentation by someone has for its object something to be presented, and this is possible only when there is difference. (Madhavananda, 2004, 518)

Ultimately, Śankara maintains that the best way to think of *Brahman* is without any qualifying characteristics (viz., as *nirguna Brahman*). As in the cases noted previously where he utilizes the "I" with a double-reference, here we see such analogies as the rope-snake gain rhetorical power because they focus attention not on any specific quality predicated of *Atman/Brahman,* but instead because they focus attention on the *process* of negating superimposed qualities of any sort. One cannot talk about *Brahman,* perhaps, but one can talk in such a way as to evoke the experience of what it is like to *remove* false talk about *Brahman.*

At this point, one can note a divergence in emphasis in how Śankara's story could proceed. His emphasis of all being *Brahman* could lead one to deny the illusion of the individuated world, or it could lead one to deny the *psychological importance* of that world. I prefer the latter reading, since it does appear that Śankara is more concerned in his teaching and rhetorical practice with *reorienting* the individual's approach to this world of seemingly diverse and individuated phenomena than with "winning" a certain ontological claim. It is the individual's *ori-entation* that is targeted—what the individual thinks is truly real and what is of value. This is what Deutsch captures in his concept of "sub-ration," which he describes as "the mental process whereby one disval-ues some previously appraised object or content of consciousness be-cause of its being contradicted by a new experience" (Deutsch , 1973, 15). In this case, the "new" experience would be the one provoked by Śankara's argumentative employment of the analogy. His Indian audi-ence presumably has had previous experience with snakes, as well as with perceptual error (perhaps even such error in identifying snakes); what is novel is his *combination* of this sort of experience with his radi-cal claim about the ultimate unity of *Brahman.* The new experience is the experience of seeing the act of superimposition and its negation in both the old instance and the new (viz., in seeing *Brahman* without qualities).

If all goes according to Śankara's purposes, this experience will result in the individual *subrating* the beliefs she has about the indi-viduated world; such a world does not disappear, but the individual is radically and psychologically reoriented toward it. Śankara emphasizes just such an orientational point in his commentary on *Brahmasūtra* III.ii.21:

> What is meant by this sublation of the universe of mani-festations? Is the world to be annihilated like the destruc-tion of the solidity of *ghee* by contact with fire; or is it that the world of name and form, created in Brahman by nescience like many moons created in the moon by the eye-disease called *timira,* has to be destroyed through knowledge? (Gambhirananda, 1965, 620)

Śankara answers this question with the surprising answer of "no." Why? He indicates that such an extirpation of the existent would be too difficult for one person, and that the task would be complete upon the enlightenment of the first individual. What seems to be his point is that *psychologically,* knowledge dawns when the individual reori-ents herself to what exists and what value it has; this reorientation, for Śankara, is comprised of the act of knowing *Brahman,* or the act of removing superimposed qualities that comprise the state of igno-rance (*avidya*). The rope-snake analogy is powerful precisely because it evokes a subjective, psychological experience of just this sort of re-orientation.

Possibility-Instantiating Examples:
The Dreamless Sleep Example

Śankara commonly employs another tactic, which I will refer to as the dreamless sleep example. Many commentators find this example problematic in a similar way to the rope-snake analogy. I will argue, however, that it serves an important rhetorical purpose in being a *possibility-instantiating example*—an example that calls upon an experience or evokes an experience in an audience to demonstrate the possibility of some state. In Śankara's case, he will call upon various states of human ontology (including sleep states) to show the possibility of realizing nondual states of being (viz., knowledge of *Atman/Brahman*). In various places, Śankara analyzes the states of human being into four states—the states of waking (*jāgrat*), dreaming (*svapna*), dreamless or deep sleep (*susupti*), and pure consciousness (*turīya*). The latter state is the pure instantiation of *Atman/Brahman* without limiting qualities, whereas the previous three are held to be states most individuals have experienced in everyday life. The rhetorical employment of this division of types of experience is simple—Śankara uses it to *show* us what enlightenment is like with its lack of duality and subject/object separation. A characteristic evocation of this division occurs in the *Upad*, where he claims that "Sense-perception should be known as the waking state, memory as the dreaming state, the absence of both as the state of deep sleep, and one's own *Atman* as the highest state" (*Upad*, I.17.24). The key point to this strategy is that the first two states (waking and dreaming) imply a separation between objects. In the first case, it is objects of sense experience; in the second, it is remembered objects of sense experience. Thus, one has certain "experiences" in life concerning her car; in a dream, such a subject may imagine owning and driving a car she has only seen in action movies. Both cases involve a certain relation between an object and a subject, and in Śankara's scheme, both would involve a sort of fundamental superimposition of individuating qualities on *Atman/Brahman*. The third state, dreamless or deep sleep, is a key part of this argument as it shows that one has experienced a state of being that is close to that of the (enlightened) fourth state—a state with no objects, no subjects, and no activity driven by ideas and desires. One remembers the blissful night's sleep not because of her experiencing it as a subject (as she would remember a vivid dream and its "objects"), but instead as a period of nonduality in the midst of individuated waking and dreaming states. Śankara is assuming that his audience has had such a deep, dreamless sleep, but the source of this argument's power is evident—it draws on an instantiated state that individuals have likely had, and this state is used as a pointer toward the non-intuitive endpoint of Śankara's nondual system.

Śankara uses this series of states that most have experienced in another way as well. Dreamless sleep is not merely used to show the possibility of a state of nondual experience; it is also used in an argument to show the unreality of the waking world—it is a result of superimposition of non-necessary qualities upon *Atman/Brahman*. This is part of his overall strategy to show the world of individuated objects and subjects to be an illusion, an ontological state between something that is real and something that is unreal. As in the rope-snake analogy, the key point about an illusion is that under certain conditions, it will disappear. For Śankara, the conditions under which the world and its enticements will be subrated deal with knowledge of *Atman/Brahman*. In reference to the dreamless sleep example, he argues that the objects and individuation in the dream state *and* waking state are conditionally real:

> Both of them are adventitious [and] not your nature. If [they] were your nature [they] would be self-established and continuous like your nature, which is Pure Consciousnesses. Moreover, the dreaming and waking states are not your nature, for [they] depart [from you] like clothes and so on. It is certainly not experienced that the nature of anything, whatever it may be, departs from it. But the dreaming and waking states depart from the state of Pure Consciousness-only. (*Upad*, II.2.89)

Much is built into this argument that could be objected to, foremost of which is the criterion of the real—that which can never be contradicted. This connects to the standard *advaitin* criterion of the unreal or false—that which can be contradicted or shown to be something else. The problem for Śankara with the dream state is that upon waking, its objects, actions, and accomplishments are shown to be unreal. Nothing was really seen, nothing was really done. The waking state sublates the supposed reality of the dream state by showing its objects and subjects to be of a lesser status than what one took them at in the dream itself. This much is agreeable to most individuals. The difficult point comes in his next move—that the waking state, with all its objects, subjects, and individuation, is also shown to be ultimately unreal because it is sublated by the experience of nonduality in deep or dreamless sleep. This shows that the fundamental quality of individuation is not an essential part of our experience (viz., part of "your nature"). Śankara makes this point in such verses as "Everything comes from nescience. This world is unreal for it is seen by one who has nescience and is not perceived in the state of deep sleep" (*Upad,* I.17.20). One remembers that time as nondual, thus putting the ultimate reality of dualistic experience of waking life into question, much like the reality of one's dreams are put into question upon waking.

This major argumentative resource is drawn upon in many of Śankara's works, and I cannot analyze all of its dimensions here. What I would like to highlight, though, is how it functions rhetorically. It is an *experiential* argument insofar as it draws on common experiences that the audience could be expected to have, and insofar as it calls upon them to imaginatively evoke and reflect upon such experiences upon attending to Śankara's argument. As was the case with the rope-snake analogy, the argumentative force of the dreamless sleep example is often missed by commentators who view it as an airtight "proof" of some vedāntic point. For instance, Charles Hartshorne objects to Śankara's dream-based arguments against realism because "It is simply false that the real physical world we all share is entirely absent from our dreams" (Hartshorne , 1989, 100). He takes Śankara's argument to be incorrect insofar as our dreams and the "real world" of waking states interpenetrate—noises in the room will affect our dreams, and our dreams will affect our bodily states in an observable fashion. Of course, what is left out of his account is the part that Śankara finds so important—the third state of dreamless sleep. This is what furnishes the experiential "proof" that convinces one to view the waking state as one views the dream state after waking.

Of course, one could object that what one is remembering is false—one actually had dreams but simply doesn't remember them upon waking, and thus judges that night of sleep to be "dreamless." This is an epistemological objection to Śankara's dreamless sleep example, and is similar to the arguments against his position given by H. S. Prasad. Prasad writes that Śankara asserts his claims about the sleep state and the deep sleep state "on the basis of *a priori* arguments, scriptural statements, and empirical analogues which are all guided by metaphysical and religious presuppositions." This leads Prasad to claim that they are "epistemologically and empirically impossible to establish" (Prasad, 2000, 66). As was the case in the rope-snake analogy, one who thinks of this device as a logical *proof* of some descriptive point about the world will be disappointed. If one sees the dreamless sleep example as a rhetorical device and as an experiential argument, then one can see how and why it operates Śankara's writings. It calls upon the auditor to remember a supposed case in her experience that comes close to this state that Śankara is describing. This is important not because it proves that this state exists, but insofar as it makes the unreal and far-flung seem possible—in other words, insofar as it ameliorates or improves how one orients herself toward the world. In addressing his audiences that subscribe to some sort of individuation, this tactic is powerful since it shows that a common experience of sleep without dreams is closely related to this goal of enlightenment—it shows that non-individuated experience could be possible, and thus individuated experience may not be the ultimately reality it was taken to be.

Whether or not one was dreaming and failed to remember it upon Śankara's request is beside the point; in the act of imaginatively evoking one's memory of such a state, one sees the sort of experience Śankara is discussing. Śankara then can integrate these two experiences in relation to the goal of enlightenment:

> He who, in the waking state, like a man in the state of deep sleep, does not see duality, though [actually] seeing, because of his nonduality, and similarly he who, though [in fact] acting, is actionless—he [only] is the knower of Atman, and nobody else. (*Upad*, I.10.13)

Once one sees that the existence of a state of nondual being is not impossible, one can then begin to understand and accept the point Śankara pushes in terms of being enlightened here in this world. Like one sleeping in a dreamless state, one could appear to be individuated, yet not really be experiencing a world of objects and subjects. Likewise, one who appears to be going through this world of subjects and objects may not really be experiencing such a world of individuation—this would be the enlightened individual. Śankara's point in using the dreamless sleep example is not so much to apodictically prove a certain claim about the world; indeed, he calls the examples at one point "merely verbal handles," and that the "triad, namely, the state of deep sleep, etc. are unreal" (*Upad*, I.17.65). This is necessary, of course, insofar as his position on what is ultimately real is a nondualistic *Atman/Brahman*.

This educative point of such examples can be missed by commentators focused on descriptive issues. A similar oversight is noted by William Kirkwood (1985) in his analysis of how commentators take religious stories and examples. Kirkwood highlights the tendency in many interpreters to demean the epistemic value of everyday examples (such as the use of stories in religious texts), and to privilege the use of rarified metaphors. For instance, he claims such interpreters conceive of examples as expendable, as merely reinforcing existing knowledge, and as not involving cognitive activity on the part of the audience. In other words, the tendency is to take examples as not doing any important or unique work in argument. Metaphors, supposedly being much more removed from the everyday (compared to parables), are said to hold the opposite qualities. Yet, as Kirkwood perceptively illustrates with religious parables, simple examples can expand one's knowledge—specifically in regard to what Kirkwood calls an "exemplar of states of awareness" (1985, 431). His point is that the experience of such a story by an attending auditor instantiates a certain state of mind, which then has educative value. This is rhetorical insofar as it is guided by a rhetor, directed at some sort of audience, and has some persuasive or educative end that is desired.

In a similar fashion, one must not be too quick to criticize the dreamless sleep example for failing in a theoretical or descriptive employment. One comes closer to Śankara's educative purposes when one sees the example as an exemplar of what it is like to experience the world in a nondual fashion—just as one sees the difference when imaginatively recounting the states of being connected with waking life, dreaming, and dreamless sleep. Like many of Śankara's arguments, this description of various states of waking and sleeping life is really used as an educational tool to enlighten his audience, and to encourage them to subrate or devalue the world of individuation to the world of *Atman/Brahman*. The dreamless sleep example serves this rhetorical purpose by proving *to an audience* that his nondual position fits the experiences of their supposedly individuated lives, as well as the imaginative activities they could undertake now in remembering instances of dreamless sleep. It thereby illustrates that such an endpoint is not completely removed from the audience's range of actual or possible experiences, an important rhetorical accomplishment for Śankara's philosophical project. Whereas the rope-snake analogy gave the audience an experience of what it is like to remove superimpositions, the dreamless sleep example experientially illustrates the possibility of nondual experience. Both of these are vital moves in securing the educative ends that Śankara has in relation to his audiences, and both function in a reorienting fashion to the activities and objects that one has previously taken to be real and really of value.

CONCLUSION

It is safe to say that not all of Śankara's argumentative efforts utilize such experiential arguments. It is defendable to claim that his use of such experiential methods holds an important role in his rhetorical strategy, precisely because his ultimate point seems to be less of a theory of the world to be accepted and more of an individual reorientation toward the real. One must never forget the point that much of Śankara's writings were directed at tearing down rival systems (Potter, 1999, 165), and that he left little of a positive system that was free from paradoxes and conflicts that his later disciples would struggle to explain and elaborate. Perhaps Śankara's point was not to leave any such complete, positive system, but to show what he claims at a variety of points—that *Atman/Brahman* is beyond words, and that our task is to remove the concretized qualities we have added to it. Such a task is largely psychological, but if Śankara is right, the psychological *is* the cosmological. At any rate, his frequent use of analogies and examples can be seen as ways of evoking experience, a point I have discussed in regard to the rope-snake analogy and dreamless sleep example. His manipulation of pronouns (such as the "I" of speaker and hearer) is another way to bring this counterintuitive claim of monism into discursive reality. All of these bring the point of Śankara's system closer to the lived experience of his audience, both in their recollected past and in the imaginative experiences his arguments evoke in the present. It seems that part of Śankara's continuing intrigue and power to captivate rests partially in his unique position, as well as in the unique ways he chooses to convey that position. If he is correct, the content and method of his "system" may be integrally fused and indivisible, just as the realization of one's true nature *is* the realization that one was unified with *Brahman* and the world all along.

NOTES

1. This is not a challenge faced only by the Indian tradition—the Japanese Zen tradition also sought ways around issues with the conceptualization of self and enlightenment through such devices as *kōans*. For more on how *kōans* can be used in such a fashion, see Stroud (2006).

2. For more on Śankara's rhetorical activities, see Pande (1994, 99–100); Hirst (2005, 16). For more on the general rhetorical activities of ancient India, see Kennedy (1998).

3. From the *Upadeśāhasrī*, translated in Sengaku Mayeda (1992). I will cite the *Upadeśāhasrī* by "*Upad*" and book, chapter, and verse number. The bracketed insertions are Mayeda's additions.

4. As stated in his introduction to the *Brahmasūtra Bhāsya*, in Gambhirananda (1965, 2).

5. For instance, see *Chāndogya Upanisad* Chapter 6, translated by Gambhirananda (1997).

6. *Brhadāranyaka Upanisad* I.iv. 10, in Madhavananda (2004, 100).

7. Śankara uses a bevy of other analogies, as well, such as ones involving crystals appearing a certain color, ones referring to foam and waves, magicians and illusions, mirages of water, space and jars, magnetism, and the ever-popular analogy of waking states, dreaming states, and deep sleep states. For more on these analogies, see Potter (1999, 164–65).

8. III.ii.20, *Brahmasūtra Bhāsya of Shankaracharya* in Gamghirananda (1965, 616).

9. Sankara's commentary on *Brhadāranyaka Upanisad* I.iv.10, in Madhavananda (2004, 102).

10. Sankara's commentary on *Bhagavad Gita* 13.13, in Gahbhirananda (2000, 532).

WORKS CITED

Bader, Jonathan. *Conquest of the Four Quarters: Traditional Accounts of the Life of Śankara.* Delhi: Aditya Prakashan, 2000.

Cenkner, William. *A Tradition of Teachers: Śankara and the Jagadgurus Today.* Delhi: Motilal Banarsidass Publishers, 1983.

Deutsch, Eliot. *Advaita Vedānta: A Philosophical Reconstruction.* Honolulu: U of Hawaii P, 1973.

Gambhirananda, Swami, trans. *Brahmasūtra Bhāsya of Shankaracharya.* Calcutta: Advaita Ashrama, 1965.

—, trans. *Chāndogya Upanisad.* Calcutta: Advaita Ashrama, 1997.

—, trans. *Bhagavat-Gita with the Commentary of Śankarācārya.* Calcutta: Advaita Ashrama, 2000.

Hartshorne, Charles. "Śankara, Nāgārjuna, and Fa Tsang, with some West-
  ern Analogues." *Interpreting across Boundaries: New Essays in Comparative
  Philosophy.* Ed. Gerald Larson & Eliot Deutsch. Delhi: Motilal Banarsi-
  dass, 1989.
Hirst, J. G. Suthren. *Śamkara's Advaita Vedānta: A Way of Teaching.* London:
  Routledge, 2005.
Isayeva, Natalia. *Shankara and Indian Philosophy.* Albany: SUNY P, 1993.
Kaplan, Stephen. "*Vidyā* and *Avidyā:* Simultaneous and Coterminous?—A
  Holographic Model to Illuminate the Advaita Debate." *Philosophy East &
  West* 57 (2007): 178–203.
Kennedy, George A. (1998). *Comparative Rhetoric: An Historical and Cross-
  Cultural Introduction.* New York: Oxford UP, 1998.
Kirkwood, William G. "Parables as Metaphors and Examples." *Quarterly
  Journal of Speech* 71 (1985): 422–40.
Madhavananda, Swami, trans. *The Brhadāranyaka Upanisad with the Com-
  mentary of Sri Śankarācārya.* Calcutta: Advaita Ashrama, 2004.
Mayeda, Sengaku, trans. *A Thousand Teachings: The Upadeśāhasrī of San-
  kara.* Albany: SUNY P, 1992.
Oliver, Robert T. *Communication and Culture in Ancient India and China.*
  Syracuse, NY: Syracuse UP, 1971.
Pande, Govind Chandra. *Life and Thought of Śankarācārya.* Delhi: Motilal
  Banarsidass Publishers, 1994.
Potter, Karl H. *Presuppositions of India's Philosophies.* Delhi: Motilal Banar-
  sidass, 1999.
Prasad, H. S. "Dreamless Sleep and Soul: A Controversy between Vedānta
  and Buddhism." *Asian Philosophy* 10 (2000): 61–73.
Solomon, Esther A. *Indian Dialectics: Methods of Philosophical Discussion,* vol.
  1. Ahmedabad, India: B.J. Institute of Learning and Research, 1976.
—. *Indian Dialectics: Methods of Philosophical Discussion.* Vol 2. Ahmedabad,
  India: B. J. Institute of Learning and Research, 1978.
Stroud, Scott R. "Multivalent Narratives: Extending the Narrative Paradigm
  with Insights from Ancient Indian Philosophical Texts." *Western Journal
  of Communication* 66 (2002): 369–93.
—."Multivalent Narratives and Indian Philosophical Argument: Insights
  from the *Bhagavad Gītā.*" *Journal of Indian Philosophy & Religion* 7
  (2002): 45-78.
—."Narrative as Argument in Indian Philosophy: The *Astāvakra Gītā* as
  Multivalent Narrative." *Philosophy and Rhetoric* 37 (2004): 42–71.
—."How to Do Things with Art." *Southern Journal of Philosophy* 44 (2006):
  341-64.
Thibaut, George, trans. *Vedanta-Sutras, with the Commentary by Śankarācārya.*
  Part 1. Delhi: Motilal Banarsidas, 1992.
Verma, Satya Pal. *Role of Reason in Śānkara Vedānta.* Delhi: Parimal Publica-
  tions, 1992.

An Ancient Western Non-Greek
Rhetoric: Ancient Ireland

11 Orality, Magic, and Myth in Ancient Irish Rhetoric

Richard Johnson-Sheehan

Ancient Irish culture provides us an interesting opportunity to explore a rhetoric that was European but not significantly influenced by Greco-Roman culture and rhetorical practices. Unlike most Europeans, the Irish were able to keep Roman culture at arm's length until the fifth century CE, and Ireland was not conquered until England's Henry II subjugated the island in 1172 CE. This isolation kept Roman influences to a minimum, while giving the Celtic Irish the ability to preserve and practice their own unique civic rituals and forms of rhetoric. Perhaps even more intriguing, though, is that the ancient Irish may have preserved elements of an even older Celtic rhetoric that existed before the arrival of Roman legions and, later, Roman Catholic clergy.

In Irish mythology and literature, we find ample evidence that a distinctive rhetoric was practiced in Ireland and Celtic Europe. One of our most important clues is that the Celts and the Celtic Irish included a god of eloquence, poetry, and rhetoric, named Ogma, in their trinity of major gods. Ogma was described by the second-century Greek satirist, Lucian of Samsota, in the following way: "he draws a willing crowd of people, fastened to him by slender golden chains, the ends of which pass through his tongue" (Scherman 1981, 35). Meanwhile, Irish legends and sagas consistently feature the predominant role of speech, poetry, and symbol-usage in the lives of the ancient Irish. In Celtic Ireland, oral and symbolic forms of language were a means for wielding power, especially magical power, and for passing along cultural norms and practices. Druids—ancient Celtic priests—and bards were masters of poetry, rhetoric, and magic, occupying similar roles in Irish culture as did poets and early sophists in ancient Greece. Moreover, in Irish mythology, gods and heroes are honored as much for their eloquence with language as their dexterity in battle. In one notable example, any warrior who wished to join the Irish hero Finn and his entourage would need to first be "versed in the Twelve Books of Poetry, and . . . versed in the rime and metre of the masters of Gaelic poesy" (Rolleston 1990, 264).

Studying ancient Irish rhetoric offers us a window into an ancient European rhetoric that differs from the Greco-Roman tradition we find in the works of Plato, Aristotle, Cicero, and Augustine. Though there are notable parallels between ancient Irish rhetoric and the rhetorical elements found in the Homeric poems of pre-literate Greece, these parallels are most likely due to material conditions of an oral culture and not due to influences of the Greeks on Irish culture. In this article, my aim is to offer a brief introduction to Irish mythology, highlighting some of the major rhetorical elements and themes. I will then begin to reconstruct the narrative-based, oral rhetoric that might have existed in Ireland and perhaps Celtic Europe before the arrival of Roman culture and Roman Catholicism.

Sources: Cycles of Irish Mythology

Traditionally, the ancient Irish canon of mythology has been divided into four *cycles,* or collections of stories. The cycles are chronological and they retain many of the same gods and themes. Each cycle features a different cast of human characters, and each is set in a different province of Ireland:

- The *Mythological Cycle* includes a disparate collection of myths and legends, beginning with Irish creation myths and ending with the arrival of the Milesian Celts in about the seventh century BCE. Stories in this cycle tend to be set in the provinces of Leinster or Meath in central-eastern Ireland.
- The *Ultonian Cycle* centers on the reign of King Conor mac Nessa of the northern province of Ulster in about the first century CE. Featured prominently in this cycle are Ulster's champion, Cuchulain, and his adversary, Queen Maeve, from the western province of Connacht.
- The *Ossianic Cycle* features the exploits and adventures of the Irish king Finn mac Cumhal and his circle of champions. These stories are set in the provinces of Munster and Leinster in the

third century CE, and they are similar in character and spirit to Britain's Arthurian legends. However, the stories of Finn and his entourage are unique to the Irish and do not show crossover with stories of Arthur, which are also Celtic in origin.

- The *Historical Cycle* is a broad collection of histories, romances, and fairy tales that do not fit into the other three cycles. The Historical Cycle lacks the organizing center found in the other three cycles; however, this cycle does, importantly, include legends from other provinces of Ireland.

The sources for these stories are twofold. First, an assortment of medieval codices have survived, which provide a significant collection of stories. Second, in the nineteenth century, the poet William Butler Yeats and his contemporaries carefully collected oral versions of Irish stories as they were told in the countryside. Their efforts added many stories to the Irish canon, while filling out and adding coherence to medieval versions.

Scholars have tended to give primacy to the surviving medieval manuscripts in which these stories survived. The oldest existing text in Irish is the *Book of Armagh,* which dates to the year 812 and contains stories involving St. Patrick. The medieval texts that contain Irish legends and mythology include the *Lebor na hUidre* (c. 1100), the *Book of Leinster* (c. 1150), the *Lebor Gabála Érenn* (twelfth century), the *Yellow Book of Lecan* (1391 and 1401), and the *Cath Maige Tuired* (sixteenth century). The narratives recounted in these books were almost certainly transcribed from earlier medieval texts; however, these manuscripts are the ones that have survived. Unfortunately, the vast majority of ancient Irish texts did not survive history's tragic fires, floods, and destructive invasions by the Vikings, Normans, and English.

The nineteenth-century versions collected by Yeats and his contemporaries do not have the historical ethos of medieval codices, but they are equally important to a study of ancient Irish rhetoric. In the nineteenth century, as the Irish people regained and reclaimed their identity after centuries of English domination, Irish poets and mythologists began collecting myths, histories, and legends told in the countryside. Prominent among these collectors were Yeats, Lady Gregory, Ella Young, T.W. Rolleston, and Jeremiah Curtin. With some alarm, Yeats and his contemporaries realized that Irish myths, oral histories, and fairy tales were at risk of being lost as Ireland modernized and became more literate and urban. Besides adding new stories to the Irish canon, their efforts allowed mythologists to fill out and clarify the versions of the stories found in medieval texts. These important nineteenth-century renditions are far more poetic and vibrant than are the medieval versions, most likely because they reflect the full oral versions of the tales. Meanwhile, the reputations of Yeats and Lady Gregory heighten the gravitas and standing of these nineteenth-century versions. Today, most books that are published on Irish mythology are reprints of these nineteenth-century texts or retellings of the stories found in them.

When researching Irish mythology and rhetoric, it is tempting to give automatic primacy to the medieval manuscripts; however, some important limitations of these texts should be kept in mind. First, it is almost certain that the stories in these books are not the complete oral versions and do not accurately reflect how the stories would have been told in ancient Ireland. These medieval versions were probably synopses of the stories written down by court scribes, or perhaps they were plot outlines that apprentice bards would use to help them memorize the stories. Apprentice bards, after all had so much to learn. The *Book of Leinster* lists out all the kinds of stories that a bard would need to know:

> Of the qualification of the poet in stories and deeds, here follows to be related to kings and chiefs: Seven times fifty stories—five times fifty prime stories, and twice fifty secondary stories—and these are the Prime Stories: Destructions and Preyings, and Courtships and Battles and Caves and Navigations and Tragedies and Expeditions and Conflagrations. (Slavin 2005, 28)

The *Book of Leinster* also includes a seventh-century list of the titles of 187 prime stories that any bard would need to know. So plot outlines would have been very helpful to an apprentice, if available.

My point is that these medieval codices do not contain full renderings of the stories. Bards would have memorized these brief versions and then extemporaneously filled out the stories in front of their audiences (Gantz 1981, 19). A major Irish legend probably took several evenings to recite. Since bards were travelers who told stories for room and board, it would be a hungry and homeless bard who stuck to the brief versions we find in medieval texts.

A second limitation of the medieval texts involves the fact that scribes and monks, not poets or bards, were probably the persons who wrote down the versions found in medieval manuscripts. Court scribes or monks were likely commissioned to feverishly scribble down the stories as they were told at a banquet or at a village festival. Or perhaps a bard visited the monastery and told stories for the monks to copy. Granted, the surviving medieval versions are entertaining and beautifully composed, but they are not the works of master storytellers or poets (Gantz 1981, 19). Instead, they seem to be shorthand versions written by scribes or monks, who likely reconstructed them from notes and their own understandings of the stories. For this reason, as graceful as these medieval versions are, they lack the full force and color of the oral versions. We can, however, witness the full force and color in the nineteenth-century versions of the stories.

Third, the medieval texts offer only particular versions of each story, not *the* version of the story. Many versions of the stories circulated, and there was never a single version from which others derived. In our post-printing press era, we tend to assume that a primordial text existed from which other versions were taken. In ancient manuscripts, however, the versions that survive are simply that—the ones that survived. Other written versions existed that did not survive, and even more oral versions perished with the bards who sang them.

Thus, I believe we cannot restrict ourselves to medieval sources when researching ancient Irish rhetoric. Without a doubt, the surviving medieval manuscripts are vitally important to the reconstruction of an ancient Irish rhetoric, but the nineteenth-century sources and even contemporary sources are also vitally important. A skeptic might point out that the ancient stories have evolved over the centuries, having been shaped to suit Christian themes, but one could also point out that such evolution occurred also before and during the Middle Ages. The medieval versions are not *the* originals to which we can turn for the "true" or originating accounts of these stories. Instead, they are brief versions passed down from previous generations. The stories from the nineteenth century—and even the stories as they are told now in Ireland—hold importance for our study.

Therefore, since our goal is to look for elements of rhetoric in ancient Irish myths, we should avoid getting caught up in debates about the exact meanings of specific phrases or dialogue in medieval texts. Research in ancient rhetorics occasionally requires a scholar to blur close vision to see the larger patterns and themes at the core of these stories. In the case of ancient Irish rhetoric, sources from the Middle Ages and nineteenth century can complement each other to reveal and bring important rhetorical patterns and themes to the surface.

ORALITY, RHETORIC, AND ANCIENT IRISH CULTURE

Before recounting two archetypal stories that are among the best-known legends in the Irish canon, I want to preface these works by forecasting some of their rhetorical features. That way, readers can be aware of these rhetorical features as they occur. Many of these features are likely due to the material conditions of an oral culture. Other features, which I will discuss after the recounting of these two legends, seem distinctive to the ancient Irish.

In an oral culture like that of the ancient Irish, rhetoric would have had a different civic role and purpose than the rhetorics we are familiar with in Western literate cultures: where rhetoric tends to be overtly persuasive. The aim of a speaker or writer is to "see the available means of persuasion," as Aristotle states in his definition of rhetoric (Kennedy 1991). Once the available means have been identified, the rhetor can then use artistic and inartistic proofs to invent an argument that is designed to win over the audience.

The purpose of rhetoric in a pre-literate culture such as that of ancient Ireland, would have been quite different. As Kennedy suggests,"*Traditional* rhetoric is rhetorical practice as found in traditional cultures that do not use writing and have been relatively untouched by western civilization . . . rhetoric in traditional societies is primarily a means of attaining consensus. . ." (1997, 4). Specifically, persuasion would have been less direct, relying primarily on the repetition of familiar narratives to reinforce core values and beliefs. In other words, storytelling in oral cultures was essential to transmitting and preserving cultural norms, values, and civic practices. In *Comparative Rhetoric,* Kennedy explains this function of oral rhetoric when he states, "Both in chiefdoms and in egalitarian societies, public speaking serves to establish and renew social ranking within the society and to reinforce traditional values" (64).

The characters we meet in ancient Irish stories do argue and they occasionally try to persuade one another, as do the characters in the Homeric poems of pre-literate Greece. However, as I will show in the stories themselves, their primary intent at these moments is the restoration of consensus or the reinforcement of traditional values. The characters use repetition and formulaic speech to coax other characters back into consensus. In situations where consensus cannot be restored, the characters typically resort to magic or violence to restore the natural order as the ancient Irish would have perceived it.

On a larger scale, the repetition of stories was crucial to building consensus in pre-literate Irish society, much as it was in ancient Greek culture. In an oral culture, as Ong argues, repetition and redundancy would have been vital to the preservation of knowledge and values (1982, 78). Words themselves were transitory in nature and immediate to the rhetorical situation in which they were used. Knowledge and values that were not repeated over and over would be lost (Havelock 1963, 91–93). As Ong writes,

> in an oral culture, to think through something in non-formulaic, non-patterned, non-mnemonic terms, even if it were possible, would be a waste of time, for such thought, once worked through, could never be recovered with any effectiveness, as it could be with the aid of writing. (35)

The orators in Irish society responsible for repetition of stories and redundancy of themes were the bards and druids who traveled widely throughout Ireland, telling stories, reciting poetry, and singing songs. As entertainment, these stories, poems, and songs were the nectar that attracted audiences to the bards' and druids' performances, but the cultural narratives and common themes at the core of these stories would have had a pollinating effect on Irish society. In these legends, we observe how narrative can be used in an indirect way to build consensus in an oral culture.

So what distinguishes ancient Irish rhetoric from other oral rhetorics? Such distinguishing qualities mostly involve the civic practices and the values that the stories repeat. Repetition and redundancy did more than help the bard remember how to tell the story. They also helped instruct the audience and reinforce common Irish beliefs, values, and practices. For this reason, we find a specific set of beliefs and values repeated over and over in these stories.

Historian Thomas Cahill argues that four core values dominate much of Irish storytelling and mythology: courage, loyalty, generosity, and beauty (94). Dialogues in ancient Irish stories predictably and routinely pivot on issues involving these values. When characters are shown to embody these qualities, they are triumphant in word and deed. However, when they contravene any of the core values, they are inevitably defeated or disgraced. In ancient Irish rhetoric, I believe, these core values were similar to common *topoi* in Greek rhetoric. They are places from which characters speak and maneuver. For this reason, we find them repeated over and over throughout the Irish canon of stories.

Two Archetypal Narratives

Many stories could be used to illustrate ancient Irish rhetorical practices, but I will recount two of the best known. The first legend, popularly called "The Coming of the Milesian Celts," is from the Mythological Cycle and it offers a mythic account of the Celts' arrival in Ireland. The second story is the *Táin Bó Cúalgne,* which describes a battle between the Irish province of Connacht and the province of Ulster. Set in the Ulster Cycle, the *Táin* is the most famous and revered Irish tale. After relating these two stories, I will highlight and explain their rhetorical elements, showing how a broad sense of Irish rhetoric can be developed from disparate rhetorical elements.

The Coming of the Milesian Celts

The first story describes the arrival of the Milesian Celts in Ireland. "The Coming of the Milesian Celts," recounted in the *Lebor Gabála Érenn,* is set around 700 BCE. The saga implies a singular invasion of Ireland by the Celts, but historians and archeologists believe the migration of the Celts occurred gradually over a few centuries, possibly beginning in 1000 BCE (Ó Corrain 1989, 1–3). More than likely, the Celt colonizers of Ireland came from a variety of European homelands, including Britain, France, and Spain. The Milesian Celts were likely one tribe of Celtic colonizers, but in "The Coming of the Milesian Celts," they are featured as the sole and original Celtic conquerors of Ireland.

The story begins with Ith, the leader of the Milesian Celts. On a clear winter day in northern Spain, Ith comes down from the Tower of Breogan and begins talking excitedly about a mysterious green shore he had glimpsed to the north. Ith is determined to explore this new land as soon as possible. So, he gathers up ninety of his best warriors and they set sail.

The Milesian Celts arrive in Ireland at an opportune time. The current inhabitants of the island are the Danaans, a race of people with magical powers. Neit, the king of the Danaans, has just been slain in a battle with the Fomorians, an ogre-like race of cruel, evil giants. With the Fomorians finally defeated, Neit's three sons, Mac-Cuill, MacCecht, and MacGrene, hold a conference to decide how to divide up the kingdom, but their negotiations devolve into quarrels. So, when Ith and his warriors arrive, the Danaan kings decide to ask him, as an impartial judge, to mediate their claims and help them decide upon the partitioning.

According to the legend as told in the *Lebor Gabála Érenn*, "Ith surpassed the judges of Ireland in cunning (*amainse*) and in argument (*thachra*); and he settled every matter and every dispute that was before them" (1956, 17). Then, at a concluding event, Ith brings the process to a close by offering a speech in which he expresses his awe and veneration of the Danaans' fertile green land. He urges the brothers to live in peace. He says, "It is right for you to maintain good brotherhood; it is fitting for you to be of good disposition. Good is your island, plenteous its honey, its harvest, and its wheat, its fish and its corn. Moderate is it in heat and in cold. Within is all that ye need" (17). With his work complete, Ith then leaves to return to his ship and sail back to Spain. While listening to Ith's speech, however, the Danaan kings begin to wonder whether these visiting Celts might not be so harmless after all. So, the Danaan kings send troops to pursue and kill Ith in cold blood before he can reach his ship. Ith's warriors retrieve his body and set sail back to their homeland in Spain, their minds set on vengeance.

In Spain, the Celts muster a force commanded by thirty-six chieftains, and they sail back to Ireland. At this point, a Celtic druid and poet named Amergin takes a leading role in the saga. In the *Lebor Gabála Érenn*, the word used to describe Amergin is *filé*, which is a word commonly used for poets, bards, and druids. In Celtic culture, poetry was a form of magic, and Amergin takes on the role of a powerful user of magic in this tale.

As the Celtic invasion force draws near Ireland, the Danaans see the Celts' ships on the horizon and rush down to the shores to fend them off. The Danaans are not strong militarily, but they are a magical people. So, they use their magic to enshroud the island in mist and clouds. They whip up the winds. But these artifices only serve to slow the landing of the Celts, who ultimately come ashore further up the coast. As the Celts land on Irish shores, Amergin takes over as the leader of the invasion force. He and a landing party march inland. While advancing, they separately meet and "had colloquy" with each of the three Danaan queens of Ireland: Banba, Fotla, and Eriu. Recognizing the superiority of the Celts, each queen requests that her name be used as a name for Ireland after it is conquered. Amergin grants the requests and lets them go. The third queen, Eriu, then pronounces a prophecy: "Long have soothsayers had knowledge of your coming. Yours shall be this island forever; and to the east of the world there shall not be a better island. No race shall there be, more numerous than yours" (35).

The Celts finally reach Tara (also called Teamhair), which is the traditional seat of power in Ireland, set in the north-central part of the island. Even before the Celts arrived, Tara had long been a power center in Ireland. The Hill of Tara still contains the ruins of a large oval fort that was built in the Iron Age (approximately the eighth century BCE) and a passage tomb at Tara dating to 2500 BCE. Irish "high kings" traditionally ruled from Tara before and after the arrival of the Celts, and St. Patrick eventually used Tara as his base of power, building his first major church on this site.

When the Celts arrive in Tara, both sides of the conflict seem to recognize that the Celtic invaders will have the upper hand in a battle. The Bronze Age Celts are technologically further advanced and more battle-hardened than are the Danaans. So, Amergin gives the Danaan kings an ultimatum. He demands that they immediately relinquish their rule over Ireland and live peacefully with the Celts. The loss of their kingdoms by capitulation or battle, Amergin argues, would compensate the Celts for the unprovoked murder of Ith.

The Danaan kings, as one might expect, are not pleased with the offer. So they decide to stall by asking Amergin to give them three days to muster their forces. Amergin grants this request, fully intending to take the land fairly through right of battle. Amergin and his landing party return to their ships to prepare for armed conflict. He orders the fleet to draw back "nine waves from the shore."

At this point, the accounts of what happened diverge. In one account, the Danaans launch a surprise magic attack on the Celtic fleet, using spells to enshroud the ships in mist and conjuring up a vicious storm that scatters the fleet on the ocean. They also call up demons to block the harbors. In another account, Amergin seems to challenge the Danaans to a duel. He agrees with the Danaan kings that if they have enough magical power to impede the fleet from landing again, then the Celts would sail away and never return. But if the Celts are able to come ashore, Amergin states, they would be the new masters of Ireland.[1]

The legitimacy of their invasion and occupation of Ireland seems to have been an important issue for the Celts. In the first account, the Celts give the Danaans a fair chance to muster their forces, but the deceitful Danaans decide instead to employ underhanded tactics and subterfuge. In the other account, the invasion is presented as a trial by combat in which the odds are equalized—Danaan magic and monsters versus Celtic technology and brute force. Both accounts seem designed to legitimize the taking of the island by portraying the Celts as a people destined to inhabit Ireland.

The Danaan's magic storm wreaks havoc on the Celtic fleet, scattering their ships on the ocean with significant loss of life. Several chieftains and five of Amergin's own brothers are killed in the storm, leaving him only two brothers alive. Eventually, Amergin uses his own poetry to counter the storm, chanting the following spell:

> I seek the land of Ireland,
> Coursed be the fruitful sea,
> Fruitful the ranked highland,
> Ranked the showery wood,
> Showery the river of cataracts,
> Of cataracts the lake of pools,
> Of pools the hill of a well,
> Of a well, of a people of assemblies,
> Of assemblies the kind of Temair;
> Temair, hill of peoples,
> Peoples of the Sons of Míl,
> Of Míl of ships, of barks;
> The high ship Eriu,
> Eriu lofty, very green,
> An incantation very cunning,[2]
> The great cunning of the wives of Bres,
> Of Bres, of the wives of Buainge,
> The mighty lady Eriu,

> Erimón harried her,
> Ir, Eber sought for her—
> I seek the land of Ireland (*Lebor,* 117).

As Amergin finishes the poem, the winds fall and the ocean grows still. Perhaps most interesting though, is that the spell itself is an interesting blending praise for and connection to nature, the Milesian Celts, and even the Danaans. Amergin says at the beginning and end, "I seek the land of Ireland," thus expressing the purpose of the spell. Then, as he recites the poem, he weaves together land and peoples. The immediate purpose of the spell is to calm the seas, but its larger purpose seems to legitimize the taking of Ireland by the Celts. Amergin seems to be notifying nature itself that he and the Celts "seek the land of Ireland." Therefore, if it is the Celts' destiny to have Ireland, he seems to say, then nature itself should cooperate in their conquest. Ultimately, Amergin's spell seems to put into action the prophecy of Eriu, the Danaan queen they met earlier.

The scattered Celtic fleet regroups and approaches the coast. Stepping first onto shore, Amergin then chants the Rann, which is one of the most important poems in the Irish canon:

> I am the Wind that blows over the sea,
> I am the Wave of the Ocean,
> I am the Murmur of the billows,
> I am the Ox of Seven Combats,
> I am the Vulture upon the rock,
> I am the Ray of the Sun,
> I am the Fairest of Plants,
> I am the Wild Boar in valor,
> I am the Salmon in the Water,
> I am the Lake in the plain,
> I am the Craft of the artificer
> I am the Word of Science,
> I am the Spear-point that gives battle,
> I am the god that creates in the head of man the fire of
>   thought,
> Who is it that enlightens the assembly upon the mountain,
>   if not I?
> Who telleth the ages of the moon, if not I?

Who showeth the place where the sun goes to rest, if not I?
(De Jubainville translation, reprinted in Rolleston 1990,
134).

The Rann gives us a sense of what it meant to be a poet or druid
(*filé*) in ancient Ireland. It also gives us a sense of the rhetorical power
of magic in this culture. On its surface, line by line, the meaning of
the Rann is not obvious. But when taken as a whole, as the mytholo-
gist Rolleston points out, we sense a blurring of the boundaries that
separate nature from humanity from gods (1990, 134). These three
elements unite to give Amergin, acting as a *filé*, an amalgam of natural
power and god-like knowledge. The chanted rhythm of the text, with
the emphasis on the repeated "I am," blends his own power as a human
with that of nature and God. The spell becomes the point of the spear
that the Celts will use to invade Ireland and defeat the Danaans. Its
rhetorical power seems intended to remake the natural order, realign-
ing the relationships of nature and god and the people of Ireland.

The battle between the Celts and the Danaans commences soon
afterward at Tailltin. The Danaans find themselves overwhelmed by
the strength and superior weaponry of the Celts. Moreover, the Celts
are fueled by their desire to avenge the death of Ith. All three Danaan
kings are killed in combat or by plague, depending on the version of
the legend. Soon, the Tuatha de Danaan, or "people of Danaan," realize that they have lost Ireland. They are forced to withdraw and cede
Ireland to the Celts.

Interestingly, though the Danaans decide to withdraw, they do not
leave the land completely. Instead, they use their magical powers to
make themselves and their homes invisible. They take up residence in
the spiritual realm of Ireland. This otherworld, called the *Síde* (pronounced "shee"), is not a form of heaven but rather a parallel existence to reality. Living in the Síde, the Danaans inhabit faery mounds,
ruins, hills, and valleys, and continue their existence hidden among
the Celts. In other Irish tales, they reveal themselves for purposes of
mischief, love, or to impart knowledge to craftspeople or druids. The
Danaans are the faeries, sprites, and leprechauns who are the principal
characters in Irish fairy tales. Also, curiously, the original Celtic gods
brought over from Europe are referred to as Danaans in many Irish
tales.

The Táin Bó Cúalgne

The most famous Irish legend is the *Táin Bó Cúalgne* from the Ulster Cycle, set in about 100 CE. The oldest version of the story is found in the *Lebor na hUidre,* which is also popularly called the *Book of Dun Cow.* Other versions from medieval texts have been used to fill out the one found in *Lebor na hUidre.*

The *Táin* introduces us to two archetypal Irish characters, Cuchulain and Queen Maeve, who represent the masculine and feminine ideals of power (Bitel 1996, 214). Cuchulain is a great warrior, speaker, poet, and musician. He is sexually promiscuous, quick to violence, vicious in battle, and he occasionally falls victim to his passions. Queen Maeve is a multifaceted character who is as beautiful and ruthless as Cuchulain. She commands her armies deftly and uses her own sexuality to great effect. Maeve is the most prominent female character in Irish mythology, which hosts a unique assemblage of complex, powerful, and independent women.

The *Táin* begins, interestingly enough, in the bedroom of Queen Maeve and her husband King Ailell. In the "pillowtalk scene," Maeve and Aillel begin discussing something that would be familiar to most married couples. Here is how Lady Gregory presents their conversation:

> "It is what I am thinking," said Ailell, "it is a true saying, 'Good is the wife of a good man.'" "A true saying indeed," said Maeve, "but why do you bring it to mind at this time?" "I bring it to mind now because you are better today than the day I married you." "I was good before I ever had to do with you." (1970, 141)

Maeve's sneer in that last line is palpable. Clearly irritated, she goes on to point out that before marriage, she was the ruler of the western Irish kingdom of Connacht, which she inherited from her father: "I was the best and the one that was thought most of. As to dividing gifts and giving counsel, I was the best of them, and as to battle feats and arms and fighting, I was the best of them" (141). Her ire growing, Maeve reminds Ailell that she refused many offers of marriage before his:

> "For it was not a common marriage portion would have satisfied me, the same as is asked by other women of Ireland," she said; "but it is what I asked as a mar-

riage portion, a man without stinginess, without jeal-
ousy, without fear. For it would not be fitting for me
to be with a man that would be close-handed, for my
own hand is open in wage-paying and in free-giving;
and it would be a reproach of my husband, I to be a
better wage-payer than himself. And it would not be
fitting for me to be with a man that would be cowardly, for I myself go into struggles and fights and battles
and gain the victory; and it would be a reproach to my
husband, his wife to be braver than himself. And it
would not be fitting for me to be with a husband that
would be jealous, for I was never without one man
being with me in the shadow of another." (142)

In Maeve's list of desired characteristics for herself and her husband, we see the four key core values of Irish culture: generosity, courage, loyalty, and desirability (Cahill 1995, 94). Maeve points out that
she chose Ailell because he was the kind of man she sought, and also
that her wedding gifts provided him much of what he owns now.

Ailell, now feeling insulted, puffs himself up and reminds her that
he was the third son of the king of Leinster and Tara. He claims he
would have been king of those kingdoms if he didn't have two older
brothers. (Irish audiences would likely have seen such a statement as
humorous, because he was so far removed from the kingship.) He
claims he owned more than Maeve before marriage, and still owns
more than her now.

To resolve the quarrel, Maeve proposes that they tally up all their
possessions to see who owns more. When Ailell agrees, they begin
bringing forward all their possessions, from servants to cups to jewelry
to horses and sheep. (No doubt, this scene in the *Táin* is meant to be
funny, as the two of them haul out all their stuff.) In every way, however, they find that they are equal in wealth. Soon, though, as they
continue to parade out all their possessions, Maeve realizes that Aillel
possesses one thing that she cannot match. He owns a great white-
horned bull that was born in Maeve's herd but that she had allowed to
go over to Ailell's herd when it was uncontrollable in hers.

Maeve is beside herself at the possibility of losing the argument, so
she asks her advisors if they know of a bull that will better Aillel's. One
of her advisors tells her about a bull in Cuailgne, in the province of
Ulster, that is twice as good as Aillel's bull. So, Maeve sends a delega-

tion to negotiate borrowing the bull for a year. The delegation offers
the owner of the bull, a chieftain named Daire, a large amount of land
and many head of cattle as interest for the loan. Very pleased with the
offer, Daire agrees to lend the bull.

Later that evening, Maeve's delegation dines at Daire's house. As
they wait, they begin talking among themselves about the loan of the
bull. Daire's steward overhears them saying that Maeve was planning
to take the bull by force if Daire did not lend it, so it was wise of him
to agree to the loan. When the steward passes this information along
to Daire, he becomes angry, deciding not to loan the bull after all. He
sends the delegation back to Connacht empty-handed. Having failed
in their mission, the delegation returns to Maeve with the bad news.
She is not surprised: "They did not intend to let us get the bull at all;
but now we will take him from them by force" (Gregory 1970, 144).

The *Táin* then turns abruptly from light humor to grave serious-
ness. To invade Ulster and capture the bull, Maeve assembles a large
army from the western kingdom of Connacht and calls up her allies
in the south-central kingdom of Leinster. Meanwhile, the overking of
Ulster, Conor mac Nessa, hears of Maeve's plans to invade his kingdom and he begins to collect his own troops to defend against the
invasion. However, Maeve's army is superior to the army of Ulster,
primarily because the men of Ulster are under a curse that makes them
groggy and lethargic. Conor mac Nessa has an equalizer, though—his
17-year-old champion, Cuchulain. Though young, Cuchulain is portrayed as the ideal Irish hero, shown to be generous, courageous, loyal,
and beautiful. Cuchulain agrees to delay Maeve's army until the men
of Ulster are released from their curse.

Besides being a relentless warrior and an eloquent speaker, Cuchulain also has the ability to use magical symbols to slow the march of
Maeve's army. In one scene, he braids an oak sapling into a circle. Then
he uses Ogham, an ancient Irish form of writing named after Ogma,
the god of eloquence, to carve an explanation of how he made the circle
into the braided sapling. Doing so, he places a *geiss* on Maeve's army
until one of them could match the feat. A *geiss* (pronounced 'gaysh'; pl.
geise or *gessa*, pronounced 'gaysha') is a spell or magical sanction that
cannot be violated without great misfortune (Rolleston 1990, 164). In
Irish legends, *geise*—often in the form of written symbols—are commonly used by druids or bards to hinder or restrain warriors. They are
sacred obligations that others must obey or suffer misfortune. Eventu-

ally, Fergus, who is Maeve's main military advisor and a former mentor to Cuchulain, is able to match the feat and break the *geiss*.

Cuchulain uses a variety of *geise* and tricks to keep Maeve's army at bay. His antics kill off many of her soldiers, but Cuchulain grows exhausted by his single-handed struggle against Maeve's army. Seeing that he is tiring, Maeve asks him to meet with her, and she tries to persuade him over to her side. As they negotiate, Maeve and Cuchulain "chant a lay" (*doringni laíd*), a two-sided poem set in four-line stanzas that is usually agonistic in tone. Here is a translation of Maeve and Cuchulain's lay from the *Book of Leinster* version of the *Táin* (Maeve begins and Cuchulain, in italics, responds):

> O Cú Chulainn renowned in song, ward off from us your sling. Your fierce famed fighting has overcome us and confused us.
>
> *O Medb from Múr mac Mágach, I am no inglorious coward. As long as I live I shall not yield to you the driving of the herd of Cúailnge.*
>
> If you would accept from us, O triumphant Hound of Cúailnge, half your cows and half your womenfolk, you will get them from us through fear of you.
>
> *Since I, by virtue of those I have slain, am the veteran who guards Ulster, I shall accept no terms until I am given every milch cow, every woman of the Gael.*
>
> Too greatly do you boast, after slaughtering our nobles that we should keep guard on the best of our steeds, the best of our possessions, all because of one man.
>
> *O daughter of Eochu Find Fáil, I am no good in such a contention. Though I am a warrior—clear omen!— my counsels are few.*
>
> No reproach to you is what you say, many-retinued son of Deichtere. The terms are such as will bring fame to you, O triumphant Cú Chulainn. (*Táin* 1967, 177–8; italics added)

In this lay, Maeve's attempts to flatter and bribe Cuchulain are not persuasive. His loyalty to his kingdom cannot be undermined or bought off.

The lay illustrates the work of rhetorical practice in this oral culture. The lay itself is, as Kennedy would point out, a form of "formal deliberation" (64), which Kennedy describes as requiring "the use of special etiquette, designated seats by social rank, traditional rhetorical topics, and a special style of language and delivery" (1997, 64). Kennedy points out that "The primary and explicit function of both formal and informal meetings in traditional societies is to achieve group consensus on some important issue" (64). The recitation of the lay, as part of the bard's telling of the mythical narrative, serves to bring the bard's audience to consensus on the cultural issues involved, primarily loyalty and courage.

In this lay, we see both Maeve and Cuchulain appealing to consensus on ways to proceed to resolve the situation. Maeve, who has disrupted the status quo with her attack on Ulster, turns to flattery and bribery, promising Cuchulain a new social order in which he is wealthy, famed, and essentially made king of Ulster. Cuchulain reminds Maeve of his duty as a warrior and his loyalty to his people. Specifically, Maeve argues that Cuchulain should reach consensus with her in the leadership of Ulster, while Cuchulain seems to be reminding her that consensus can only be reached through loyalty to his kingdom. Since Maeve and Cuchulain cannot reach consensus, they return to violence and magic to resolve their differences.

Eventually, Maeve's lieutenant Fergus chants a lay with Cuchulain that persuades his former apprentice to meet one champion per day in single combat. Cuchulain agrees on the condition that Maeve's army can only march toward Ulster as long as the daily champion stays alive. When Cuchulain defeats the day's champion, Maeve's army must stop, set up camp, and stay put until the next day. Each day's melee is highlighted by conversations between Cuchulain and the champion sent against him. Each conversation stresses the core Irish values—particularly of courage, generosity, and loyalty. Cuchulain prevails in each melee because his foes slip up or are found lacking in one or more of these qualities.

The melees continue day after day until Maeve, having lost too many of her best warriors, decides to send her best young warrior Ferdia, who is a good friend of Cuchulain's and his only equal as a fighter. Both Ferdia and Cuchulain had trained with Skatha, a warrior woman, and pledged as young men never to fight each other. Citing his promise to Cuchulain, Ferdia rejects Maeve's attempts to persuade him to fight his friend. Maeve then threatens to have her druids use the *glámma dícend,* a form of public satire and lampooning, to force Ferdia to fight. The *glámma dícend* had magical power that allowed druids and bards to control their victims. This threat changes Ferdia's mind. Curiously, Ferdia agrees to fight Cuchulain, who will almost certainly kill him, to avoid being satirized by the *glámma dícend.*

It is unclear why the *glámma dícend,* as a form of satire, would be so powerful. Were its victims simply afraid of being publicly shamed? Or, did it contain a magical power that would bend them to its will? To give a sense of its power, we can look to a later Irish legend, "The Death of Cuchulain," where enemy bards use the *glámma dícend* to force Cuchulain against his will to give up three of his magic spears, which they use against him.

The climax of the *Táin* is the melee between Ferdia and Cuchulain, which lasts a few days. The two begin with insults, as Cuchulain reminds Ferdia of their oath not to fight each other. Soon, though, they begin to exchange compliments and sorrows. Each evening, they help bind each other's wounds and share healing salves. Eventually, on the third day, Ferdia wounds Cuchulain, which causes that latter to go into his signature "warp-spasm." In his rage, Cuchulain pulls out the Gae Blog, a unique spear-like weapon, which only he has mastered. The Gae Blog completely fills the victim's body with barbs. Using this weapon, Cuchulain slays Ferdia and then weeps for his fallen friend.

With the death of Ferdia, Maeve's army advances into Ulster. Cuchulain is too injured to impede Maeve's army further. However, the army of Ulster finally awakens from its curse to defend its kingdom. The *Táin* ends with a great battle between the two armies. The tide is turned when an injured Cuchulain returns to the field of battle and forces Maeve and her army to retreat.

RECONSTRUCTING ANCIENT IRISH RHETORIC

Reconstructing an ancient rhetoric is similar to studying an archeological site. While sifting through ancient texts, we begin to unearth isolated rhetorical artifacts that at first appear to have little meaning on their own. But, as we contextualize these artifacts with other texts and historical evidence, patterns of rhetorical behavior start to emerge.

In the two Irish legends related above, many rhetorical artifacts can be reconstituted into a rough understanding of ancient Irish rhetoric. Much of ancient Irish rhetoric seems in accord with the descriptions of pre-literate rhetorics offered by Havelock, Kennedy, and Ong. There are also some distinctive qualities that set ancient Irish rhetoric apart.

Narrative and Core Celtic Values

A first observation is the importance of narrative as a rhetorical means for building cultural consensus and reinforcing core Celtic values: courage, generosity, loyalty, and beauty. Certainly, these values are important in other cultures, especially the Greeks, but, as Cahill points out, ancient Irish narratives put an acute weight on them. These core values become places out of which the stories are told and characters shape their behavior. Their repetition across the Irish canon seems to make them similar in function to common *topoi* in Greek rhetoric.

Examples of these core values are found throughout the legend of the Milesian Celts and the *Táin*. In the legend of the Milesian Celts, the Danaans kings are shown to be selfish, disloyal, deceitful, as well as cowardly. Due to their deficiencies, it is almost inevitable that these kings will be deposed by the Celts. To an ancient Irish audience, the idea of leaving such people in control of Ireland would have been unacceptable. So, the taking of Ireland by the Milesian Celts would have appeared predestined and almost compulsory. Likewise, in the *Táin*, when Maeve lists off the qualities she sought in a husband, she was essentially highlighting the core values of Irish culture: she sought a husband who would be courageous, loyal, generous, and beautiful—much like herself, of course.

As Cahill points out, these four core values are repeated over and over in Irish stories (1995, 94). Sometimes, they are exhibited in the deeds and misdeeds of the main characters, but often enough we find them reinforced strongly in their dialogues. When characters in the *Táin* chant lays together, they are often specifically reinforcing these values. Then, when they engage in combat, the lack of one of these values—even temporarily as in Ferdia's case—brings about the character's downfall or ruin. Cuchulain is repeatedly shown to be successful against his foes because he always exhibits the qualities of a classic Irish hero. He is courageous, loyal, generous, and attractive. His adversaries, like Maeve, Fergus, and Ferdia, are shown to possess many of these qualities too, but each is found to be lacking in some essential way. For this reason, each of them eventually meets defeat. In a literate culture, the repetition of these core values might seem tedious and the use of cliché to describe characters can seem trite, but as Ong argues, the repetition of core values and familiar phrasings would have been essential to an oral culture.

Ultimately, though, consensus is the aim of ancient Irish rhetoric, which Kennedy would call a "traditional rhetoric." The repetition of core values within the stories and the reiteration of the narratives themselves were rhetorical means for preserving and restoring consensus in a pre-literate society dealing with understandings of how to behave in complex situations. In ancient Irish stories, we witness how a narrative-based oral rhetoric worked.

The Purveyors of Rhetoric and Values

A second observation about ancient Irish rhetoric is the importance of poets (*filé*) in this culture. In ancient Ireland, the poets were bards (*filid*) and druids (*faithi*). Describing the role of druids and bards among the Gaulish Celts, Julius Caesar wrote the following:

> They preside over sacred things, have charge of public and private sacrifices, and explain their religion. To them a great number of youths have recourse for the sake of acquiring instruction, and they are in great honor among them. For they generally settle all their disputes, both public and private; and if there is any transgression perpetrated, any murder committed, or any dispute about inheritance or boundaries, they decide in respect of them. (*De Bello Gallico*, VI, 13–18, quoted in Matthews 2001, 15)

Bards and druids were travelers and rhapsodes, moving from village to village in the Irish countryside, telling stories, educating youth, and acting as jurists. Commoners were not allowed to travel outside their kingdoms (*tuath*), so bards and druids played a critical role in pollinating and norming the Irish culture. The entertainment value of their stories certainly attracted their audiences, but it was the educational themes at the heart of these stories that would be most important to preserving Irish culture.

Because the Irish bards and druids did not write down their rituals and beliefs, even after the advent of literacy in Ireland, it is hard to determine exactly what they believed or taught. Nevertheless, the function of bards and druids in Irish society seems to have been similar to that of the poets and older sophists in ancient Greece. Much like Gorgias, Protagoras, and other sophists, they were traveling educators and ambassadors. They entertained people and taught (see Gagarin 2001). They acted as advisors, and they were believed to have magical powers due to their verbal acumen.

Rhetoric and Magic

An unmistakable feature of ancient Irish rhetoric, as in almost any oral culture, would be the role of magic. In Irish stories, we see spells used regularly, as in the story of the Milesian Celts. We see written symbols being used to impede others, as in the story of Cuchulain's braiding an oak sapling into a circle and thus placing a *geiss* on Maeve's army. We see magical forms of satire, as in the story of Maeve's threatened use of the *glámma dícend* against Ferdia to force him into combat with Cuchulain.

In *Magic, Rhetoric, and Literacy,* William Covino defines the relationship between magic and rhetoric in the following way:

> Magic is not the instant and arhetorical product of an
> otherworldly incantation; it is the process of inducing
> belief and creating community, with reference to the
> dynamics of a rhetorical situation. Magic is a social act
> whose medium is persuasive discourse, and so it must
> entail the complexities of social interaction, invention,
> communication, and composition (1994, 11).

Later, he writes, "Magic takes place, for the exorcist and the orator, the witchdoctor and the psychiatrist, when the parties involved agree to agree, when they enact what E. Fuller Torrey calls 'a shared world view'" (12).

As Covino suggests, in an oral culture like that of ancient Ireland, rhetoric and magic would have been yet another way to preserve or restore consensus. In both the story of the Milesian Celts and the *Táin,* we observe that order has broken down. In these situations, rhetoric and magic are employed to restore natural order (i.e. what Kennedy calls "consensus" or what Torrey calls "a shared world view"). After Amergin casts his spells, the Celts are able to defeat the Danaan kings. In the *Táin,* Cuchulain's magic helps him hinder Maeve's invasion of

Ulster because if Maeve ignores Cuchulain's *giesse*, she would break the cultural and natural consensus—with dire consequences. Even in situations in which magic is being used to do evil, such as Maeve's threatened use of the *glámma dícend* against Ferdia, there is a sense that magic is being used to maintain the traditional hierarchy. Ferdia must obey, because Maeve is his superior in social rank. To resist her would mean breaking consensus with her and her army. Ferdia must comply because magic like the *glámma dícend* would ultimately force him back into consensus with his queen and his people.

In a literate culture, the role of magic tends to be greatly diminished. The ability to write ideas down allows a level of analysis that can demystify most forms of magic and superstitions. However, in an oral culture, magic would be an essential feature of language usage. In ancient Greek writings about rhetoric, for example, we see flavors of magic, such as Gorgias' argument in "Encomium of Helen" in which he argues that *logos* has magical or drug-like powers. In *Magic and Rhetoric in Ancient Greece,* Jacquiline de Romilly argues that the sophists directly drew from a tradition in which poets were "superhuman creatures and whose powers, in all sorts of matters, were both mysterious and great" (1975, 4). Gorgias, deRomilly writes, drew from this tradition of magic in his arguments for the power of *logos.* Covino expands on de Romilly's argument by tracing the relationship between magic and rhetoric from antiquity to the present. As Covino suggests, it is only with the rise of science, which used reason to legitimize practices from natural magic, that the bonds between magic and rhetoric are weakened (1994, 8). But for the ancient Irish, the bonds between rhetoric and magic would have seemed unbreakable.

In ancient Irish texts, we see magic fully displayed as a cornerstone of their rhetoric. In the saga of the Milesian Celts, Amergin uses magical poetry to calm the waters and draw forward the power of nature into himself. Similarly, Cuchulain uses symbols, written in Ogham, to place *geisse* on Maeve's army. And, Maeve's threat to use the *glámma dícend* on Ferdia, shows the essential importance of magical language in ancient Irish rhetoric. In ancient Irish rhetoric, the magical use of language was a way to get things done with words, a means for taking action.

Because magic is such an important feature of nearly all oral cultures, I don't want to make too large a claim for the exceptionality of magic to the Irish and the Celts. However, it is notable how vitally related language and magic seem to be in Irish mythology. Magical acts are routinely accompanied by poetry. Spells are regularly used as ways to influence events in agonistic situations. Indeed, it seems that the use of magic in ancient Irish stories must be accompanied by some kind of rhetorical act. In other words, language and magic seem inseparable as though magic would be impossible without utterance. The *glámma dícend* is an especially curious rhetorical artifact. Here, we observe satire being used in a completely magical way. In Irish stories, the use of satire to impel characters to do things against their will is an important element.

The Irish had great faith in the magical ability of language to move people to do things. In these ancient Irish legends, I believe we witness how integrated magic would have been with words in an oral rhetoric. The use of spells and *geisse* are critical plot elements in the stories, but they are also not exceptional. Rather, they seem to be central characteristics of the rhetoric itself.

Conclusion: Myth and Rhetoric

Let me conclude by raising issues, rather than attempting to bring closure to this line of research. In this article, I have only offered a sampling of the possible areas of exploration in ancient Irish rhetoric. Certainly, the catalog of Irish myths offers many more sites to be explored. "The Coming of the Milesian Celts" and the *Táin bo Cúalgne* are canonical stories in ancient Irish literature, but there are many more texts to be studied and many more rhetorical artifacts to be unearthed.

A few projects seem immediately available to us. In this article, I have explored issues of orality, the uses of rhetoric by bards and druids, and the centrality of magic to ancient Irish rhetoric. These issues could be explored further in other texts, and many other issues could be studied to broaden our understanding of ancient Irish rhetoric.

Perhaps more challenging, though, would be exploration of the parallels between mythology and rhetoric. While working on this article, I looked mostly in vain for materials that explained and elucidated these rather obvious parallels. The shared elements between mythology and rhetoric seem so obvious and undeniable, yet little has been done in this area, except with the Greeks. A broader study of mythology as a form of rhetoric could be a vital undertaking, especially when we explore ancient rhetorics. After all, much of an ancient culture's rituals and practices can be found reflected in its mythology, thus making mythology a doorway to understanding the roles that rhetoric played in that culture. In an oral culture, a mythology is, at its core, a rhetoric. Myth is the way an oral culture verbally maintains its knowledge, rituals, and beliefs (Campbell 1949, 10–11; Doty 2000, 135). Myth serves a vital role to preserve evidence of cultural and rhetorical practices and values. A comprehensive study relating mythology and rhetoric is needed that looks at cultures other than the Greeks.

Finally, Irish rhetoric seems to offer us a window into the workings of pre-Roman oral cultures. We are fortunate that these stories survived in their current form. The rapidity with which literacy was thrust onto the Irish seems to have preserved many of the oral traits of these stories. It would be valuable to look for other ancient cultures like the ancient Irish, where the advent of literacy allowed the preservation of oral legacies. Then, we could perhaps develop a broader sense of how rhetoric might have operated in oral cultures.

Notes

1. The difference in these accounts probably depends on what would be considered fair play by Celtic audiences listening to the saga. More than likely, the real Celtic arrival on Ireland took centuries. The contagious germs the Celts brought from Europe may have formed their real front line, mowing down the pre-Celtic inhabitants who were not immune to them. Indeed, in one version of the Milesian Celt legend, the Danaan kings were actually killed by a plague, not the Celtic invaders (*Lebor* 29). That may explain why no pre-Celtic people seem to have survived after the arrival of the Celts. The few pre-Celtic people spared by plagues probably assimilated into the new dominant culture.

2. Here, we also observe the use of "cunning" in a positive light, much as it was to describe Ith's earlier performance in mediating the land dispute among the Danaan kings. These usages bring to mind the frequent descriptions of Odysseus as someone who was cunning in word and action.

Works Cited

Aristotle. *On Rhetoric: A Theory of Civic Discourse*. Trans. George Kennedy. New York, NY: Oxford UP, 1991.

Bitel, Lisa. *Land of Women: Tales of Sex and Gender from Early Ireland*. Ithaca, NY: Cornell UP, 1996.

Cahill, Thomas. *How the Irish Saved Civilization*. New York: Random House, 1995.

Campbell, Joseph. *Hero with a Thousand Faces*. New York: Pantheon, 1949.

Cath Maige Tuired. Ed. Elizabeth Gray. Dublin: Irish Texts Society, 1983.

Covino, William. *Magic, Rhetoric, and Literacy: An Eccentric History of the Composing Imagination*. Albany: SUNY P, 1994.

Curtin, Jeremiah. *Myths and Folklore of Ireland*. New York: Wings Books, 1975.

de Romilly, Jacqueline. *Magic and Rhetoric in Ancient Greece*. Cambridge, MA: Harvard UP, 1975.

Doty, William. *Mythography: The Study of Myths and Rituals*, 2nd ed. Tuscaloosa: U of Alabama P, 2000.

Foster, Roy. *The Oxford Illustrated History of Ireland*. Oxford, UK: Oxford UP, 1989.

Gagarin, Michael. "Did the Sophists Aim to Persuade?" *Rhetorica* 19 (2001): 275–91.

Gantz, Jeffrey. *Early Irish Myths and Sagas*. New York: Penguin, 1981.

Gregory, Lady. *Cuchulain of Muirthemne*. Gerrards Cross, UK: Colin Smythe, 1970.

Havelock, Eric. *Preface to Plato*. Cambridge, MA: Harvard UP, 1963.

Kennedy, George. *Comparative Rhetoric*. Oxford, UK: Oxford UP, 1997.

Lebor Gabála Erenn. Ed. R.A. Stewart MacAlister. Dublin: Irish Texts Society, 1956.

Matthews, John, ed. *The Druid Source Book*. London: Caxton, 2001.

Ó Corrain, Donnchadh. "Prehistoric and Early Christian Ireland." *The Oxford Illustrated History of Ireland*. Ed. Roy Foster. Oxford, UK: Oxford UP, 1989. 1–54.

Ong, Walter. *Orality and Literacy*. New York: Routledge, 1982.

Polkinghorne, Donald. *Narrative Knowing and the Human Sciences*. Albany: SUNY P, 1988.

Rolleston, T. W. *Celtic Myths and Legends*. New York: Dover, 1990.

Rutherford, Ward. *Celtic Mythology*. New York: Sterling, 1987.

Scherman, Katherine. *The Flowering of Ireland*. Boston: Little, Brown, 1981.

Slavin, Michael. *The Ancient Books of Ireland*. Montreal: McGill-Queen's UP, 2005.

Swartz, Dorothy. "Repetition in the Book of Leinster *Táin Bó Cúailnge* and in Neo-Classical Rhetoric." *Proceedings of the Harvard Celtic Colloquium* 4 (1984): 45–81.

Táin Bó Cúalnge from The Book of Leinster. Ed. Cecile O'Rahilly. Dublin: Dublin Institute for Advanced Studies, 1967.

Yeats, W. B. *Irish Fairy and Folk Tales*. New York: Barnes and Noble, 1983.

Young, Ella. *Celtic Wonder-tales*. New York: Dover, 1995.

Contributors

Roberta Binkley received her PhD from the University of Arizona. She left a position as Assistant Professor at the University of Tennessee in Chattanooga to return to Arizona, where she teaches as a lecturer at Arizona State University. She is working on a book and has published two articles on the prophetess Enheduanna. In addition, Roberta co-edited a 2004 collection of essays with Carol Lipson, entitled *Rhetoric Before and Beyond the Greeks*.

Richard Johnson-Sheehan is Associate Professor of English at Purdue University, where he teaches courses in classical rhetoric and professional writing. He received his PhD at Iowa State in 1995, in Rhetoric and Professional Writing. He has published two texts on technical communication, as well as a number of articles and chapters on issues of scientific rhetoric, particularly focusing on metaphor as well as on visual rhetoric. Of late, he has begun to investigate ancient Irish rhetoric.

Steven B. Katz is the Roy Pearce Professor of Professional Communication at Clemson University, having received his PhD in Communication and Rhetoric from RPI in 1988. He has published on the rhetoric impulse of the Hebrew alphabet (*Journal of Communication and Religion*, 2003), as well as a book on the epistemic music of rhetoric (1996, SIUP). His scholarly interests include ancient alternative rhetorics (Biblical, Jewish/sophistic, kabbalistic), as well as material rhetorics and rhetorics of ethics and style.

Carol Lipson is Professor of Writing and Rhetoric, and immediate past chair of the Writing Program at Syracuse University. She received her PhD in English at the University of California – Los Angeles, where she began the study of Egyptology. She has published on ancient Egyptian medical rhetoric, on the multimedia nature of ancient Egyptian public texts, and on the central Egyptian value of *Maat* in relation to the culture's rhetorical principles. Carol co-edited a collection entitled *Rhetoric Before and Beyond the Greeks* with Roberta Binkley (SUNY Press, 2004).

Arabella Lyon, Associate Professor at the State University of New York–Buffalo, was awarded the 1999 W. Ross Winterowd Prize for her book entitled *Intentions, Negotiated, Contested, and Ignored*. She has written a number of essays on ancient Chinese rhetoric and on comparative-rhetoric methodology, including a collaborative essay with Sue Hum entitled "Advances in Comparative Rhetorical Studies" (Lunsford, Wilson, and Eberly, eds. *The Sage Handbook of Rhetorical Studies*, 2009).

Yichun Liu is Assistant Professor in the Foreign Language Center at National Chengchi University in Taiwan. Having received the PhD in 2004 from Purdue University, specializing in ESL, Yichun has supplemented work in second-language issues and on writing in China today to include collaborative essays with Xiaoye You on ancient Chinese rhetoric, including one on Confucian policy arguments.

Mari Lee Mifsud is Chair of Rhetoric and Communication Studies and Associate Professor of Rhetoric at the University of Richmond. She serves on the editorial board of *Rhetoric Society Quarterly*. She has published on the history of rhetoric, and most recently, on rhetoric as gift giving (*Philosophy and Rhetoric*, 2007).

Scott Stroud earned his PhD in philosophy from Temple University in 2006. He is Assistant Professor in the Department of History and Philosophy at the University of Texas—Pan American. His research interests and publications range from pragmatism to Asian and comparative philosophy, as well as to the intersection of aesthetics and rhetoric.

James W. Watts is Professor of Religion at Syracuse University. He received his PhD at Yale University in 1990. At Syracuse, he teaches Hebrew Bible and ancient Near Eastern textual traditions. Among his publications are *Ritual and Rhetoric in Leviticus: From Sacrifice to Scripture* (2007) and *Reading Law: The Rhetorical Shaping of the Pentateuch* (1999).

Kathy Wolfe is Assistant Professor of English at Nebraska Wesleyan University, having received her PhD from Texas Christian University in 1994. Kathy teaches rhetoric, writing, linguistics, history of English, and liberal arts seminars. She is active in curriculum reform, development and assessment, and co-directs a minor in peace and justice studies. She has presented papers on Japanese rhetoric at several national and international conferences; her publications include an essay on language as an instrument of change for women in Japan (*Women and Language*, 1995).

Xiaoye You is Assistant Professor of English and Asian Studies at Penn State University. He received his PhD at Purdue in 2005, where he specialized in ESL and Rhetoric. He has published several articles and chapters on English instruction in China. A second area of his work involves historical development of Confucian rhetoric; in 2006, he published an article in *Rhetoric Society Quarterly* on the rhetoric in Confucius's *Analects* as multimodal rhetoric. With Yichun Liu, he is preparing new work on essay writing in ancient China.

Index

Lightning Source UK Ltd.
Milton Keynes UK
UKOW04f1956050915

258106UK00001B/76/P